Proto-Indo-European Syntax

Proto-Indo-European Syntax

by Winfred P. Lehmann

UNIVERSITY OF TEXAS PRESS, AUSTIN AND LONDON

Library of Congress Cataloging in Publication Data

Lehmann, Winfred Philipp, 1916-
Proto-Indo-European syntax.

1. Proto-Aryan language–Syntax. I. Title.
P671.L4 417'.7 74-10526
ISBN 0-292-76419-7

Printed in the United States of America

CONTENTS

FIGURES

PREFACE

Syntax, the study of sentences, is generally held to be the heart of grammar. Whether or not, with students of language like Rudolf Carnap and Noam Chomsky, one takes semantics to be interpretive, phonology must be so viewed; and morphology deals with a subcomponent of syntax. Morphological and phonological studies must therefore be provisional unless carried out on the basis of a syntactic description. Yet most investigations dealing with the early Indo-European dialects and the reconstructed parent language are concerned with these subsidiary components of grammar. *Proto-Indo-European Syntax* has been written to remedy this shortcoming of Indo-European linguistics and to provide a syntax of the parent language.

Yet *Proto-Indo-European Syntax* is itself only a preliminary work. In spite of Berthold Delbrück's excellent monographs and his syntax in the first edition of the Brugmann-Delbrück *Grundriss,* and in spite of excellent discussions of syntactic problems, such as those in Jacob Wackernagel's *Vorlesungen,* no syntactic description of Proto-Indo-European has yet been written. In this situation a large-scale treatment did not seem desirable, but rather one which can lead to examination of major problems and individual syntactic constructions.

In attempting to understand and describe Indo-European grammar a linguist must rely on scholars in many disciplines besides linguistics. One of his chief debts is to the editors and interpreters of texts and to the producers of dictionaries. It would be impossible to give individual credit to even the most important such scholars. Moreover, even basic scholarly materials, like the transcribed Hittite texts, cannot be cited. If an Indo-Europeanist wishes to contribute to a field which attracted some of the best minds of the nineteenth and early twentieth centuries, he must draw not on such detailed, fundamental philological accomplishments but rather on the widely available editions of texts in the various dialects. Moreover, in order to provide accessibility for judgments of his linguistic interpretations, he must refer to standard, readily available editions. Nonetheless Indo-Europeanists are greatly indebted to the dedicated philologists who are making accessible the materials in the Anatolian, Tocharian, and other dialects that have been made known recently, such as Mycenaean Greek; they are also greatly in debt to their painstaking predecessors who produced the basic texts, grammars, and dictionaries for the various Indo-European dialects.

The debt this book owes to other scholars is evident on every page. I would like especially to thank R. P. Lehmann and Ladislav Zgusta, and students who investigated particular problems, H. S. Ananthanarayana, Eugene Grace, Solveig Pflueger, Carol Raman among others. I also acknowledge research support, in large part for such investigations. A grant from the American Council of Learned Societies provided the initial support for a computerized concordance of the Rigveda and other materials. Grants RO-5120-72-128 from the National Endowment for Humanities and GS-3081 from the National Science Foundation supported numerous individual studies in Indo-European linguistics and related fields. I owe special thanks to the Guggenheim Foundation for the grant which provided the opportunity to complete *Proto-Indo-European Syntax*.

W. P. Lehmann

ABBREVIATIONS USED

AB: Aitareya Brahmāna
Ab.: ablative
Acc.: accusative
Act.: active
Adj.: adjective
Adv.: adverb
Aor.: aorist
Aux.: auxiliary
C: consonant
Caus.: causative
Comp.: complement
Conj.: conjunction
Cont. continuative
Dat.: dative
Dec.: declarative
Det.: determiner
Enc.: enclitic
esp.: especially
F: first consonant
f.: feminine
Gen.: genitive
Gk.: Greek
Goth.: Gothic
Hitt.: Hittite
IE: Indo-European
Imper.: imperative
Imperf.: imperfective
Inj.: injunctive
Int.: interrogative
Iter.: iterative
K: kāraka, case category
k: case indicators; terminations or pre/postpositions
KBo: Keilschrifttexte aus Boghazköi (Leipzig)
KUB: Keilschrifturkunden aus Boghazköi (Berlin)
L: last consonant
Lat.: Latin
Lith.: Lithuanian
Loc.: locative
M: middle consonant
m.: masculine
ME: Middle English
MHG: Middle High German
Mid.: middle voice
Mod.: modifier
Mom.: momentary
N: noun
n.: neuter
NE: New English, Modern English
Nec.: necessitative
Neg.: negative
$N^{Mod.}$: nominal modifier
$N^{Obj.}$: noun obj.
Nom.: nominative
NP: noun phrase
O: object
Obj.: object
Obl.: obligative
OCS: Old Church Slavic
OE: Old English
OHG: Old High German
ON: Old Norse
Opt.: optative
OSV: object-subject-verb order
OV: object-verb order
P rules: phrase-structure rules
Pass.: passive
Perf.: perfective
PIE: Proto-Indo-European
Pl.: plural
Pred.: predicate
Pres.: present
Pron.: pronoun
Prop.: proposition
Ptc.: particle
Q: qualifier
Recip.: reciprocal
Refl.: reflexive
Rel.: relative
RV: Rigveda. References are to book, poem, and stanza; e.g., 5.1.3.=Book 5, Poem or Hymn 1, Stanza 3.
S: subject
ŚB: Śatapathabrāhmaṇa
S.C.: structural change
S.D.: structural description
sg.: singular
Skt.: Sanskrit
Slav.: Slavic
SOV: subject-object-verb order
Subj.: subjunctive
SVO: subject-verb-object order
TB: Taittirīya Brāhmaṇa
TS: Taittirīya Saṁhitā
V: verb
Vb.: verbal
VO: verb-object order
Voc.: vocative
Vol.: volitional
VP: verb phrase
VSO: verb-subject-object order
Σ : initial node for sentence
1: first person
2: second person
3: third person
$\rightarrow$: rewrite as
$\Rightarrow$: transform to

Proto-Indo-European Syntax

1. The Syntactic Framework

1.1. Earlier Syntactic Treatments of PIE.

When we concern ourselves with the syntax of Proto-Indo-European (PIE), our best treatment is still Berthold Delbrück's section on syntax in the first edition of the Brugmann-Delbrück *Grundriss der vergleichenden Grammatik der indogermanischen Sprachen* (1886–1900). Although Delbrück's three volumes on syntax in the *Grundriss* were completed in the last year of the preceding century, they have not been superseded. They were based on many detailed studies on syntactic phenomena in individual dialects, some by Delbrück himself.

The syntactic studies of the nineteenth century were carried out by scholars who had achieved virtually unsurpassable mastery of the important Indo-European (IE) dialects. Their mastery may be most strikingly evident in detailed syntactic descriptions, such as those of Latin and Greek in the grammars of the Handbuch der Altertumswissenschaft; the current editions, by Anton Szantyr of Latin (Leumann 1963–1965) and Eduard Schwyzer for Greek (1939–1953), provide huge compendia of the syntactic data as well as comprehensive bibliographies which alone would fill a large volume. Valuable syntactic treatments were also produced for other IE dialects, such as J. S. Speyer's for Sanskrit (1885), Franz Miklosich's for Slavic (1868–1874:IV), Jacob Grimm's for Germanic (1870–1898). In addition, numerous important handbooks for in-individual dialects included treatments of syntax; and excellent monographs, such as Carl Gaedicke's on cases (1880) and Hermann Jacobi's on compounds (1897), dealt with individual topics. All of these provided resources for a comprehensive treatment of PIE syntax. Such a treatment was planned by Karl Brugmann for the second edition of the *Grundriss* (1897–1916) but it resulted only in his posthumously published discussion of the simple sentence: *Die Syntax des einfachen Satzes im Indogermanischen* of 1925.

And Hermann Hirt's two final volumes of his *Indogermanische Grammatik, Syntax I* and *Syntax II* (1921–1937:VI, VII) seem almost a result of his determination to complete his grammar rather than of a conviction that he had advanced beyond Delbrück. For his prefaces to the two volumes on syntax reflect the same plaintive self-doubt that he expressed in his preface to the syntax volume of his *Handbuch des Urgermanischen:* "In my opinion [the basis for the absence of participation in syntactic study] lies in the fact that in many instances we find no explanations in the area of syntax. One assembles a series of facts but doesn't know what to do with them" (1931–1934: III, vi). In keeping with this pessimistic conclusion Hirt wrote in the preface to his *Syntax I,* "I hope that I have now reached a certain definite point of view and that I can offer [others] the possibility of approaching study of the many details which still await explanation" (ibid.:v) (my translations).

As the following decades showed, this hope was premature. Explanations were offered for sporadic phenomena, such as those accounted for by "attraction" or assimilation (Wackernagel 1926:49–59) and those accounted for by borrowing (ibid.:8–12). By attraction, syntacticians explained such patterns as the accusative *hoîon Peiríthoon* in Homer:

1. Iliad 1.262-263.	ou	gár	pō̄	toíous	ídon	anéras	oudè	ídōmai,
	not	for	ever	such	I-saw	men	nor	I-will-see
	hoîon	Peiríthoón	te	Druántá	te			
	such-as	Peirithous	and	Dryas	and			

'For never did I see such men, nor will I, as Peirithous and Dryas.'

Jacob Wackernagel explained this construction as one assimilated from *hoîos Peiríthoos ȇn* 'as Peirithous was' (1926:54). Among examples of borrowing he cited the use of the nominative *deus* 'God' as a term of address in Church Latin; this syntactic pattern was based on the Greek *ho theós,* which in turn was "borrowed" from Hebrew, in which there was no vocative. The explanation was buttressed by the observation that only Christians used a term of address for 'god' (1926:10). But apart from such occasional syntactic constructions, there was no attempt to explain syntactic patterns. Recent syntactic studies however have given us the possibility of providing syntactic explanations based on syntactic universals, and accordingly it is now possible to undertake an explanatory syntax of PIE. That is the aim of this book.

In seeking to carry out this aim I view PIE as a language spoken by a specific community around 3000 B.C. Thanks to remarkable advances in archeology during the past decades, this community can be identified with the peoples of the Kurgan culture situated north of the Black Sea at this time, as the excellent essays of Marija Gimbutas and Ward H. Goodenough in the collection *Indo-European and Indo-Europeans* indicate, with differences in details that may well be expected because of the recency and complexities of the archeology concerned (Cardona, Hoenigswald, and Senn 1970:155–197, 253–265). The view that we must reconstruct the syntax of a language spoken around 3000 B.C. requires the application of other methods than those applied in earlier syntactic treatments of PIE.

Most notable among these additional methods is the reconstruction of syntactic patterns in accordance with a syntactic framework which has been developed on the basis of typological study. Moreover, our conception of syntax is determined by a specific theory of language. For a concise statement of the various views of syntax in IE studies, Wackernagel is unsurpassed (1926:1–4). The eminent Slavist Miklosich viewed syntax as the study of word classes and word forms. For the Latinist Christian Karl Reisig, syntax was the study of the joining together *(Verbindung)* of words. For the Greekist Karl Krüger, syntax included two subdivisions: analysis, which corresponds to the syntax of Miklosich, and synthesis, which corresponds to the syntax of Reisig. Subsequent to such statements, John Ries published in 1894 his influential book *Was ist Syntax?* His conclusions that syntax involves only "synthesis" and that the meaning of word classes and word forms must be treated in connection with morphology had a decisive influence on Brugmann and the second edition of the *Grundriss.* Criticizing this point of view, Hirt proposed that syntax need not be rigorously defined; but he saw as its task the determination of the "words and combinations of words used to express feelings and thoughts" (1921–1937:VI:6–7). Hirt then returned to the views maintained before the publication of Ries's book, views that are in Wackernagel's *Vorlesungen* (1926–1928). These views were also adopted by Hans Krahe (1972:11). Accordingly, the general treatments of IE syntax view it as "the study of the sentence and its parts" and are essentially descriptive.

1.2. The Bases of an Explanatory Syntax.

An explanatory syntax is now possible because of two recent developments in linguistics: the study of syntax for its underlying patterns, which owes much of its impetus to the work of Noam Chomsky (1965), and the typological framework for syntax, which is based in great part on an important essay of Joseph Greenberg (1966). While our data are taken from surface manifestations, syntactic study is concerned with the abstract patterns underlying these–in Ferdinand de Saussure's term, with *langue;* in Chomsky's, with a theory of competence.

When studied for their underlying patterns, the "series of facts" that Hirt and his predecessors could not handle can be interrelated; a syntax can be produced which describes a languages by means of ordered rules. Such rules are written in accordance with a framework of syntactic universals, which typological study has yielded. Our conclusions about the syntax of PIE can be presented within this framework; we will be able to test the IE data against this framework in much the way we would a language spoken today. In this way we can explain the syntactic patterns we find, not merely list and describe them.

The recent advances in syntax have resulted from an approach which is referred to as generative. By *generative* we mean that all linguistic patterns are fully specified. Such specification is sought by proceeding from the assumption that the sentence is the unit of language (see Brugmann 1925:1). We assume that every sentence can be accounted for through a series of rules which represent expansions from an initial node of *sentence.* In syntactic rules this initial node is often symbolized by S; but because S is also used to symbolize "subject," I use the label Σ. From Σ then, any sentence in any language can be derived, by means of carefully determined rules. These rules, of which the first are phrase-structure or P rules, determine the grammatical form and, together with the selected lexical entries, the meaning of the sentence.

The assumption that the sentence is the fundamental unit of language does not exclude consideration of longer sentences. In longer sentences we commonly find such syntactic processes as substitution and deletion more widely than in simple sentences. But we account for the resulting phenomena in much the same way as we account for the phenomena of simple sentences. The following sequences therefore present similar problems.

2*a*. John and I went to town yesterday. 2*b*. We went in his car.
3. John and I went to town yesterday in his car.

Substitutes like *we* and *his* must be accounted for, whether they occur in two separate sentences like those of Example 2 or within one sentence. We account for them by equating all such sequences with simple sentences and then noting modifications. Thus, in the examples above, the second sentence of Example 2 has the substitute *we* for *John and I;* it also has the substitute *his* for *John's,* as does the last phrase in Example 3. In Example 2*b* the embedded sentence expressed by:

4. John and I went to town in John's car.

is reduced further than it is in Example 3. Neither Example 2*b* nor Example 3 can be accounted for without starting from underlying patterns like that represented in Example 4. Linguistics accordingly follows the strategy of accounting first for the patterns underlying "simple sentences" and subsequently for those underlying complex and compound sentences and successive sentences like those in Example 2 which contain substitutes and deletions. Although this strategy is based on the assumption that the sentence is the basic unit of language, it does not exclude consideration of longer sequences of discourse; such sequences are merely reserved for subsequent consideration, and are treated under study labeled "discourse analysis," *Textlinguistik,* or even stylistics. The problems concerned will not be discussed in this book.

In forming sentences, phrase-structure rules are selected by the speaker in accordance with the lexical content he wishes to include. For example, if a speaker wishes to produce the sentence *The man saw the sheep,* he must select from his repertoire of lexical items the one referring to a male adult human and the one referring to a woolly quadruped as well as the verb *see.* An understanding of language requires a theory in which the two ingredients of language, grammatical rules and lexical items, are accounted for.

Currently there are two competing theories among transformational grammarians, labeled generative syntax and generative semantics. Generative syntax proposes that the syntactic component is central to language and that sentences are produced by adducing syntactic rules and interpreting these by means of appropriate semantic conventions. Generative semantics, on the other hand, proposes that the semantic component is central and that in the production of a sentence speakers put selected semantic material in a correct syntactic structure. The two theories are often contrasted by means of frameworks illustrating their treatments of the various constituents of language (see Figure 1).

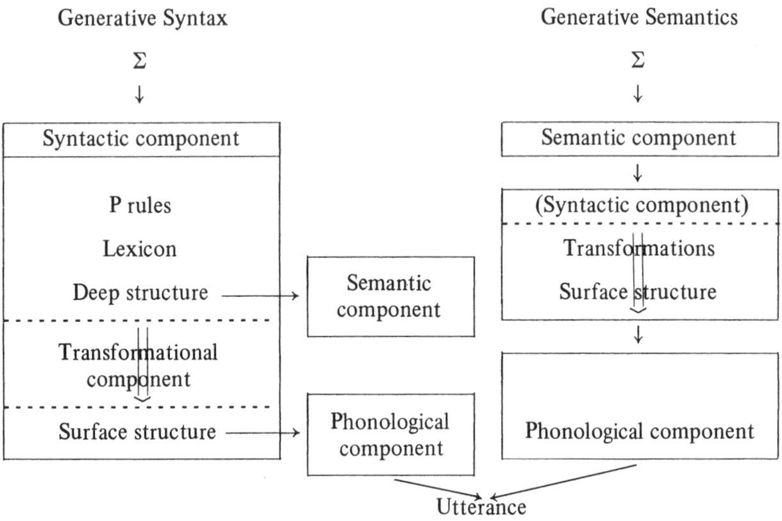

Figure 1. Sentence generation in generative syntax and generative semantics.

Arguments advanced in favor of each theory are inconclusive, and indeed some scholars state that the two approaches are essentially notational variants. Points of conflict have to do largely with psycholinguistic concerns regarding the functioning of the brain in the use of language. In dealing with these concerns a reconstructed language will make few contributions, especially since we no longer hold that PIE is so close to the beginnings of human speech that it may disclose fundamental data about language through its great antiquity.

Moreover, while in IE studies we cannot carry out the detailed investigations necessary for statements in generative semantics, we can determine the sentence patterns of PIE. Accordingly my treatment of PIE will follow the position of generative syntax, though with modifications as described here. The semantic component is then interpretive, relating the syntactic component to the outside world. And I will discuss the PIE language in terms of a traditional definition of the sentence, that given by Hermann Paul in his *Prinzipien:* "The sentence is the linguistic expression, the symbol for the fact that the union of several concepts or groups of concepts has been completed in the mind of the speaker, and the means for arousing the same union of the same concepts in the mind of the hearer" (Paul 1920:121). While Paul's statement could be and has been discussed at length, only a few points will be noted here concerning this definition, which has been fundamental for much of the linguistic work carried on during the almost one hundred years since Paul first published his book. First, the sentence is defined as a symbol, an abstraction; accordingly Paul proposed to deal with underlying syntactic forms as well as surface forms. Further, a sentence is a linguistic expression of a union of concepts; for the understanding of a sentence Paul takes the treatment of these concepts into consideration as well as their linguistic forms. Generative syntax does so by means of the lexicon as well as grammatical rules. Elements of the lexicon as well as the grammatical rules are abstract constituents.

Each of these elements conveys meaning, as do combinations of them. Thus New English (NE) *red* conveys a set of meanings, as does *neck;* and the combination *redneck* conveys its own additional meaning: 'one who has a red neck, an ordinary, generally reactionary laborer'. The determination of units of meaning for any such elements and combinations is one of the most difficult areas in the study of language. And the identification of such units will occupy students of language for some time to come. In past study, various labels have been given to "units of meaning," such as *sememe, noeme, semon;* the units as well as the labels proposed by one linguist often differ from those proposed by another. Here the term *sememe* will be used. It will apply to the smallest unit of meaning expressed by a lexical item, a qualifier, a pattern of order, an intonation pattern, or a modification pattern. Thus, the central meaning of **derk-* 'see' is a sememe, as is that of the negative qualifier, of the order pattern in *Hé did?* versus *Díd he?;* likewise that of the intonation pattern in *Did he leáve?* and the modulation pattern in Sanskrit (Skt.) *ihā́sti* < *ihá asti* 'he is here'. A sememe may be expressed by any lexical or syntactic device, although sememes referring to objects are likely to be expressed lexically and sememes referring to relationships between elements are likely to be expressed syntactically. To illustrate the variety of expression of a sememe, we may recall that the interrogative sememe may be expressed with a lexical element, as in Japanese *ka;* with an order pattern, as in *Did he?;* with an intonation pattern, as in *He did?;* or with a selectional indicator, as in Turkish *mi.* I view the interrogative sememe as a primitive. Yet sememes like those of such items as *sheep, man, γowi,* and **derk-*

are composites of semantic features, such as *animate, quadruped, woolly*. Such features may be combined in various ways in specific languages. Notably, features like *animate* may be found in lexical elements, as in English, or in grammatical elements, as in Bantu. In a grammar of any language, the lexical elements and the syntactic elements are generally treated as the basic units, with no thoroughgoing attempt to specify all the features of which they are composed. Here too we will deal with the lexical elements of PIE, like *man, sheep, see,* as basic elements, and will only pursue a complete analysis of composite inflectional elements when they occur, e.g., *-mi,* which is a first-person singular, primary ending, expressing accordingly at least three sememes.

If now a sentence like *The man saw the sheep* is to be generated, in keeping with Paul's definition the abstract elements which yield the lexical items *man, see, sheep* are combined with the rules for the syntactic unit, sentence. We will deal with lexical items in Chapter 6. At this point we will only note that in producing a linguistic description we must avoid duplication. For example, if we include the feature *animate* among our lexical elements, we will not assume distinct grammatical elements based only on this feature. That is to say, if we have a lexical class of animate nouns, we will not incorporate the feature *animate* as a distinctive feature in the set of grammatical elements labeled underlying cases. Accordingly we will not distinguish between two potential underlying cases, *dative* and *factitive,* on the grounds of the feature *animate.* As we will see below in the discussion of sentences, lexical and syntactic features are combined in various patterns to yield different meanings. Moreover, in different languages, specific features like those expressing time or place or sex may be incorporated in one or the other ingredient of language. In this way they contribute to the richness of language with economy of means.

The phrase-structure rules proposed here are assumed to be universal. Such an assumption is made for various reasons, not least that any child can learn any language whatsoever. This capability of children leads us to conclude that the sentences of every language are initially generated in accordance with a small number of rules; the differences ascertainable among languages are a consequence of transformational and lower-level rules.

The grammar proposed here generates nouns through abstract syntactosemantic categories which have been called cases but which I will refer to as K, from Panini's term *kāraka* for underlying case categories. In this way it resembles the Sanskrit grammar ascribed to Panini. In recent discussions grammars of this kind have been labeled case grammars (Fillmore 1968; Ananthanarayana 1970*b*).

1.3. The Phrase-Structure and Transformational Rules.

P Rule 1. $\Sigma \rightarrow$ Conj. Σ^n (optional; $n \geqslant 2$)

This rule permits coordination of two or more sentences by means of conjunctions.

P Rule 2. $\Sigma \rightarrow$ Q Prop.

This rule generates on the one hand those abstract elements which qualify the entire sentence; hence the abbreviation Q, for qualifier. On the other hand it generates the propositional elements, verb and K categories (see Rule 4 below). For the Lisu language of Thailand, Burma, China, and India, Edward R. Hope includes in this rule categories for presupposition and focus (1972). Rules for these functions are included elsewhere in the present grammar.

P Rule 3. Q $\rightarrow$ [± Dec.] [± Int.] [± Neg.] [± Mid.] [± Nec.] [± Vol.] [± Perf.] [± Mom.] [± Iter.] [± Caus.]

By means of this rule the sentence is determined to be either a factual declarative sentence or not. Similarly it is determined to be or not be interrogative, negative, middle, necessitative, volitional, perfective, momentary, iterative, and causative.

P Rule 4. Prop. $\rightarrow$ V (K categories)

By means of this rule a verb or a nominal predicate is produced for every sentence, optionally accompanied by a substantive in one of eight K categories:

Target (Complement)	Time
Receptor	Place
Agent	Source
Means (Instrument)	Manner

P Rule 5. $K \rightarrow \begin{Bmatrix} NP\ k^n \\ \Sigma \end{Bmatrix}$

By means of this "case-conversion" rule, K generates either a complement Σ or an NP (noun phrase) accompanied by k, that is, by preposed or postposed function words or by inflections selected in accordance with the lexical entries for V.

P Rule 6. NP → (Det.) N (Σ) (optional)
This rule permits embedding. Like all of the P rules it is governed by the order principle stated below. Thus, in OV languages the Σ is embedded before the noun (N); in VO languages it is embedded after N.

At this stage in the generation of sentences, lexical material comes to be associated with the grammatical rules. It must be remembered however that the "lexical material" is still in the form of lexical features, not surface manifestations of "words." The same is true for the prepositions, postpositions, or inflections generated by K.

For example, if the PIE sentence 'He saw the sheep = He has seen the sheep' were to be generated, at this point the lexical features underlying the verb stem **derk-* would be incorporated with the grammatical rules. Besides introducing the semantic features of **derk-*, this step would require the selection of a target from the set of K and the rejection of all other potential K categories. In this way the P rules are constrained by lexical features which subsequently would be expressed by the surface sentence:

5.	PIE	γówim̥	dedorke
		sheep	he-saw

In addition to the requirements exercised by the lexical constraints, at this stage in the generation of a sentence the principle must be applied which produces the fundamental order in the sentences of each language. This principle may be stated as follows:

$$\#\, Q\, V\, (N^{Obj.})\, (N^{Mod.})\, \# \rightarrow \left\{ \begin{array}{l} \#\, Q\, V\, (N^{Obj.})\, (N^{Mod.})\, \# \\ \#\, (N^{Mod.})\, (N^{Obj.})\, V\, Q\, \# \end{array} \right\}$$

By this principle noun objects ($N^{Obj.}$) are placed either before or after verbs. If objects are placed before verbs, the verb is followed by the categorial markers for qualifiers. If objects are placed after verbs, the Q categorial markers precede the verbs. Further, nominal modifiers ($N^{Mod.}$) are placed on the opposite side of nouns from that on which verbs stand with regard to their objects. This principle brings about the distinguishing characteristics of verb-object (VO) and object-verb (OV) languages.

As with any feature or characteristic of language, the features of the language governed by the principle may be undergoing change. When they are, the language in question is not a consistent language, though it may be predominantly VO or OV.

These rules are followed in application by a series of transformational rules which in large part determine the individual characteristics of any given language. The order of these and other rules is determined intrinsically rather than extrinsically; that is to say, the rules are selected throughout for their specific applications rather than by a sequence regulated by their position in the grammar. The transformational rules will accordingly only be identified in general here. In accordance with general theory, transformational rules apply to the output of the phrase-structure rules, that is, to P markers. In the generation of sentences a P marker based on phrase-structure rules accompanied by lexical entries appropriate for a given sentence is constructed after the application of P Rule 6, which in turn was applied after application of the lexical-entry constraint and the principle determining order. If then the PIE sentence for 'He saw the man who carried the sheep' were to be generated, a gross statement of the lexical and propositional features would be as follows:

6.	wīro-^{Agent}	γowi-^{Target}	bher-$^{\text{Perf.}}$	wīro-^{Target}	derk-$^{\text{Perf.}}$
	man	sheep	carry$^{\text{Perf.}}$	man	see$^{\text{Perf.}}$

The appropriate inflections result after application of the transformational rules.

Transformational rules are included for the following processes:

- Topicalization
- Complementation
- Deletion, as of equivalent noun phrases
- Agreement
- Relativization and relative-clause reduction
- Transportation of elements, such as the negative qualifier

In addition there are numerous rules which bring about the correct sequences and patterns in the surface structure; these are often referred to as "housekeeping rules."

After the application of such transformational rules, phonological rules produce the actually occurring forms, that is, the utterance. These processes will be sketched below as they apply to PIE. In most respects the surface forms of the individual PIE words will not differ from those which have been proposed during the past generation, as in Lehmann 1952. The major subsequent advances in our understanding of PIE grammar have to do with the order of constituents in the sentence and with the type of syntactic constructions found with characteristic orders that are generally labeled VO and OV.

1.4. A Syntactic Framework Based on Typological Study.

The syntactic framework used by Brugmann, Delbrück, and other Indo-Europeanists was based on Classical Greek and Latin. Since these languages were similar in the type of their syntactic constructions, the framework for all of the previous syntactic statements on PIE is distorted. It assumes constructions like those in languages in which objects consistently follow verbs, the VO languages. Earlier Indo-Europeanists did not take into account the syntactic patterns characteristic of OV languages, that is, languages in which objects consistently precede verbs, as may be illustrated by their comments on the OV comparative structures in the various dialects (Brugmann 1911:489). Moreover, they had no understanding of the relationship which exists between various syntactic patterns. The deficiencies in their descriptive and theoretical statements are due in great part to their limited attention to languages. The most likely non-Indo-European languages with which they dealt were Finnish and Hebrew or another Semitic language, all of which are VO. Accordingly their understanding of language was determined by information drawn from only one of the two basic types.

Such a restricted basis for linguistic theory is unfortunately not limited to our predecessors. The theoretical statements which are issued by members of the most vigorous school of transformationalists are based on the assumption that languages are VO in underlying structure. In accordance with this assumption the first P rule is commonly written

$$S \rightarrow NP^\frown Aux.^\frown VP$$

implying that every underlying sentence string (5) consists of a noun phrase, an auxiliary, and a verb phrase (Chomsky 1965:68). This rule brings about the further erroneous assumption that the subject is a major constituent of the underlying sentence. This assumption is also found in nineteenth-century syntactic studies influenced by Kant (Wackernagel 1926:28). Thus for Gottfried Hermann every sentence consists of a subject, predicate, and copula. Yet, as sentences in the early dialects illustrate and as studies by linguists dealing with non-Indo-European languages indicate, subjects are not essential components of sentences, especially in OV languages. Accordingly many of the transformational rules devised to place subjects appropriately or to delete them, especially from embedded sentences, are unnecessary in the grammars of many languages. These rules are required primarily for SVO languages, that is, languages which, like English, must have a subject as well as a verb and an object. The assumption that subjects are essential components of P rules has led to great misunderstanding of language and to much unnecessary work in recent linguistic study.

A set of simple sentences from a consistent VO language and a consistent OV language will illustrate the essential patterns, also referred to as stigmata, of the two basic types of language. The patterns illustrated will also illuminate the syntactic framework which we have proposed above in § 1.3, and indicate why we must assume for language generally a set of P rules in which the constituents are unordered.

1.4.1. Basic Sentence Patterns. The VO language used here is Arabic; the OV language is Turkish.

7. Relation of object to verb: 'He saw the dog.'

VO		OV	
šāhada	lkalb	köpegi	gördü
saw-he	the-dog	dog	saw-(he)

Further constructions involving "objects":

8. Comparatives: 'The dog is bigger than the cat.'

lkalb	akbar	min	lqiṭṭa	köpek	kediden	daha	büyük
the-dog (is)	bigger	than	the-cat	dog	cat-than	more	big

9. Prepositions versus postpositions: 'He saw the dog from the window.'

šāhada	lkalb	min	iššibak	pencereden	köpeği	gördü
saw-he	the-dog	from	the-window	window-from	dog	saw-(he)

For typological purposes the comparative construction and prepositional/postpositional constructions are to be regarded as verbal. In each of these constructions a constituent governs another constituent in much the same way as a verb governs an object. Accordingly in their underlying pattern of arrangement the three constructions *verb-object, adjective-pivot-standard,* and *preposition (postposition)–object* are identical. It may also be assumed that in the underlying structure V symbolizes an element much more general than is usually included under the rubric *verb.* For this reason the order of the three constructions illustrated in Examples 7, 8, and 9 is identical in consistent languages.

Examples of these constructions in Hittite, Vedic Sanskrit, and additional IE languages are given in Chapter 2 and subsequent chapters.

1.4.2. Nominal Modifying Constructions.

10. Relative constructions: 'He saw the dog which ate the meat.'

šāhada	lkalb	allaðii	'akala	'allaḥm	eti	yiyen	köpeği	gördü
saw-he	the-dog	which	ate-he	the-meat	meat	eating	dog	saw-(he)

11. Adjectival constructions: 'He saw the big dog.'

šāhada	lkalb	lkabir		büyük	köpeği	gördü
saw-he	the-dog	the-big		big	dog	saw-(he)

12. Genitival constructions: 'He saw the dog of his neighbor.'

šāhada	lkalb	ǰarih		komşunun	köpeğini	gördü
saw-he	the-dog	of-neighbor		his-neighbor's	dog	saw-(he)

As these examples illustrate, nominal modifiers consistently occupy the same position; this is the position, with regard to the noun, opposite that of the verb. This consistent placement of nominal modifiers can be understood when language is examined from a generative point of view. For adjectival and genitival constructions are derived from relative constructions. Accordingly, if relative constructions are placed either to the left or the right of nouns, adjectives and genitives will follow the same placement.

The placement of relative constructions can also be understood from a generative point of view. For the placement of objects with regard to their verbs is one of the fundamental rules of order, as noted in § 1.3. Subsequent constituents, such as modifiers, are accordingly so placed that they do not disrupt this relationship.

Examples from selected IE languages are given in Chapter 2 and subsequent chapters.

1.4.3. Verbal Modifying Constructions. The placement of nominal modifying constructions has long been understood. Recently it has become clear that verbal modifying constructions follow the same principle (Lehmann 1973*a*). Just as nominal modifiers are placed on the side of the noun opposite the verb, so verbal modifiers are placed on the side of the verb opposite the noun.

This understanding is so recent that the verbal modifiers concerned have not yet been completely identified. It is clear that the interrogative constituent and the negative constituent of the *qualifier* are two of these modifiers. Others must be identified and incorporated in our grammars. In such study the surface forms are often misleading. Thus the English nominal construction *the late president* seems parallel to *the big dog,* and accordingly *late* might be labeled adjectival and derived from a relative construction like *big.* But obviously *the late president* or *the former president* cannot be derived from *the president who is late* or *the president who is former.* In these phrases, then, *late* and *former* cannot be identified as adjectives in the same sense as is *big* in *the big dog.* In this way, the generative analysis concerned can be used as a discovery procedure for identifying structural classes in language. By such analysis, interrogation and negation can be viewed as primary verbal modifiers, but tense cannot, as the position of the tense marker in the Turkish examples below indicates.

13. Interrogative verbal modifiers: 'Did he see the dog?'

hal	šāhada	alkalba	köpeği	gördümü
?	saw-he	the-dog	dog	see-Past-(he)-?

14. Negative verbal modifiers: 'He didn't see the dog.'

ma	šāhada	alkalba	köpeği	görmedi
not	saw-he	the-dog	dog	see-not-Past

15. Interrogative, negative verbal modifiers: 'Didn't he see the dog?'

amo	šāhada	alkalba	köpeği	görmedimi
?-not	saw-he	the-dog	dog	see-not-Past-?

These examples may illustrate that verbal modifiers are placed in accordance with a specific hierarchy. The constituent for interrogation is placed closer to the beginning or end of the sentence than is the constituent for negation; that for negation is placed next, between the interrogative constituent and the verb. But other elements than the verb may be negated or questioned. When qualifiers are attached to such elements, the markers for them may be placed elsewhere in the sentence.

In contrast with the widespread similarity of order in expressions for the interrogative and negative qualifiers, expressions for tense follow idiosyncratic patterns. In these Turkish examples, the past marker *di* is not ordered in accordance with the same hierarchical principle as are those for the interrogative and negative. And, in the Arabic examples, tense is indicated by a different selectional device than are interrogative and negative. Because of such differences in indications of tense in many languages, I do not include tense among the verbal qualifiers (Lehmann 1973*a*). Problems having to do with verbal qualifiers will be examined in Chapter 3, as will the identification and placement of additional verbal modifiers besides those commented on here.

1.4.4. Pronominalization and the Expression of Reflexivization. For purposes of IE studies it must still be mentioned here that "pronominalization" is highly important. Like the role of the subject in language, pronominalization has been greatly misunderstood. Its description in many grammatical statements has been based on the subtype of VO languages which are known as SVO (subject-verb-object). This limited source of data has led many linguists to the erroneous opinion that pronouns are basic constituents of language and that basic grammatical processes like reflexivization are pronominal. The falsity of these opinions may be illustrated by examining examples of both VSO and SOV languages.

Surface pronouns may be used in both Arabic and Turkish, but, as the sentences in Example 7 illustrate, they are by no means mandatory. Both languages disclose the order of subjects with regard to objects if a specific subject must be expressed, as in 'John saw the dog.'

16.	šāhada	John	lkalb	John	köpeği	gördü
	saw-he	John	the-dog	John	dog	saw-(he)

Moreover, when the pronominal subject is emphasized, a specific pronoun can be used in both Arabic and Turkish, to correspond to a sentence like 'It was he who saw the dog.'

17.	šāhada	huwwa	alkalba	o	köpeği	gördü
	saw-he	he	the-dog	he	dog	saw-(he)

It should also be noted that the third person of the verb is an unmarked form. When other categorial information is to be conveyed in the verb form, such as number, person, or gender, this information is overtly expressed, often by special inflections. Some languages, however, like Japanese, have no verbal expression for these categories. The overt expression of such categories in the IE languages has obscured the linguistic significance of deixis, that is, the use of deictic elements, as categories which might be indicated in combination with verbs.

For our understanding of IE syntax it is particularly important to examine the expression of reflexivization in language. Both in VSO and in SOV languages reflexivization is indicated by means of verbal markers. Thus, in Turkish, the suffix *-in/ün-* is used to express the reflexive, as in *görünmek* 'to let oneself be seen, to appear'; as this gloss for *görünmek* illustrates, reflexives often have an intransitive meaning. They also have a meaning of "carrying out the action of the verb with regard to oneself," that is, a meaning category often referred to as "middle," as in Turkish *giyinmek* 'to get dressed' as opposed to *giymek* 'to dress'. We may compare the Sanskrit *vaste* 'get dressed', which is consistently inflected in the middle. The Greek cognate has an active form with a nasal suffix with the meaning 'to dress': *hénnumi,* but the middle form means 'get dressed', as in the following example from the Iliad:

18. 10.334. héssato d' éktosthen rhinòn polioîo lúkoio
he-got-dressed but outside pelt of-gray of-wolf
'but he dressed himself on the outside in the pelt of a gray wolf'

As these preliminary observations may suggest, the presence of a middle inflection in the early IE dialects, characterized by verbal suffixes, provides strong evidence that PIE was OV.

For our general understanding of language it is also noteworthy that the middle inflection was lost as the IE languages became VO. By the time of the *koinḗ* the middle was relatively infrequent in Greek. While some uses of middle forms have a reflexive use in the New Testament, it is curious that these are found in the writers with a native Semitic language, such as Matthew, Mark, and Peter; the native speakers of Greek, Luke and Paul, on the other hand have introduced reflexive pronouns, as in Luke 9:23.

19. arnēsásthō heautón
let-him-deny himself

This development to expression of reflexivization by means of a pronoun may be observed in all the IE dialects. An indication of its lateness is given by the diverse forms of the reflexive pronoun from dialect to dialect.

To illustrate the position of reflexivization in the hierarchy of qualifiers we may compare the following Arabic sentences; as the last indicates, the order of qualifier markers is Int., Neg., Refl. (reflexive). (Compare the expression for interrogative—*hal, a*—in Examples 13 and 15 and that for the negative—*ma*—in Example 14; *ta* expresses the reflexive).

20. adaba alwalada 'He educated the boy.'
educated-he the-boy

21. taʔadaba 'He educated himself > he behaved [himself].'
Refl.-educated-he

22. hal taʔadaba 'Did he behave?'
? Refl.-educated-he

23. ma taʔadaba 'He didn't behave.'
not Refl.-educated-he

24. ama taʔadaba 'Didn't he behave?'
?-not Refl.-educated-he

This discussion of the reflexivization qualifier may illustrate the problems concerned with the less adequately investigated verbal qualifiers, as well as their means of expression in the various types of language. To be sure, contemporary Arabic also has reflexives with a specific object, as in:

25. adaba nafsahu
educated-he soul-his
'He educated himself.'

This usage is an indication of development towards an SVO structure. In this way, the expression of qualifiers undergoes change, as do other characteristic features of languages besides the qualifiers. Other qualifiers will be discussed in the pertinent chapters of this book.

1.4.5. Postposed Coordinators and Absence of Verbal Prefixes as Characteristics of OV Languages. We may still note two further characteristics of OV languages: the absence of verbal prefixes and the position of coordinating conjunctions.

The absence of verbal prefixes can be accounted for by the principle expressed above, in § 1.3. Since in OV languages there is a strong bond between the object and the verb, elements modifying verbs in OV languages are placed in other positions than initially before verbs. OV languages are characteristically suffixing (Lehmann 1973*a*); and when verbal modifications like those associated with adverbs are introduced, the adverbial element is placed separately in the sentence, at some point before the object. The well-known absence of prefixes in PIE (Delbrück 1888:49–51; 1893:648–653; Meillet 1937:151) is in accordance with this situation and provides further strong evidence that PIE was OV.

While prefixes were gradually introduced, even in the early dialects, the further OV characteristic of postposed coordinating conjunctions was long maintained, even in late dialects like Latin. In consistent OV languages, coordinating conjunctions are placed after the conjoined nouns, as in Japanese:

26. zasshi to shimbun to o yonda
magazine and newspaper and Obj.-Ptc. (he)-read
'He read magazines and newspapers.'

We may compare Homeric expressions such as:

27. patḕr andrôn te theôn te
father of-men and of-gods and
'the father of men and gods'

Also the Latin:

28.	sēque	remque	pūblicam	cūrābant
	self-and	affair-and	public	they-took-care

'They took care of themselves and of the public welfare.'

(Delbrück 1897:512–513; 1900:49–50). When one of the conjunctions was omitted, it was the first, as in the well-known *senātus populusque* 'senate and people' of Latin. We may conclude from the survival of this usage in Vedic Sanskrit, Greek, and other early dialects that coordination provides further evidence of the OV structure of PIE.

1.5. Marked versus Unmarked Patterns in Language.

The syntactic patterns we have examined so far are those normally expected. In recent linguistic study there has been a great deal of attention to nonnormal patterns. Carrying a special meaning or mark, these have come to be known as *marked* in contrast with the normal or unmarked patterns. As the term *normal* suggests, unmarked patterns carry no special connotation or heightened feeling. When however such meanings are intended, the nonnormal or marked pattern is commonly used. It is particularly favored in poetry or elevated prose, as examples from Milton may indicate, such as the opening line of the concluding stanza in *Lycidas,* with the subject following the verb:

29. Thus sang the uncouth Swain to th' Okes and rills

In much the same way, the earliest materials in Indo-European abound in marked patterns, for they follow literary conventions, as in the third stanza of the eminent hymn to soma:

30.	Rigveda (RV) 8.48.3.	ápāma	sómam	amŕ̥tā	abhūma
		we-have-drunk	soma	immortals	we-have-become
		áganma	jyótir	ávidāma	devā́n
		we-have-approached	the-light	we-have-found	the-gods

'We have drunk soma; we have become immortals; we have come to the light; we have found the gods.'

The three-sentence-initial verbs in these lines of exhilaration illustrate the marked use of word order which we find in the Veda, in Homer, and in much else of the earliest surviving material. Because of the characteristic use of marked order in such materials, we must be careful in our choice of typical material when carrying out linguistic analysis.

We must also be careful in our choice of the characteristic patterns, or stigmata, of OV and VO languages. Among the patterns discussed in § 1.4, some are susceptible to rearrangement for marking, such as the basic sentence pattern and the position of adjectives and genitives with regard to their nouns. Others are rearranged with difficulty, such as comparatives; it is unlikely that an English poet would produce an OV comparative construction such as *the oaks house from high* to express *the oaks are higher than the house.* Still other characteristic patterns can be rearranged relatively readily, such as the shift of a postposition to prepositional order, as was common in Classical Sanskrit and Greek. For this reason we ascribe great importance to constructions like the comparative in determining the basic patterns of individual languages. Other patterns, however, often reveal the trend of development in a language if it is undergoing change of syntactic type. In the course of time, then, marked patterns may become predominant in a language and in this way contribute to its change in basic type.

1.6. Consistent and Inconsistent Languages.

Obviously languages change in their syntax as in their phonology. When they do, we may expect to find a combination of OV and VO patterns, as we do in Classical Sanskrit, Greek, and Latin. It is rare that we find a highly consistent language. Even French and Spanish, which have all the patterns of VO languages, show the OV word order with a small group of common adjectives. English is less consistent, inasmuch as it shows the OV word order of adjectives generally. Besides determining the consistency of type for languages, linguists must attempt to determine characteristic features of inconsistent languages. When languages are even less consistently regulated in order, so that constructions like adjectives and nouns or genitives and nouns show no characteristic order, I have labeled such languages ambivalent. In this book I will not include studies of patterns to be expected in inconsistent or ambivalent languages; but some characteristic constructions of such languages will be noted here briefly.

Absolute constructions are a characteristic of ambivalent languages. We account for them by assuming that when languages are neither OV nor VO, embedding can occur either before the OV constituent of complex sentences or after it. The embedded sentence cannot then be consistently placed with reference to a noun, in the normal way for relative constructions. Accordingly a nonrelating, or absolute, construction develops (Lehmann 1972*b*).

Possibly one more characteristic of languages undergoing syntactic change is the development of a grammatical form which is both verbal and nominal, the so-called verbal noun. Like absolute constructions, verbal nouns are reduced forms of sentences, often sentences without objects. But most of the details concerning their situation in the structure of specific language types have not been determined.

The situation of nominal compounds presents similar difficulties. Jacobi suggested that they were equivalent to subordinate constructions (1897). Unfortunately his views, like those of many earlier linguists, are colored by the notion that PIE (his *Grundsprache*) and pre-IE (his *Ursprache*) were primitive and that for this reason the prior element of nominal compounds did not show inflection. We now assume that PIE was by no means primitive or in any grammatical way inferior to languages in use today. Our treatment of its compounds must accordingly be comparable to our treatment of compounds in contemporary languages.

Morphologically we derive nominal compounds from simple sentences, like those presented in Chapter 2. But in compound formations the "case-conversion rules" do not apply, and hence we do not find inflection of the prior element. This assumption however does not solve the syntactic problem of their origin or their presence in a language. Compounds made up of nominal plus verbal elements seem to be relatively infrequent in OV languages, as in Hittite, where we find few such compounds. Further study is necessary, however, to support this assumption.

Further study is also necessary with regard to the phenomenon of apposition. Apposition, in contrast with relative constructions, does not seem to be regulated by the principle given above for the order of modifiers. On the other hand, it also seems to follow different order rules from those applying to titles. As the Japanese *Tanaka-san* in contrast with English *Mr. Middleton* may indicate, titles are treated like the heads of nominal constructions. For this reason they are placed closest to the verb in an object-verb sequence:

31. Tanaka-san o mita
'I saw Mr. Tanaka'

They maintain this position in all nominal constructions.

But appositives are not placed on such a basis. Unfortunately most studies of apposition are restricted to a single language or to a single type of language. Until more general studies are undertaken, our treatment of apposition in an explanatory syntax can only be preliminary.

1.7. Aims of a Syntactic Treatment of PIE.

A new syntactic treatment of PIE, as mentioned above, cannot merely be descriptive, that is, merely a summary of the data. Rather, it must analyze and present the data in accordance with a specific framework and relate the various constructions. That is to say, it must be explanatory.

On the other hand it is unnecessary to list scores of examples representing each dialect. We know that the various dialects are related, and if a variety of evidence is desired it can be found in the works of Delbrück, Brugmann, and many others whose materials are readily accessible. A large number of examples, especially if they are taken from texts as widely separate as those of the second millennium B.C. and the second millennium A.D., will do little but obscure an attempt to present the syntax of PIE.

In the aim to be explanatory any grammar must take into account the various processes or means of syntax. These have been grouped by Leonard Bloomfield under four headings: selection, arrangement or order, modification, and modulation or intonation (Bloomfield 1933:184; Lehmann 1972*c*:111). These four groups make up a coherent set of the processes or means *(Mittel)* enumerated by Paul (1920:123–124); see also Brugmann, who takes into account only selection, arrangement, and modulation (1925). Of these four processes of syntax, IE studies of the nineteenth century have dealt exhaustively with selection, so exhaustively that little can be added to their descriptions except for the subsequently discovered materials, such as the Anatolian and Tocharian. Arrangement however was inadequately understood until very recently, as noted in § 1.4, and accordingly is poorly treated in earlier syntactic statements. A current description of arrangement in accordance with the findings of typology will also bring about reinterpretations and improved statements of the principles of selection in PIE. These improved statements will draw heavily on previous work, as on Delbrück's three volumes of the *Grundriss* and the various "case grammars" published near the end of the century, such as Gaedicke's (1880), Heinrich Winkler's (1896), and M. J. van Meer's (1901).

Modification, or sandhi, has also been well described. An excellent basis for these descriptions was available in Indic grammar. Again, a current grammar draws heavily on earlier statements.

Our least adequate description is in the field of intonation. We are fortunate in having early texts that are accented, in Vedic Sanskrit. And the information we derive from these texts can be supplemented by data gleaned from phonological information gathered from other dialects, as from patterns of alliterative verse in Proto-Germanic and its dialects. But, as for any language known only from written records or from reconstructions based on these, the intonation of sentences in PIE is difficult to reconstruct. The statements on the role of intonation in IE syntax are accordingly much more tentative than are those on the other three syntactic processes.

For an understanding of PIE syntax, the role of each of these processes must be related. A sentence in PIE is generated by selection of word classes and inflected subsets of these arranged in various patterns, which are subject to sandhi changes and delimited by specific patterns of intonation. We must attempt to determine the operations carried out under each of these processes as fully as the selection classes in earlier grammars were determined. Such an aim requires thorough analysis of our data and accurate evaluation of the chronological layers in the various dialects.

This aim also requires a different use of the methods of historical linguistics than was made by nineteenth-century scholars. Their syntactic analyses rely heavily on the comparative method. Use of this method can however lead to contrastive statements rather than reconstruction of earlier stages of the language. An example is the "reconstructed" relative construction (Delbrück 1900:295–406). In spite of the variety of relative particles and relative constructions from dialect to dialect, scholars assumed "that the stem **i̯o-* was relative already in PIE and that it was the only relative particle of this period" (Delbrück 1900:405). Moreover, they paid little attention to the arrangement of the relative clause with regard to its antecedent. When Hittite with its preposed relative constructions was investigated, the nineteenth-century view was modified but by no means abandoned (see Raman 1973 for details). Interpreting properly the Hittite data and taking into consideration the many preposed relative constructions of Vedic as well as other details that will be examined below, we must conclude that the PIE relative construction was like those of OV languages; the variety of particles and relative constructions indicates that each dialect developed its own VO type relative construction as these dialects came to be more and more VO in structure. But relying only on the comparative method we would arrive at the same results reported by Delbrück. Rather than a reconstruction of the PIE phenomena of 3000 B.C., the proposed *yo-* relative clause represents a contrastive construction of the situation in the archaic dialects around 1000 B.C. We can reconstruct the earlier phenomena only if we analyze the various attested constructions in accordance with a framework based on universals.

Such reconstructions are made under the assumption that PIE was a changing language much like those languages for which we have texts. I do not assume that it was consistently OV, especially in its later stages. Further, the syntax described here represents only one stage in the development of the reconstructed language from which the various dialects developed. Moreover, this syntactic description is by no means complete, though the majority of the constructions are described, as may be determined from the adequacy of the syntax in analyzing and generating characteristic sentences as illustrated at the conclusion of Chapter 5.

1.8. Bases of Our Data.

Among the data available from the various dialects we must still draw heavily on those monuments which were of greatest importance to our predecessors, notably Vedic Sanskrit and Homeric Greek. The prose texts in Vedic provide some of our best evidence; fortunately for syntactic studies, these have been comprehensively studied by Delbrück. His definitive statement was published in his *Altindische Syntax* of 1888, the conclusions of which were used in his syntax of PIE (1893, 1897, 1900). Our improvements with reference to these materials consist largely in greater awareness of the chronological strata in the Rigveda; the evidence for determining such strata, as well as the sorting out of the various poems, we owe in large part to E. Vernon Arnold's *Vedic Metre* of 1905. After his study we give our greatest credence to evidence taken from the two oldest periods of Rigvedic hymns, named by him Archaic and Strophic. Yet recent philological studies, particularly the insights into epic tradition opened up by Milman Parry, indicate that ancient linguistic patterns may be preserved as part of a poet's stock; the late layers of the Rigveda may accordingly contain very archaic patterns. In short, we must evaluate our materials sensitively, with all the assistance we can find in careful editions and interpretations of the ancient texts.

Such procedures are not less important for the materials which have become available since our standard syntactic treatments were produced, notably those in the Anatolian languages, the Greek of Linear B, and Tocharian. Of these, the Tocharian texts are the least valuable for studies in the syntax of Proto-Indo-European, because they consist largely of translations and because they are so late. The texts of Linear B unfortunately are short and comparable rather to the files of a tax accountant than to the type of material which is especially valuable for syntactic studies. On the other hand the Anatolian documents, notably the Hittite texts, are of the greatest importance. They provide us with materials which are at least of the age of the Archaic Rigvedic hymns and the inscriptions in Linear B. But we must also use them with care.

First of all, we must attempt to sort out influences of other languages. Apparently in various periods of the Hittite empire the Hittite scribes knew Akkadian, possibly even Sumerian, and also some languages which need considerably more philological and linguistic study, such as Hurrian and Hattic. All of these languages may have influenced the literary Hittite and the bureaucratic Hittite which make up most of our texts. As in the use of Vedic Sanskrit and Greek texts, we must rely heavily on the few specialists who have mastered the various disciplines necessary for a proper understanding of the documents.

One of the results of their study is a demarcation of the various strata of Hittite materials. Hittite scholars now distinguish between Old Hittite and Late Hittite texts. Obviously Indo-Europeanists will find the Old Hittite texts of greatest importance for their purposes. Thanks to scholars like Johannes Friedrich, Annelies Kammenhuber, and Heinrich Otten, these texts have been identified and are being made available in excellent editions. They have added an important new perspective to our sources of evidence, and their availability would of itself require the production of a new syntax of PIE, apart from the demands aroused by our greater understanding of syntax.

Without the careful philological work of numerous specialists, IE studies would be impossible. Yet unfortunately we cannot give appropriate credit to all of these specialists, for the list of their writings would yield an annotated bibliography far longer than this book. Not even all the syntactic treatments can be listed, though brief reference may be made here to standard works in which the characteristic constructions are discussed. For Indic the grammars of Speyer, as well as the works of Delbrück and more recently those of Jan Gonda are essential. As noted above, the grammars of Schwyzer for Greek and Leumann-Hofmann-Szantyr for Latin provide huge compendia on the scholarship as well as the data. For Anatolian the best resume of syntactic data is that in Johannes Friedrich's grammar; Hans Jensen provides similarly compact data for Armenian. For Slavic the treatments of Miklosich and Wenzel Vondrák are standard; for Lithuanian, that of Alfred Senn. There are unfortunately no comprehensive syntactic statements for Tocharian and Celtic; data on the interpretation of syntactic constructions must be gleaned from handbooks, monographs, and articles. For Germanic, Grimm's grammar is important, especially when supplemented by the excellent syntax of Jean Fourquet. These and a severely restricted list of monographs and articles are listed in the bibliography, though the editions of texts and dictionaries, without which IE linguistic study would be impossible, cannot be included, for reasons of space. But virtually any of the works cited, or Wackernagel's justly celebrated *Vorlesungen über Syntax,* will provide access to further studies and will illustrate the extent of our debt to many earlier Indo-Europeanists and general linguists.

1.9. Outline of the Book.

This treatment of PIE syntax will consist of a chapter on the syntax of simple sentences, followed by two chapters on complex sentences, two further chapters on syntactic categories and lexical entries, and a final chapter outlining some of the developments from the parent language to related dialects.

Chapter 2 on the syntax of simple sentences will deal largely with surface patterns. The essential constituent of the sentence is the verb, as I have demonstrated in my paper entitled "Converging theories in linguistics" (Lehmann 1972*a*). The simple sentence may consist minimally of a verb, or of a verb accompanied by a mandatory nominal element and in addition by optional nominal elements. The four syntactic processes will be examined preliminarily for their use in PIE sentences.

Chapter 3 will deal with nominal modifiers. These are largely introduced by embedding, through P Rule 6. The chapter will therefore have to treat more extensively than does Chapter 2 the underlying patterns of syntax.

Chapter 4 will deal with verbal modifiers and with complements. These may be introduced by embedding, through P Rule 5, or by coordination, through P Rule 1. As in Chapter 3, a great deal of attention must be given to underlying patterns.

Chapter 5 will deal with the syntactic categories of PIE which are used in the constructions of its sentences. Besides coordination and subordination or embedding, these are involved in the syntactic devices of substitution, the use of function words, and the patterns of congruence and government. At the conclusion of the chapter, the adequacy of the grammar will be demonstrated with selected sentences.

Chapter 6 will present selected lexical entries, indicating those elements which are represented in lexical items and their interrelationship with the elements expressed in grammatical categories.

In Chapter 7 the developments of syntactic patterns in selected dialects will be sketched, particularly to illustrate the changes involved in the shift from an OV to a VO structure. In this way the study of IE syntax will illuminate the use of language generally. For by the examination of changes we can gain insights into the structure of language, such as the fundamental importance of some syntactic patterns, like that of the sentence, and the dependence on this of many other syntactic patterns, such as arrangements of subordinate constructions and even morphological structure (Lehmann 1973*a*). Since the materials which we have available for the study of the IE languages span an extent equal to that available in Sino-Tibetan and Afro-Asiatic, but far greater than for most language families, the examination of their syntactic changes provides some of the best evidence we have for insights into man's use of language and particularly into the processes and causes involved in its change.

2. The Syntax of Simple Sentences

2.1. The OV Structure of PIE as Demonstrated by Vedic.

Linguists have generally maintained that the sentence is the basic unit of language (Brugmann 1904*a*:623, Paul 1920:121). Linguistic analysis, whether of attested or reconstructed languages, must therefore concern itself in the first instance with the sentence. This chapter examines the forms of the simple sentence in PIE. It will be followed by chapters dealing with modifiers of its constituents, with syntactic categories, and with selected lexical entries.

As noted in Chapter 1, the fundamental order of sentences in PIE is OV. Support for this assumption is evident in the oldest texts of the materials attested earliest in the IE dialects. The fundamental order of sentences in these early dialects cannot be determined solely by frequency of sentence patterns. For, like other linguistic constructions, sentence patterns manifest marked as well as unmarked order. Marked order is expected in literary materials. The documents surviving from the earliest dialects are virtually all in verse or in literary forms of prose. Accordingly many of the individual sentences do not have the unmarked order, with verb final. For this reason conclusions about the characteristic word order of PIE and the early dialects will be based in part on those syntactic patterns that are rarely modified for literary and rhetorical effect: comparative constructions, the presence of postpositions and prepositions, and the absence of prefixes, as well as the other patterns discussed in § 1.4. All of these constructions, as well as the basic sentence pattern, provide evidence that PIE was OV in structure.

Berthold Delbrück, the great syntactician of IE, assembled the pertinent data for Vedic Sanskrit and arrived at conclusions about these syntactic patterns which would lead to the characterization of PIE as OV. But he did not discuss the interrelationships between the individual syntactic constructions or the importance of fundamental sentence order, whether VO or OV. Yet, since the data for Vedic Sanskrit were given by him, evidence in Indic for the word order of PIE will be cited first.

2.1.1. Basic Sentence Pattern and Further Verbal Constructions (Delbrück 1888:17).

1. Śatapathabrāhmaṇa (ŚB) 1.3.2.15.	víśaḥ	kṣatríyāya	balíṃ	haranti
	villagers	to-prince	tax	they-pay

'The villagers pay taxes to the prince.'

Comparative constructions, with the pattern *standard* ('ghee')-*pivot* (ablative)-*comparative* ('sweeter') (Delbrück 1888:113):

2. RV 8.24.20.	ghṛtā́t	svā́dīyaḥ
	ghee-from	sweeter

'sweeter than ghee'

In many of Delbrück's examples this construction is breaking down, for they exhibit the order *comparative-pivot-standard,* as in:

3. Taittirīya Saṁhitā (TS) 5.1.2.3.	pā́pīyān	áśvād	gardabháḥ
	lesser	horse-from	donkey

'A donkey is less valuable than a horse.'

But even though the order typical for OV languages is being abandoned, there are few examples in Vedic Sanskrit of a comparative construction expressing the pivot with a particle, as in VO languages like English (Delbrück 1888:196). Accordingly, evidence in Indic suggests that the inherited pattern of the comparative construction was OV. This assumption is supported by evidence from Hittite, Greek, and other dialects which will be given below.

Postpositions Rather than Prepositions. Delbrück states as a general principle that the genuine prepositions "traditionally stand behind the case form they govern" (1888:21). His section on these (1888:440–470) contains many examples, of which the first is:

4. ŚB 1.2.1.12.	yád	imā́ṅl	lokā́n	áti	caturthám	ásti
	what	these	worlds	beyond	fourth	it-is

'What is fourth beyond these [three] worlds.'

The evidence in Vedic for postpositions accordingly supports strongly the conclusion that the word order of PIE was OV.

2.1.2. Evidence from Nominal Modifying Constructions, Such as Relative Clauses. Since relative clauses will be discussed at length in the following chapter, Delbrück's conclusions may simply be noted here about the position of the relative clause with regard to its antecedent in Vedic. Both in poetry and in prose relative clauses commonly precede their antecedent when it is *tá* (Delbrück 1888:559, 564). John Avery (1881) found that relative clauses preceded main clauses in more than 50 percent of the "nearly 4,000" passages in the Rigveda.

5. RV 2.13.2.	yás	tā́kṛṇoḥ	prathamáṃ	sā́sy	ukthyàḥ
	who	these-things-you-did	first,	that-you-are	to-be-praised

'You who did these things first are to be praised.'

(The literal translation given here is clumsy; actually the *sa* introducing the second clause is a reflex of a sentence-introductory particle rather than a pronoun, as we came to know when Hittite was analyzed.) Another of Delbrück's examples shows the same construction in the plural:

6. Aitareya Brahmāna (AB) 3.34.1.	ye	'ṅgārā	āsaṅs	te	'ṅgiraso	'bhavan
	who	coals	were	these	Angiras	became

'Those who were coals became Angiras.'

As might be expected from the position of relative clauses, descriptive adjectives also precede their nouns (Delbrück 1888:19–20):

7.	mānuṣī́	vā́k
	'human	voice'

Attributive genitives also precede the nouns they modify (Delbrück 1888:19–20):

8.	devā́nāṃ	hótā
	of-the-gods	priest

'priest of the gods'

Nominal modifying constructions accordingly support the conclusions concerning OV word order.

2.1.3. Evidence from Absence of Prefixation, from Conjunctions, and from Gapping. Three further characteristics of arrangement described by earlier scholars provide evidence of OV word order. The first is the absence of prefixes. Antoine Meillet states flatly that PIE did not contain prefixes (1937:151). Delbrück concludes that "prepositions" are not combined with verbs (1888:44–51). For often they follow the verb; but when they precede it, other words may stand between the "preposition" and the verb.

9. TS 2.1.10.3. ápa támaḥ pāpmā́naṃ hate
away darkness evil she-drives
'She drives off darkness and sin.'

Vedic accordingly provides evidence that there were no prefixes in PIE, in keeping with Meillet's conclusion.

Conjunctions follow rather than precede the second or further word of a conjoined series (Delbrück 1888:22). For the most frequent of these, *ca,* Hermann Grassmann gives many examples, as Delbrück indicates (1888:474).

10. RV 1.12.10. yajñáṃ havíś ca
sacrifice libation and
'sacrifice and libation'

Gapping. Patterns of gapping still require much detailed investigation. But Vedic contains examples of OV gapping, in which the identical verb is deleted from the first of two conjoined clauses and maintained in the second, as in the following example (Ptc. = particle):

11. RV 1.102.7. út te śatā́n maghavann úc ca bhū́yasa
Ptc. your 100-from O-blessed Ptc. and more

út sahásrād ririce kṛṣṭíṣu śrávaḥ
Ptc. 1000-from exceeds among-men glory

'Your glory, O blessed one, exceeds more than a hundred, even more than a thousand among men.'

The two clauses conjoined by *ca,* introduced by *úd (út, úc),* have the verb deleted in the first.

On the basis of the above-listed characteristics of OV structure, it is clear that Vedic Sanskrit was largely OV, even though VO patterns were being introduced. Moreover, the Vedic evidence strongly supports the conclusion that the earlier language was essentially OV.

2.1.4. Order of Nominal Sentences. In accordance with the OV structure of sentences containing objects and verbs, sentences containing predicate substantives may be expected to have the order *topic–predicate substantive.* This is the order in Hittite:

12. J. Friedrich 1960:117-118.
attaš aššuš
father good
'The father [is] good.'

13. J. Friedrich 1959:72, § 42.
I GÍN KUBABBAR kuššan šet
1 shekel silver reward his
'One shekel of silver [is] his reward.'

As Friedrich points out, when such sentences were in the past tense, the copula could not be omitted and had to be placed at the end of the sentence. For this reason I now consider erroneous my earlier assumption that the Sanskrit order N . . . Pred N was marked (Lehmann 1969: 10–11). For Vedic as well as Hittite and PIE, the unmarked order must have the predicate noun or adjective in final position, as in:

14. RV 8.48.15.
tvám naḥ soma viśváto vayodhā́s
thou to-us soma on-all-sides strength-giver
'Thou, soma, should be our strength-giver on all sides.'

Predicate noun and adjective sentences are accordingly parallel with sentences containing verbs in having the "verbal" element at the end of the sentence. They may also be expanded with optional substantival phrases and in this way show expansions of the types discussed below.

2.2. Evidence from Hittite for OV Structure of PIE.

In support of the assumption that OV structure must be assumed for PIE, material will be cited from Hittite, with references to similar patterns in other dialects.

For Hittite the examples included here contain evidence for six selected patterns of OV order, without having a special sentence exemplifying each, for each example contains two or more of the patterns.

Verb-final order and order of adjectives with regard to their nouns are illustrated in the following sentence (Otten and Souček 1969:18, § 14):

15. DUMU.É.GAL šuppi watar parā epzi
nobleman pure water preverb he-brings
'The nobleman brings pure water.'

A proposed genitive, *anzēl,* and the OV comparative pattern with *TI-anni* as standard are represented in the following example (J. Friedrich 1960: 127):

16. namma- kan anzēl TI-anni *UL ŠA BELU-NI* TI-tar nakki
moreover Ptc. of-us life (Dat.-Loc.) not Gen.-Ptc. lord-our life important
'Moreover, (if) the life of our lord is not more important than our life . . .'

An instance of a postposition, *piran,* and of a preposed relative clause is found in the following example; this example also illustrates the placement of verbal complements before the finite verb *akuwanna* (Raman 1973:58):

17. man LUG[A]Lwaš piran šeškanzi kuiš hazzizzi
when king before they-sleep who he-acts-appropriately

nu- šše GEŠTIN-an akuwanna pianzi
Ptc. to-him wine to-drink they-give

'When they sleep before the king, then people give wine to the one who acts appropriately.'

Accordingly, nominal modifiers, that is, relative constructions, genitives, and adjectives are consistently placed before nouns; the postpositional constructions and the order of comparative constructions and clause order are also OV. Hittite materials accordingly support the conclusion that PIE was OV.

2.3. Evidence from Other Dialects for OV Structure of PIE.

The other early dialects also support these conclusions about OV order; examples will be given here primarily from Greek, with supplementary materials in other dialects.

The basic word order of simple sentences is OV in early Greek (Schwyzer 1950:693–696), as illustrated in the first clause of the Odyssey:

18. Odyssey 1.1. ándra moi énnepe
man to-me you-tell-of
'Tell me about a man . . . '

Early Latin also has OV order (Leumann 1965:397–398), as in an example from *Archaic Inscriptions* (Warmington 1959:154):

19. Honce loucom nequs violatod
this grove no-one he-should-violate
'No one should violate this grove.'

In comparative constructions the standard is indicated by the genitive in the oldest Greek texts, and this commonly precedes the adjective (Schwyzer 1950:98–101). In this use the genitive replaces the ablative:

20. Iliad 16.722. aíth', hóson hḗssōn eimí,
Oh, to-what-extent weaker I-am

tóson	séo	phérteros	eíēn
to-that-extent	from-you	stronger	I-might-be

'I wish I were as much stronger than you as I am weaker.'

For Latin an example of the preceding standard in the ablative may be illustrated with *quō* in the following quotation (Leumann 1965:136, 162–163.

21\. Vergil, Aeneid 1.544.

Aenēās,	quō	iūstior	alter
Aeneas	from-whom	more-perfect	another

nec	pietāte	fuit
not-ever	in-piety	he-was

'Aeneas, than whom no other was ever more perfect in his piety.'

While case forms were commonly used in the earliest Greek texts to indicate nominal relationships in the sentence, they could be supplemented with particles, which subsequently developed into prepositions. As in Hittite and Vedic, these often followed their nouns, and accordingly they must be viewed as postpositions in OV languages (Schwyzer 1950:417–421).

22\. Iliad 11.50.

ásbestos	dè	boḕ	génet'	ēō̃thi	pró
unquenchable	but	cry	it-arose	Dawn	before

'But an unquenchable cry arose before Dawn.'

In Latin this position of "prepositions" was so frequent that it was given a special name, anastrophe (Leumann 1965:214–217, 692–693). It is particularly notable in frozen expressions, such as *mēcum* 'with me', *sēcum* 'with himself'.

Moreover, prepositional adverbs were used in conjunction with verbs, but not as prefixes (Schwyzer 1950:419–424; Leumann 1965:214–215). Many syntactic patterns subsequently maintained in the dialects give evidence of this situation, such as the use of "separable prefixes" in German today: *aufführen* 'produce' but *er führt . . . auf* 'he produces', and the placing of particles between the apparent verbal prefix and the verb root in some Gothic forms, such as *ga-u-laubjats* 'do you two believe' (see Streitberg 1920:161). Another such pattern is the use of a prefix with only the first of two verbs, as in Xenophon, Cyropaedia 7.1.1.:

23\. prosḗnegkan hoi therápontes empieȋn kaì phageȋn (*not* emphageȋn)
'The servants brought [things] to drink and to eat.'

As an OV language, PIE did not have prefixes. The prefixes introduced when the dialects became VO were not integrated into them for some time, as these examples demonstrate.

Relative constructions in an OV language may have finite or nonfinite forms preposed to nouns. Japanese formerly had a special attributive verb form which was used before nouns and particles, but in contemporary standard Japanese the normal finite forms are used attributively to provide relative constructions. In Turkish, on the other hand, special forms are used in relative constructions and are called participles. When the IE dialects were becoming VO, only this participial construction was found in place of relative constructions, as in Greek:

24. Odyssey 9.259.

hēmeȋs	toi	Troíēthen	apoplagkhthéntes	Akhaioì
we	indeed	from-Troy	returning-back	Achaeans

'We are Achaeans who are returning from Troy.'

As is well-known, such participial constructions could be placed either before or after the nouns they modified, as in the following example:

25. Iliad 24.3.

autàr	Akhilleùs
but	Achilles

klaȋe	phílou	hetárou	memnēménos
he-wept	dear	friend	remembering

'But Achilles wept, remembering his friend.'

Such participial constructions came to be widely used in the various IE dialects and eventually were not associated with relative constructions. Yet in early materials they cannot simply be treated as adjectival participles, as in the following example cited by Schwyzer (1950:392, also 618–619):

26. Odyssey 5.6.

méle	gár	hoi	eȍn	en	dṓmasi	númphēs
it-worried	for	to-her	being	in	house	of-the-goddess

'For he who was in the house of the goddess was a concern to her.'

In this example the participle *eȍn* is equivalent to a finite form of a clause, which generally was introduced by the relative pronoun *hós* in Greek.

The assumption that participles, like those in the examples cited above, were developments of PIE relative constructions with finite verbs may be supported by recalling an early use of adjectives which has long intrigued linguists (Wackernagel 1928:65–75). In this use the adjectives function as substantives modified by a relative construction:

27. Odyssey 14.257. pemptaîoi d'Aígupton eürreítēn hikómestha
as-fivers Egypt beautifully-watered we-came
'We who had traveled five days came to beautifully watered Egypt.'

Wackernagel gives further examples in his excellent discussion, in which he also indicates the puzzled attempts of previous scholars to explain this use (1928:67–68). When the adjectives are analyzed as reduced relative constructions, the use becomes clear. As Wackernagel indicates, the construction has been maintained to various periods of the dialects and is still characteristic of Slavic.

This adjectival construction in the early dialects also illuminates the view that descriptive genitives are derived from relative constructions. For many nominal modifiers are still expressed adjectivally in the early period, when later they are expressed through genitives. Again Wackernagel cites many examples (1928:68–74), such as *Nestoréē nēûs* 'Nestorian ship = Nestor's ship' and Paelignian *iouiois puclois* 'to Jovian boys = to the boys of Jupiter'. The parallelism between the adjectival and genitival attributes is nicely illustrated by one of Wackernagel's well-chosen quotations (1928:72):

28. Iliad 2.54. Nestoréēi parà nēȉ Puloigenéos basilêos
Nestorian beside ship of-Pylian-race of-king
'beside the ship of Nestor, the Pylian king'

These examples may illustrate the attributive constructions which developed in the early dialects from OV relative constructions: on the one hand, descriptive adjectives; on the other, genitives. As Wackernagel also indicates, they are further related to compounds and to patronymics (see also § 3.7).

The older pattern, of compound adjective as well as patronymic, is exemplified in:

29. Odyssey 1.30. tón rh' Agamemnonídēs tēleklutòs éktan' Oréstēs
him Ptc. Agamemnonian far-famed slew Orestes
'Him Orestes, the far-famed son of Agamemnon, killed.'

The older patronymic is combined with the younger genitive construction in:

30. Odyssey 1.429. Eurúklei', Ṓpos thugátēr Peisēnorídao
Eurycleia of-Ops daughter of-Peisenorid
'Eurycleia, daughter of Ops, the son of Peisenor.'

In time the genitive construction came to be more frequent than the adjective, which as Wackernagel states (1928:74) has come to be restricted to indicating characteristics in some dialects and no longer is used to indicate relationships.

The selected syntactic patterns discussed here illustrate that many syntactic features of PIE and the dialects can be accounted for by assuming that PIE was OV in structure and that it was developing to a VO language at the time of the early dialects. Many OV characteristics are found in the IE dialects spoken today, even those which are basically VO; such are the adjective-noun order of English and this order for a restricted number of French adjectives. The description of such patterns in their change through five millennia of history of each dialect is a task for the specialists in these dialects. A unidirectional change cannot simply be assumed, for external influences may have reintroduced OV patterns in VO languages (Lehmann 1970*a*:286–305). But on the basis of patterns such as those cited from the early dialects, PIE can be assumed to be OV. Its various sentence patterns are examined below.

2.4. The Structure of the Simple Sentence in PIE.

When the simple sentence is discussed in studies of PIE syntax it is generally assumed that the minimal sentence consists of two elements: a subject and a predicate. Moreover, in keeping with this assumption, sentences which consist of one element are considered aberrant. The so-called impersonal sentences, like those referring to natural events, e.g., Lat. *pluit* 'It's raining', are treated as fragments. At best, the second singular imperative is recognized as a complete sentence. The point of view which led to these conclusions is based on experience restricted to Indo-European languages. The scholars who characterized one-word sentences in this way did not take OV languages into account. In OV languages a sentence is characterized by a verb, accompanied or not by a substantive; if there is a substantive, it is in the first instance an object rather than a subject. Accordingly, Indo-Europeanists and linguists in general must modify their views of sentence structures in language.

In conversation between two friends the following statements are natural in Japanese.

31. Taroo o yonda
Taroo Obj. Ptc. called (past of *yobu* 'call')
'I called Taroo.'

32. Taroo o yonda ka (*ka* = Int. Ptc.)
'Did you call Taroo?'

33. Wakatta
'I understand' < 'have perceived'.

All of these sentences, like many sentences in OV languages, lack explicit subjects. The simple sentence of PIE may then be expected to consist of a verb and, depending on the lexical characteristics of the verb, one or more objects in addition. A subject, like expressions of time, place, and manner, would be optional, not mandatory. But for transitive verb forms an object would be mandatory. It is the influence of Western logic, based on the sentence patterns of Greek when it was already largely SVO, that has led linguists to assume for the simple sentence pattern of language a structure consisting of subject and predicate, whether expressed in this way or by the base rule: S → NP VP. Investigation of VSO languages as well as of (S)OV languages leads to the conclusion that the subject is far less central in the sentence than is the object, without taking into consideration the verb, which is the essential element, as we have noted in Chapter 1.

The so-called impersonal sentences accordingly exemplify the simplest form of PIE sentences. Among the best-known examples are those referring to natural events, such as:

34. Skt. várṣati, Lat. pluit, Goth. rigneiþ 'it is raining'

(For others see Brugmann 1925:22–24). As is also well known, when IE dialects became SVO in structure, so that a subject was required, the third singular anaphoric pronoun, corresponding to *it,* German *es,* French *il,* etc., was introduced as subject in such sentences. One result of this purely linguistic requirement has been a great deal of speculation on the antecedent of *it* in such constructions. The speculation is largely pointless; *it* was introduced because SVO languages must have subjects in sentences, as do intransitive verbs in any OV language.

Such verbs could be supplemented by substantives in various cases, among them the accusative. These constructions are especially prominent for verbs referring to the emotions:

35.	RV 10.34.11.	kitavám̥	tatāpa
		with-regard-to-the-gambler	there-is-pain
		'It pains the gambler.'	

Latin verbs may also be compared, such as:

36. miseret, pudet, taedet
'It makes one pitiful, ashamed, bored.'

These verbs may be accompanied by one or more nouns, as in Cicero's Oration for Milo 34, 92 (Hale-Buck 1903:186–187):

37. eōrum nōs miseret
of-them us it-makes-pitiful/there-is-pity
'We feel pity for them.'

The genitives in such impersonal sentences, like the accusatives, have meanings which are determined by the functions of these cases, and they cannot be parsed as "governed" by the impersonal verb. Presumably because of this situation Meillet included in his definition of sentences of PIE the characterization that every word was autonomous (1937:355). In keeping with this observation of Meillet's, examples of sentences like that cited from Cicero may be interpreted as typical constructions in a language which is OV, even though in Cicero's time this pattern was archaic. In PIE, verbs could be supplemented by one or more nominal elements, in accordance with the lexical properties of the verbs in question. Evidence for this assumption is found in dialects as late as Old High German, as in the following example (Erdmann 1882:167):

38. Otfrid 4.5.44. thes gánges thih nirthrúzzi
of-the way you may-there-not-be-weariness
'Do not let yourself be wearied of the way'

In this sentence the accusative *thih* cannot be taken as object of the impersonal verb *irthriazan,* but, like the genitive *ganges,* must be interpreted on the basis of the inherent meaning of the case.

Because sentences consist mandatorily of verbs, which may or may not be accompanied by nouns, the P rule for the proposition is written with the underlying nominal constituents as potential:

Prop. → V (Agent) etc.

The nominal constituent accompanying any verb will be indicated in the lexicon, e.g.:

**peγ*- 'drink' ____ Agent Target (Time) (Place) (Means)

As this lexical entry indicates, the possible further constituents are included in parentheses; lexical entries for selected roots are given in Chapter 6. The rules for surface expression of the underlying nominal constituents are also given there.

In PIE sentences various case forms could be used with verbs. Examples are given below, first for mandatory patterns and then for sentences in which the nominal elements are optional (see also Brugmann 1911:494–651).

Some verbs are accompanied by nouns in the nominative case, as is *as-* 'be', in:

39. RV 8.48.8. táva smasi vratā́s
your we-are devotees
'We are your devotees.'

Others are accompanied by the accusative, in constructions labeled "direct object," as is *rudh-* 'withhold' in:

40. RV 10.34.12. ná dhanā́ ruṇadhmi
not money I-withhold
'I do not withhold money.'

Compare Hittite *nu hurtialan harmi* 'beaker I-hold' 'I hold a beaker' (Otten and Souček 1969:18, § 7). Others are accompanied by nouns in the instrumental, as is *div-* 'play' in:

41. RV 10.34.13. akṣáir mā́ dīvyaḥ
with-dice do-not you-play
'Do not play (with) dice.'

In the dative:

42. RV 10.34.14. mṛlátā no
'Be gracious to us.'

In the ablative:

43. RV 10.34.5. parāyádbhyo áva hīye sákhibhyaḥ
from-departing behind I-am-left from-friends
'I am left behind by the departing friends.'

In the genitive:

44. RV 8.48.8. tásya viddhi
'Know that.'

In the locative:

45. RV 10.34.13. vitté ramasva
'In property rejoice.'

As illustrated by these examples, which are complete sentences in the passages from which they are taken, Vedic simple sentences may consist of verbs accompanied by nouns in seven of the eight cases; only the vocative is not so used. The nouns fill the role of objects or, possibly better stated, of complements. Besides the simple sentence which consists only of a verb, a simple sentence in the early dialects and in PIE could consist of a verb accompanied by a noun or pronoun as complement. A subject however was in no way mandatory. Nor were other constructions which may seem to be natural, such as indirect objects with verbs like 'give'. The root **dō-* or in its earlier form **deγ-* had in its simplest sense the meaning 'present' and was often unaccompanied by any nominal expression, as in:

46. RV 2.30.7.	yó	dádad
	who	he-gives
	'who makes presents'	

In the same way, other roots which may seem to require more than one noun to accompany them are found in their simplest constructions with a simple noun, if they have any complement whatsoever.

When subjects are explicitly expressed, the nominative is the case employed, as in:

47. RV 10.34.1.	prāvepā́	mā	bṛható	mādayanti
	dangling-ones	me	of-the-high-tree	they-please
	'The dice (consisting of the nuts of the vibhī́daka tree) please me.'			

Expression of the subject is the most prominent extension of simple sentences to include more than one substantival expression.

Besides such explicit mention of the subject, predicates may consist of verbs accompanied by two or more nouns, in cases which supplement the meanings of the verbs. Such constructions must be distinguished from the inclusion of additional nouns whose case forms indicate adverbial use. Since the use of cases in the dialects and in PIE is among the best-described features of their syntax, the various uses of cases will not be discussed here (see for example Krahe 1972:56–108). For our concern is the set of basic sentence patterns.

Few verbs are mandatorily accompanied by two nouns. Of such constructions the most frequent with simple verbs is the use of the dative in addition to the accusative, as in:

48. RV 10.14.11.	tā́bhiām	enaṃ	pári	dehi
	to-those-two	him	over	you-give
	'Give him over to those two.'			

Yet even in such sentences the additional case forms are not mandatory for the verb and accordingly are not essential in the sentence. Rather, the additional substantive may be viewed as supplemental or adverbial. This problem is found also for other cases than the dative, such as the instrumental and ablative as in the following examples:

49. RV 1.32.5. áhan vṛtrám . . . índro vájreṇa
he-killed Vṛtra . . . Indra with-bolt
'Indra killed . . . Vṛtra with his bolt.'

50. RV 7.5.6. tváṃ dásyūm̐r ókaso agna ājaḥ
you enemies from-house O Agni you-drove
'You drove the enemies from the house, O Agni.'

While the addition to these sentences which is indicated by the nouns in the instrumental and the ablative is essential for the meaning of the lines in their context, it does not need to be included in the sentence for syntactic reasons. In view of such uses, all instances of more than one noun in sentences may be taken as facultative or a result of embedding or of other complex constructions. A further example is the causative accompanied by two accusatives:

51. RV 2.37.6. devā́n̐ uśataḥ pāyayā havíḥ
gods desiring you-cause-to-drink libation
'Make the desiring gods drink the libation.'

In such sentences the agent-accusative represents the object of the causative element: as Arthur A. Macdonell indicated (1916:305), in a corresponding simple sentence this noun would have been given in the nominative:

52. devā́ havíḥ pibanti
gods libation they-drink
'The gods drink the libation.'

Accordingly a simple verb in PIE was at the most accompanied by one substantive, unless the additional substantive was complementary or adverbial. Complementary elements are introduced by means of embedding, as noted in greater detail below.

2.5. Simple Sentences Accompanied by Two or More Substantives.

Nonmandatory case forms are found in great variety, as may be determined from the studies of substantival inflections and their uses (Delbrück 1893:173–400, Brugmann 1911:464–651, Macdonell 1916:298–328, and many others). Such extended sentences will be exemplified below with five groups of adverbial elements: (1) circumstance, purpose, or result; (2) time; (3) place; (4) manner; (5) means.

2.5.1. Circumstance, Purpose, or Result. Additional case forms may be used to indicate the purpose, result, or circumstance of an action, as is the instrumental in the following sentence:

53. RV 8.48.8. mṛḷáyā naḥ suastí
be-gracious to-us for-well-being
'Be gracious to us for our well-being.'

The dative was commonly used in this sense, as in the widely discussed infinitival forms:

54. RV 8.48.4. prá ṇa ā́yur jīváse soma tārīḥ
ahead our years for-living soma you-cross
'Extend our years, soma, for our living [so that we may live long].'

Compare the Hittite dative noun form *haluki* in the example below (Raman 1973:106):

55. nu-kan ᵐNana-LUin kuin DUMU.LUGAL *ANA* ᵐNuwanza
Ptc.-Ptc. NanaLUiš whom prince to Nuwanza

haluki para nehhun
for-the-purpose-of-the-embassy away I-sent

'and the prince NanaLUiš whom I sent to Nuwanza to convey the message'

When an animate noun is involved, this use of the dative has been labeled the indirect object:

56. RV 7.71.1. riṇákti kṛṣṇī́r aruṣā́ya pánthām
he-yields black to-ruddy path
'Black night gives up the path to the red sun.'

As these examples may indicate, the dative, like the other cases, must be interpreted with reference to the lexical properties of the verbal element.

2.5.2. Time. A further adverbial segment in sentences indicates the time of occurrence. The cases in question are various, as the following example may indicate:

57. RV 7.71.1. dívā náktaṃ śárum asmád yuyotam
by-day during-night arrow from-us ward-off
'By day and during the night protect us from the arrow.'

The nominal form *dívā,* which with change of accent is no longer an instrumental but an adverbial form outside the paradigm, and the accusative *náktaṃ* differ in meaning. The instrumental, like the locative, refers to a point in time, though the "point" may be extended; the accusative, to an extent of time. Differing cases accordingly provide different meanings for nouns marked for the lexical category *time.*

2.5.3. Place. Nouns indicating place also differ in meaning according to case form. The accusative indicates the goal of an action, as in Lat. *Rōmam īre* 'go to Rome', Hitt. *tuš alkištan tarnahhe* 'and those (birds) I release to the branch' (Otten and Souček 1969:38 § 37). The instrumental indicates the place "over which an action extends" (Macdonell 1916: 306): *sárasvatyā yānti* 'they go along the Sarasvatī'. The ablative indicates the starting point of the action: *sá ráthāt papāta* 'he fell from his chariot'; and the following example from Hittite (Otten and Souček 1969:20):

58. iššaz-(š)mit lālan AN.BARaš [d]āi
from-mouth-their tongue of-iron he-takes
'He takes the iron tongue out of their mouths.'

The locative indicates a point in space, e.g., Skt. *diví* 'in heaven' or the locative *kardi* in the following Hittite example (Otten and Souček 18, § 12):

59. kardi- šmi- i̯a- at- kán dahhun
in-heart your- and- that- Ptc. I-took
'And I took away that [illness which was] in your heart.'

In addition, Hittite has a case form ending in *a* which grammars label the dative (J. Friedrich 1960:44) but which Heinrich Otten and Vladimir Souček call the directive (1969:62–63; 30, § 8):

60. teššummiuš- a takna hariemi
beakers and in-earth I-bury
'And the beakers I bury in the earth.'

Nouns with lexical features for place and for time may be used in the same sentence, as in the following example:

61. RV 10.34.10. ástam úpa náktam eti
house to night he-goes
'He goes during the night to the house.'

Although both nouns are in the accusative, the differing lexical features lead to different interpretations of the case. In this way, inflectional markers combine with lexical features to yield a wide variety of adverbial elements.

2.5.4. Manner. Among the adverbial elements which are most diverse in surface forms are those referring to manner. Various cases are used, as follows. The accusative is especially frequent with adjectives, such as Skt. *kṣiprám* 'quickly', *bahú* 'greatly', *nyák* 'downward'. The instrumental is also used, in the plural, as in Skt. *máhobhiḥ* 'mightily', as well as in the singular, *sáhasā* 'suddenly'.

Similar to the expression of manner is the instrumental used to express the sense of accompaniment:

62. RV 1.1.5.	devó	devébhir	ā́	gamat
	god	with-gods	hither	he-may-come

'May the god come [in such a way that he is] accompanied by the other gods.'

This use of the instrumental is particularly prominent with nonanimate nouns such as *javas* 'haste':

63. RV 4.22.6.	ádhā	ha	tvád	vṛṣamaṇo	bhiyānā́ḥ
	there	indeed	of-you	strong-hearted	fearful
	prá	síndhavo	jávasā	cakramanta	
	ahead	streams	with-haste	they-strode	

'There indeed fearing you, O strong-hearted, the streams strode onward hastily.'

The ablative is also used to express manner in connection with a restricted number of verbs such as those expressing 'fear':

64. RV 7.21.3.	réjante	víśvā	kṛtrímāṇi	bhīṣā́
	tremble	all	made-ones	through-fear

'All creatures tremble fearfully.'

2.5.5. Means. Adverbial expressions of means are expressed especially by the instrumental:

65. RV 1.32.5.	áhan	vṛtrám . . .	índro	vájreṇa
	he-killed	Vṛtra . . .	Indra	with-bolt

'Indra killed . . . Vṛtra with his bolt.'

As in this example, the noun involved frequently refers to an instrument. Compare also the Hittite example (Otten and Souček 38, § 26):

66. ta	kalulupuš	šmuš	gapinit	hulaliemi
Ptc.	fingers	their	with-thread	I-wind

'I wind the thread around their fingers.'

Animate nouns may also be so used. When they are, they indicate the agent:

67. RV 1.36.18.	agnínā	turváṣaṃ	yáduṃ	parāváta
	through-Agni	Turvaṣa	Yadu	from-far

ugrā́devaṃ	havāmahe
Ugradeva	we-call

'Through Agni we call from far Turvasa, Yadu, and Ugradeva.'

This use led to the use of the instrumental as the agent in passive constructions.

2.6. Some Consequences of the Use of Additional Substantives in Simple Sentences.

As the examples given above illustrate, case forms could be used independently of verbs, as well as to indicate their complements. The independent uses led to the development of adverbs from nouns which occurred commonly in one case form. The independent uses also led to the development of sentences with more than one nominal expression. In the course of time some of these uses came to be required, such as the use of the nominative to express the subject in most sentences. This use is mandatory in many contemporary languages, such as English; in contemporary English, grammars even require a subject in imperatives, such as *wash,* on the grounds that *you* must be posited at one stage of the derivation of such sentences in order to account for the reflexive in sentences like *Wash yourself.* In PIE, however, it is unnecessary to posit such a derivation, for the "reflexive" was indicated by a verbal suffix in the so-called middle, and was introduced through a Q category. Accordingly, nominative forms are not mandatory accompaniments of verbs, even of verbs in the imperative.

Like the nominative, the dative came to be mandatory with certain verbs, but only in certain uses. Next to the nominative it was the most widely used case in sentence patterns requiring the accusative, as with the root *dō-* 'give'. In this way simple sentences resulted which were accompanied by three substantives:

68. RV 1.133.7.	sunvānā́yéndro	datā̂ty	ā̂bhúvaṃ	rayíṃ
	to-the-presser-Indra	he-gives	ready	wealth

'To the soma-presser Indra gives ready treasure.'

Such sentences also resulted when other cases, such as the genitive, were used to supplement verbs:

69. RV 7.57.6.	dádāta	no	amṛ́tasya	prajā́yai
	you-give	our	of-immortality	descendants

'Give immortality to our descendants.'

As is well known, the genitive in such uses had the meaning of a partitive object. The sentence also illustrates that verbs are mandatorily accompanied by at most three nominal expressions. This restriction gave rise to the classification of case categories into two sets: the grammatical and the local cases. The local cases consisted of the instrumental, the ablative, the locative, and possibly the dative; the grammatical consisted of the nominative, the accusative, and the dative, with the genitive functioning primarily as a form expressing relationship.

In addition to the sentence consisting of verb alone or of verb with from one to three mandatory cases in late PIE, substantives in the local cases could be employed with few restrictions. In the earliest texts such sentences are far less frequent than are sentences with only one or two substantival complements. But examples can be cited, like the following:

70. RV 9.1.7.

tám	īṃ	áṇvīḥ	samaryá	ā́
him	him	delicate	for-the-festival	Ptc.
gṛbhṇánti	yóṣano	dáśa		
they-seize	maidens	ten		
svásāraḥ	pā́rye	diví		
sisters	decisive	on-day		

'Him the ten delicate maidens, the sisters [fingers], seize for the festival on the decisive day.'

In this sentence the verb is accompanied by a subject in the nominative, an object in the accusative, a dative, and a locative, to indicate the time of action.

71. RV 9.26.5.

táṃ	sā́nāv	ádhi	jāmáyo	háriṃ	hinvanty	ádribhiḥ
it	on-top	onward	sisters	golden	make-flow	with-stones

'[By crushing] it with stones the sisters make the golden juice flow on the surface.'

In this sentence the verb is accompanied by a subject and an object, plus an instrumental, *ádribhiḥ,* and a locative, *sā́nāv* (verse variant of *sā́nāu*) to indicate location. Other such examples could be cited from the early texts. They would indicate that the sentences of these texts rarely contained more than three nouns accompanying a given verb; when sentences are lengthy, the additional material generally consists of further elements coordinated with these or embedded.

2.7. Intonation Patterns of the Sentence.

As described in the previous sections, the sentence was characterized in

PIE by patterns of order and by selection. Selection classes were determined in part by inflection, in part by lexical categories, most of which were covert. Some lexical categories were characterized at least in part by formal features, such as abstract nouns marked by *-ti-*, nouns in the religious sphere marked by *-u-* and collectives marked by *-h*. In addition to characterization by means of order and categories of selection, the sentence was also delimited by intonation based on variations in pitch.

To the extent that the pitch phonemes of PIE have been determined, a high pitch may be posited, which could stand on one syllable per word, and a low pitch, which was not so restricted. The location of the high pitch is determined primarily from our evidence in Vedic; the theory that this was inherited from PIE received important corroboration from Karl Verner's demonstration of its maintenance into Germanic (1875). Thus the often cited correlation between the position of the accent in the Vedic perfect and the differing consonants in Germanic provided decisive evidence for reconstruction of the PIE pitch accent as well as for Verner's law, as in the perfect (preterite) forms of the root **deyk-* 'show.'

72.		PIE	Vedic	OE	OHG
	1 sg.	dedóika	didéśa	tāh	zēh
	1 pl.	dedikmé	didiśimá	tigon	zigum

Studies to determine the details of accentuation in PIE and its relationship with patterns of accentuation in the dialects have led to many disagreements on details. But it is generally agreed that words were characterized on one syllable by a high pitch accent, unless they were enclitic, that is, unmarked for accent.

It is also agreed that accented words could lose their high pitch accent if they were placed at specific positions in sentences. Thus, vocatives lost their accent if they were medial in a sentence or clause; and finite verbs lost their accent unless they stood initially in an independent clause or in any position in a dependent clause in Vedic. These same rules may be assumed for PIE. On the basis of the two characteristic patterns of loss of accent for verbs, characteristic patterns of intonation may also be posited for the IE sentence.

Judging on the basis of loss of high pitch accent of verbs in them, independent clauses apparently were characterized by final dropping in pitch. For in unmarked order the verb stands finally in the clause.

73. Taittirīya Brāhmaṇa (TB) 2.7.1.3. purodhā́m evá gacchati
priesthood verily he-attains
'He attains the priesthood.'

In marked order on the other hand it stands initially. H. S. Ananthanarayana investigated the accent patterns in accented Vedic texts, particularly in the Taittirīya Brāhmaṇa, and concluded on the basis of the interpretation of sentences with similar lexical material that sentences with initial verb are marked. Thus, in contrast with the previous example, the following indicates "emphasis" of the verb (Ananthanarayana 1970*c*:9):

74. TB 3.11.7.3. gácchati pratiṣṭhā́m
'He attains stability.'

Since *gacchati* in Example 73 has no high pitch accent, and since other such sentences have a similar distribution of accents, it may be concluded that sentences with normal, unmarked meaning have a final lowered pitch accent. This might be indicated with #. Clauses, however, which are marked either to convey emphasis or to indicate subordination, do not undergo such lowering. They may be distinguished with final || (Ananthanarayana 1970*c*: 9):

75. TB 1.1.9.7. yát stríyam upeyā́t || nírvīryas syāt #
if woman he-may-approach impotent he-may-become
'If he were to approach a woman, he might become impotent.'

The intonation pattern indicated by # apparently conveyed the notion of a simple, nonemphatic utterance, whether a statement, question, or command.

76. TB 2.1.1.1. kásmai nú satrám āsmahe #
why indeed sacrifice we-perform
'Why should we perform sacrifice?'

77. TB 1.1.9.7. ná stríyam úpeyāt #
'He should not approach the woman.'

The intonation pattern indicated by || apparently conveyed the notion of an emotional or emphatic utterance or one requiring supplementation, as by another clause. These conclusions are supported by the patterns found in Germanic alliterative verse. For, as is well known, verbs were frequently placed by poets in the fourth, nonalliterating, metrically prominent position in the line:

78. Beowulf 2. þeodcyninga þrym gefrūnon
of-people's-kings glory we-heard-of
'We heard of the glory of the kings of the people.'

This placing of verbs, retained by metrical convention in Germanic verse, presumably maintains evidence for the IE intonation pattern. For, by contrast, verbs could alliterate when they stood initially in clauses or in subordinate clauses.

79. Beowulf 6. egsode eorlas, syððan ǣrest wearð
he-terrified men since first he-was
'He terrified men from the time he first was [found].'

80. Beowulf 30. þenden wordum wēold wine Scyldinga
as-long-as with-words he-ruled the-friend of-the-Scyldings
'As long as the friend of the Scyldings ruled with his words.'

The patterns of alliteration in the oldest Germanic verse accordingly support the conclusions that have been derived from Vedic accentuation regarding the intonation of the Indo-European sentence, as do patterns in other dialects.

Among such patterns is the preference for enclitics in second position in the sentence (Wackernagel 1892:333). Words found in this position are particles, pronouns, and verbs, which have no accent in Vedic texts. This observation of Wackernagel's supports the conclusion that the intonation of the sentence was characterized by initial high pitch, with the voice trailing off at the end. For the enclitic elements were not placed initially, but rather they occupied positions in which unaccented portions of words were expected, as in a line quoted above (Example 47):

81. RV 10.34.1. prāvepā́ mā bṛható mādayanti
'The dangling ones of the lofty tree gladden me.'

The pronoun *mā* 'me', like other such enclitics, makes up a phrase with the initial word; in this way it is comparable to unaccented syllables of individual words, as in the next lines:

82. RV 10.34.1. pravātejā́ íriṇe várvṛtānāḥ
in-windy-place on-dice-board rolling
'[born] in a windy place, rolling on the dice-board'

A simple sentence then consisted not only of a unit accompanied by an intonation pattern, but also of subunits or phrases. These were identified by their accent and also by patterns of permitted finals.

2.8. The Role of Modification as a Syntactic Marker.

As noted in the preceding section, single words or words accompanied by enclitics were identifiable on the basis of the incidence of accent; each such syntactic unit could have only one pitch accent. Such units were also identifiable by the patterns of inflectional syllables, as in:

83. ŚB 11.1.6.8. tátaḥ saṃvatsaré púruṣaḥ sám abhavat sá prajā́patiḥ
from-it in-a year a-man together (he)-became he Prajapati
'From it there developed in a year a man, Prajapati.'

As in this sentence, syntactic units like the subject, adverbial elements, and case forms were distinguished by accents and by final syllables which, as is well known, were weakened in articulation. This phenomenon is particularly prominent in Sanskrit (Whitney 1896:34–35). But from the restricted number of finals in other languages, such as only the vowels and the consonants *n, r, s* in Greek, we must assume that the final syllables of words had a special articulation already in PIE. This assumption requires the conclusion that words, or words accompanied by enclitics, were recognized as distinct syntactic units; in many instances they were phonologically distinguished by the articulation of the final syllable.

Details on the articulation of final syllables are a concern of morphophonemics. For syntactic purposes the essential concern is the fact that syntactic units smaller than the clause were identified in PIE. In general the obstruent series were reduced to one representative. In Sanskrit this was the voiceless member: *p t ṭ k.* In Greek however all of these were lost, and *s* was the only permitted final obstruent. In Latin, on the other hand, the permitted final dental was *d,* as in the Praeneste inscription:

84. Manios med fhe fhaced Numasioi
Manios me reduplication he-made for-Numasios
'Manius made me for Numasius.'

Subsequently other final consonants were permitted, including *t* in Classical Latin *fēcit,* upon the loss of final vowels. Furthermore, in Sanskrit, final *s* and final *m* were weakened, as illustrated in Example 70 with the standard transliteration *ḥ* for this weakened *s.* The phonologically based writing system for Sanskrit provides excellent evidence for these conclusions, as do the treatments of finals in other dialects.

Patterns of modulation then suggest that syntactic units which we may call phrases and also individual words were identified in the clause. Such syntactic units will be discussed further below.

2.9. Sentence-Delimiting Particles.

Indo-Europeanists and specialists in the various dialects have long noted the prominent use of particles in the early dialects (Delbrück 1888:23–24, 215–226, 472–546); but the discussions were primarily descriptive and etymological. Only with the discovery of Hittite did the syntactic use of particles for delimiting sentences become clear. Comparing the use in Celtic of particles to introduce some sentence types, Myles Dillon and Albrecht Götze proposed that the Hittite pattern was inherited from IE (Dillon 1947:15–24). It has subsequently become evident that reflexes of these patterns survived in other dialects as well, notably Sanskrit and Greek. Presumably particles had an important function in delimiting sentences. Yet their precise use needs much additional investigation. Among other matters the kinds of clauses that were introduced by particles must be determined. The use of particles in languages generally must also be investigated; although this is a general typological problem, it is important for IE studies, especially since particles have numerous syntactic uses. Moreover the use of particles changed considerably in the history of the dialects, and varied from style to style, as J. D. Denniston pointed out in his book *The Greek Particles* (1966*a*:lxiv–lxv, lxxv). The primary concern here is the use of particles to introduce clauses.

The particles concerned are PIE *nu, so, to.* Their homonymity with the adverb *nu, nun* and the anaphoric pronoun was one of the reasons earlier Indo-Europeanists failed to recognize them and their function. Yet Delbrück had already noted the clause-introducing function of Skt. *sa* (1888:215–216), as in:

85. ŚB 1.3.3.6.

tásya	tā́ni	śī́rṣā́ṇi	prá	cicheda.	sá	yát	somapā́nam
his	the	heads	off	he-struck	Ptc.	what	soma-drinking

ā́sa	tátaḥ	kapíñjalaḥ	sám	abhavat
it-was	from-that	hazel-hen [grouse]	together	it-became

'He struck off his heads. From the one that drank soma, the hazel-hen was created.'

Delbrück identified *sa* in this and other sentences as a particle and not a pronoun, for it did not agree in gender with a noun in the sentence. But it remained for Hittite to clarify the situation.

In Hittite texts the introductory use of the particles is unmistakable (J. Friedrich 1960:147–162); *ta* and *šu* occur primarily in the early texts, *nu* in the later, as illustrated in the following Old Hittite example (Otten and Souček 1969:38, § 22):

86.

šer-a-ššan	GAD-an	pešiemi	šu-	uš	LÚ-aš	natta	aušzi
over-and-Ptc.	cloth	I-throw	Ptc.-	them	man	not	sees

'I throw a cloth over it and no one will see them.'

Besides such an introductory function (here as often elsewhere translated 'and'), these particles were used as first element in a chain of enclitics, as in *n-at-ši* 'and it to-him', *nu-mu-za-kan* 'and to-me self within' and so on. In Homeric Greek such strings of particles follow different orders, but reflect the IE construction, as in:

87. Odyssey 1.59. oudé nu soí per
not-indeed and to-you but
entrépetai phílon êtor, Olúmpie
it-turns 'dear' heart Olympian
'But your heart doesn't notice, Zeus.'

As the translation of *per* here indicates, some particles were used to indicate the relationships between clauses marking the simple sentence.

Many simple sentences in PIE would then be similar to those in Hittite and Vedic Sanskrit, such as those in the charming story taken by Delbrück from the Śatapathabrāhmaṇa (1878:63–64; see the excerpts in Chapter 3, Example 64). Among the simplest is the following:

88. ŚB 1.6.3.5. tám índro didveṣa
and-him Indra he-hated
'Indra hated him.'

Presumably *tam* is a conflated form of the particle *ta* and the enclitic accusative singular pronoun; the combination is attested in Hittite as *ta-an* (J. Friedrich 1960:63–64). The last sentence of the story shows the simple introductory particle:

89. ŚB 1.6.3.15. sa tváṣṭhā cukrodha kuvín me putrám ávadhīd íti
Ptc. Tvaṣṭhar he-got-angry whether my son he-killed Ptc.
'Tvaṣṭhar grew angry and said, "Has he killed my son?"'

Besides the use of sentence-delimiting particles, these examples illustrate the simplicity of PIE sentences. Of the fifteen sentences in the story, only two have more than one nominal form per verb, and these are adverbial as observed above, § 2.4.

90. ŚB 1.6.3.14. evámrūpaṃ hí sá tenā́śanam ā́vayat
of-such-kind Ptc. he with-it-food he-enjoyed
'For he enjoyed such kinds of food with it.'

Similar examples from the other early dialects could be cited, such as the Italic inscription of Praeneste (Example 84), or the Germanic Gallehus inscription:

91. Ek HlewagastiR Holtijar horna tawido
I Hlewagastir of-Holt the-horn I-made
'I, Hlewagastir of Holt, made the horn.'

In these late texts, as noted above, § 2.4. and § 2.6, the subject was mandatory, and accordingly two nominal forms had come to be standard for the sentence. If however the subject is not taken into consideration, many sentences contained only one nominal element with verbs, in the early dialects as well as in PIE.

3. Nominal Modifiers

3.1. Attributive Modifiers.

If, as we have assumed, PIE was OV, we would expect attributive modifiers to be embedded before nouns, in accordance with the principle of modifier placement. Relative clauses would then precede nouns, as would attributive adjectives and genitives. This chapter will survey the evidence in the IE dialects regarding these three constructions. The sections on relatives, adjectives, and genitives will be followed by sections on nominal compounds (§ 3.7), determiners in nominal phrases (§ 3.8), and apposition (§ 3.9).

According to linguistic theory used here, attributive nominal modifiers are introduced by embedding into simple sentences other sentences with equivalent NPs. The process for an OV language may be illustrated by showing the introduction of the relative clause equivalent to 'which ate the meat' into a Japanese sentence; for clarity and explicitness a subject is included in Example 1, although in Japanese and many OV languages subjects are by no means essential constituents of sentences.

1.	Taroo	wa	inu	o	mita
	Taroo	topic-Ptc.	dog	Obj.-Ptc.	saw
	'Taro saw the dog.'				

The further sentence is embedded:

2.	Inu	wa	niku	o	tabeta
	dog	topic-Ptc.	meat	Obj.-Ptc.	ate
	'The dog ate the meat.'				

Using surface order elements to represent the process, the compound sentence would have the following derivation:

3*a*. Taroo wa–inu wa niku o tabeta–inu o mita.
3*b*. Taroo wa niku o tabeta inu o mita.

As illustrated in this example, the equivalent NP is usually deleted, generally in the relative clause of the compound sentence.

The syntactic pattern may be formulated as follows: first for an OV language, then for a VO language.

(NP_2)	NP_1	V_1 +	(NP_1)	NP_3	V_2	⇒
Taro	dog	saw	dog	meat	ate	
(NP_2)	(NP_3)	V_2	NP_1	V_1	/	OV
Taro . . .	niku . . .	tabeta	inu . . .	mita		
(NP_2)	V_1	NP_1	V_2	(NP_3)	/	VO
Taro	saw . . .	dog . . .	ate . . .	meat		

Making use of formalization which indicates the requirements of an embedded sentence in relative-clause formation, we may symbolize the process as follows (letters are used to indicate the order of elements, so that the proposed OV position of the embedded NP and its Σ may be indicated [–b], as well as the postposed VO position [+b]). Parentheses around +Pron. and +Rel. indicate that these items are not mandatory.

$$
\begin{array}{llllllll}
\text{S.D.} & x & - \ [_{NP} \ NP & - \ [_{\Sigma} \ y & - \ NP & - \ w \ ]_{\Sigma} \ ]_{NP} & - \ z \\
 & a & b & c & d & e & f \\
\text{S.C.} & a & b & c & d \begin{bmatrix} \pm b \\ (+\text{Pron.}) \\ (+\text{Rel.}) \end{bmatrix} & e & f
\end{array}
$$

This rule indicates that a potential marker of relative constructions may precede (–b) or follow (+b) the equivalent NP of the matrix sentence and that it may be pronominal and a relative marker.

By this formalization intransitives as well as transitives are accounted for. The Japanese sentence:

4. Inu wa shinda
   'The dog died'

may thus be embedded in the sentence of Example 1 to yield:

5. (Taroo wa) shinda inu o mita
   '(Taro)/he saw the dog that died.'

A detailed statement of the treatment of syntactic features associated with embedded NPs would be too lengthy for a book dealing with specific languages. It may be pointed out however that relational features of the equivalent NP are not deleted. They are for example marked in the relative particle of VO languages, as in the following example:

6*a*. John met Mary. John disliked Mary's dog.
6*b*. John met Mary, whose dog he disliked.

Moreover, in such examples the relative particle may not be omitted, as has often been pointed out. Neither of the following is permitted:

6*c*. *John met Mary dog he disliked.
6*d*. *John met Mary's dog he disliked.

As these examples illustrate, a specific definition of the term *equivalent* in the expression *equivalent NP deletion* would require considerable space, especially if it dealt with OV and VO languages and their subtypes. Here the implications of such a definition will be kept in mind, but the various rules will not be formulated.

Derivation of relative clauses from embedded sentences is similar to the explanation proposed by syntacticians a hundred years ago. The term *embed* has however replaced the older term *subordinate.* Basing his statements on studies by Ernst Windisch and others, Delbrück stated in the first of the Syntaktische Forschungen, "The relative presupposes two sentences, which are to be combined" (1871:31). Delbrück's discussion is unfortunately confused by the notion that this process was evolutionary and that it reflected the development of man's ability to introduce hypotaxis or subordinate clauses in addition to the earlier parataxis (see also Delbrück 1900:412–413).

The assumption that one could determine from IE comparative linguistics the history of man's increasing control over language led to a discrediting of historical syntactic study. This assumption was combined with a theory that proposed a development from a primitive use of monosyllables in "isolating" languages through agglutination to inflection. The disillutionment which resulted when it became clear that the languages of 3000 B.C. were not "primitive" was compounded by the impossibility of verifying hypotheses about the origin of the monosyllabic markers concerned, such as the assumed deictic particle pre-IE **i,* from which the relative pronoun reflected in Skt. *yas yā yad,* Gk. *hós hḗ hó* was proposed to have originated. The unrealistic view that man began to use language only recently and the concentration on surface features like the shape of the syntactic markers may have been one of the important reasons for abandonment of syntactic studies concerning PIE. Delbrück himself did not put out a second edition of the syntactic portion of the *Grundriss,* and he had no successors. But, as noted above, in syntax as in phonology the essence of language is to be found in abstract, underlying patterns. Important features of such patterns have come to be recognized only recently through the study of the basic syntactic patterns found in languages of different types. A treatment of PIE syntax must attempt to account for its characteristics on the basis of a general theory of language, not by viewing it as a step in the development of an adequate communication system for man.

Before examining the basic nominal modifier patterns we may recall that one Indo-Europeanist made remarkable observations concerning the basic syntactic constructions in language shortly before Delbrück completed his volumes on syntax. In his important monograph of 1897, *Compositum und Nebensatz,* Hermann Jacobi studied subordination in Japanese, Tibetan, Telugu, Arabic, and Maori, among other languages (1897:26–39), assuming like Delbrück that subordinate clauses arose from coordinate clauses. In his study Jacobi pointed out that Maori simply places two sentences side by side, with no relative particle if the "nominative" is involved, as in his example:

7.	horoia	te	kaakahu	i	kawea	mai	inanahi
	washed-should-be	the	dress	was	carry	hither	yesterday

'The dress which was brought here yesterday should be washed.'

Jacobi concluded that, like Maori, early stages of PIE may not have contained a relative particle. In support of his conclusion he pointed to the *apò koinoû* constructions in Germanic, as in his English example (1897: 32).

8. Wash the clothes you brought yesterday.

Yet Jacobi's perceptive insights into syntactic patterns did not lead to an improved treatment of subordination. Jacobi himself was primarily concerned with the compounds often referred to as synthetic, such as Lat. *artifex* '[literally] art-maker = artisan'; he considered these to be developments of the relative clauses lacking relative markers. The analysis of synthetic compounds will be examined further below, in § 3.7. Jacobi's observation (1897:106–131) that PIE resembles Japanese, Altaic, and Dravidian in structure can only be applauded. Yet Jacobi lacked the insights which can now be achieved on the basis of an understanding of OV and VO characteristics. For though Jacobi discerned that PIE was OV, as are Japanese and the Altaic and Dravidian languages, he failed to interrelate the syntactic constructions expected in each of these types. This shortcoming may have resulted from the concern of his time for surface characteristics rather than for abstract syntactic patterns. For example, though Jacobi correctly saw that PIE and Japanese were similar in syntactic pattern, he confined himself to a review of morphological features (1897:111–115) without discussing syntactic patterns.

It is also unfortunate for IE syntactic study, as for the general study of syntax, that Jacobi's breadth of observation was not maintained in linguistics. His ideas foreshadow many of those presented here, though without an explicit syntactic framework and explicit formalism concerned with the underlying syntactic patterns. These ideas he based on his analyses of many languages, some of them OV. The following sections will demonstrate how the nominal modifying constructions of PIE can be accounted for by assuming that it was an OV language.

3.2. Relative Constructions in the Early Dialects.

As Delbrück observed (1871:33–34), relative clauses of various kinds are found in Vedic. Both the relative clause and the matrix clause may contain an undeleted form of the shared noun (here, 'paths'):

9. RV 1.35.11.

yé te pánthāḥ savitaḥ pūrvyā́so
which your paths O-Savitar previous

'reṇávaḥ súkṛtā antárikṣe
dustless well-made in-the-air

tébhir no adyá pathíbhiḥ sugébhi̇̄
on-these to-us today paths accessible

rákṣā ca no ádhi ca brūhi deva
you-protect and us Ptc. and you-speak O-god

'On those accessible paths, which have been yours in the past, O Savitar, dustless, well-made in the air, [come] to us today, protect us and bless us, O god.'

In other occurrences the matrix clause alone may contain the shared noun, which is called the head noun in its undeleted form:

10. RV 1.85.1. 1. prá yé śúmbhante . . .
Ptc. who they-shine

3. ródasī hí marútaś cakriré vṛdhé
worlds Ptc. Maruts they-have-made to-increase

'The Maruts, who shine, have made the two worlds increase.'

Or the relative clause alone may contain the shared noun:

11. RV 1.85.12. 1. yā́ vaḥ śárma śaśamānā́ya sánti
which to-you shelters for-striver they-are

2. tridhā́tūni dāśúṣe yachatā́dhi
threefold to-worshipper extend-towards

'Which shelters you have for the striver, extend (these) threefold [ones] to the worshipper.'

Such relative clauses containing the relative noun are, according to Delbrück (1871:34), the most frequent patterns in Vedic. As in this example, the matrix clause may express neither the head noun nor a substitute for it. Frequently however the matrix clause contains a demonstrative substitute for the head noun:

12. RV 1.91.9. sóma yā́s te mayobhúva ūtáyaḥ sánti dāśúṣe
soma which of-you beneficial aids they-are to-worshipper

tā́bhir no 'vitā́ bhava
with-those to-us helper you-be

'Soma, which of your aids are beneficial to the worshipper, with these be a helper to us.'

In addition to these examples, Delbrück cites the following passage, in which his interpretation of the relative particle *yad* and of the syntactic position of the noun *ā́yuḥ* differs from the one we can now propose.

13. RV 1.89.8. sthirair áṅgais tuṣṭuvā́ṅsas tanū́bhir
firm limbs having-praised bodies

vy àśema deváhitaṃ yád ā́yuḥ
Ptc. we-wish-to-attain god-ordained which life-power

'Having praised with steadfast limbs and bodies may we attain the length of life which is ordained by god.'

Delbrück interprets *ā́yuh* as a member of the subordinate clause beginning with *deváhitaṃ*, and states as a result that the main clause, *aśema*, contains no noun. I interpret the sentence as having marked order, so that the verb is placed before its object: *vy àśema ā́yuḥ*. Into this sentence a predicate adjective sentence is embedded, with deletion of the equivalent noun and substitution by *yad,* so that *deváhitaṃ yád* is a preposed relative construction. Such constructions were frozen into a new adjective formation in Slavic and Baltic (Lehmann 1970*c*). In other IE dialects, such as Indic, the relative particle came to be omitted, and the adjective was simply preposed in attributive constructions, with no markers except for congruence.

For Delbrück the natural position for a relative clause was that after its noun. The preponderant preposing of relative clauses in Vedic he ascribes to stylistic reasons, comparing a citation from Gotthold Ephraim Lessing; preposing in his view creates a tension and a feeling of energy which counteracts the monotony of sentence structure in Vedic (Delbrück 1871:33). While Delbrück's evaluation is an interesting commentary on possible reactions to OV sentence structure, we interpret the preposing of relative clauses and their loss in later dialects quite differently. By our view the IE dialects were changing to a VO structure from the OV structure of PIE. If this view is correct, the oldest dialects would show the clearest OV characteristics. Hittite does. As in Vedic, preposing is the dominant order; but Hittite contains relative constructions which are even more characteristic of OV languages than are those of Vedic. For as we have noted, in an OV language the relativizing verb may be preposed without a marker. Relics of such patterns may be maintained in early portions of the Rigveda, as in the following stanza from a Strophic hymn which exhibits confused word order, but they are more clearly evident in Hittite, as we shall see below.

14. RV 4.32.11.

tā́	te	gṛṇanti	vedháso
these	you	they-praise	devotees

yā́ni	cakártha	paúṅsyā
which	you-have-done	manly-deeds

sutéṣv	indra	girvaṇaḥ
in-extractings	Indra	desiring-praise

'These the devotees praise with regard to you, which are manly deeds you have done during soma sacrifices, O Indra, O praise-seeker.'

In a consistent OV language, *cakártha* alone would be a relative construction. Hittite characteristically exhibits preposed relative constructions and even occasionally such a construction without a relative marker.

The typical Hittite relative clause was marked by a form of *kuiš* and placed before its antecedent, as illustrated in § 2.2. Johannes Friedrich provides a good summary (1960: 167–169), following W. H. Held, Jr. (1957), in distinguishing between determined and nondetermined relative clauses. Determined relative clauses refer to a definite item and have the relative marker placed after its antecedent; in nondetermined clauses the marker precedes. The distinction corresponds to one between definite and indefinite elements, rather than to the widespread contrast between restrictive and descriptive clauses; see also Raman 1973.

The following is an example of a determined relative clause, taken from the Hittite Laws (J. Friedrich 1959:85, § 79).

15.

m[a]n	ta[a]n	*ABU-ŠU-i̯a*	aki	SALnann-a	kuin	
if	secondly	father-his-and	he-dies	woman-also	which	
harta	I	ŠEŠ-*ŠU*	daai	*Ú.UL*	haratar	
he-had	one	brother-his	he-takes	not	infamy	

'And if thereupon also his father dies, and the woman which he had [married] one of his brothers now marries, it is not a sin.'

The following is an example of a nondetermined relative clause according to Held's interpretation; for Raman it is definite because of the demonstrative *ape:*

16. Neu 1970:34, § 33–34.

kue	G[(AL$^{HI.A}$)]
which (Acc.pl.n.)	beakers
[(akkuš)] kizzi	ta
he-is-accustomed-to-drink	Ptc.
ape-pat	ekuzi
those (Acc.pl.n.)–Ptc.	he-drinks

'The beakers that he is accustomed to drink up, those indeed he drinks.'

Both kinds of relative clauses contain the relative noun; the matrix sentence simply contains a demonstrative, or no indication of the head noun in question, as in the Vedic sentence of Example 11. In their characteristic preposing and inclusion of the relative noun, Hittite relative clauses follow the most frequent pattern of Vedic sentences, as illustrated in Example 12. This agreement in patterning provides excellent evidence for considering preposed relative-clause order the characteristic arrangement for relative clauses in PIE.

The two Hittite sentences which are given here belong to the recently identified chronological layer of Old Hittite. In texts of this period Carol Raman has noted relative clauses which are embedded with no relative marker. Although these clauses were not earlier identified as relatives, they must be interpreted as such, because they cannot be treated as coordinate, in view of the position of the *nu* particles. The following is an example, from the Hittite Laws (J. Friedrich 1959:44, § 90):

17. takku UR.ZÍRaš I̯À ŠAH karapi B[(E.E)]L I̯À wemii̯azzi
if dog meat pig it-eats owner meat he-finds

n-an-kan kuenzi n-ašta I̯Aan šarhuuantaz-šet
Ptc.-it-Ptc. he-kills Ptc.-Ptc. meat from-stomach-his

[KAR] zi šarnikzil NU.GÁL
he-finds/takes indemnification there-is-no

'There is no indemnification when one kills a dog and takes the meat of the pig from his stomach if the owner of the meat finds the dog which has eaten the meat of a pig.'

For the interpretation of this sentence we may recall that in Hittite the shared noun as head noun is not included in the matrix sentence, but the relative noun appears in the embedded sentence. Accordingly the word for 'dog' is in the embedded sentence. In later Hittite the antecedent of the embedded sentence would be marked with a form of *ku-*, similar to the pattern in Example 15. For this stage of the language the following sequence would then be expected:

takku UR.ZÍraš kuiš I̯À ŠAH karapi *BEL* I̯À wemii̯azzi
if dog which meat pig it-eats owner meat it-finds

The interpretation of the *karapi* clause as a relative construction is supported by the position of the clause-introductory particles *nu . . . nu.* For these particles are used to mark matrix sentences, particularly when the head noun is referred to within them, as is 'dog' with the enclitic particle *an* in the first clause of the matrix: *nankan kuenzi.* In this way passages in Old Hittite texts illustrate dependent clauses of the kind found in OV languages like Japanese, as well as older forms of relative clauses like those found in Vedic.

By comparison, the other dialects show no consistency in marking relative clauses. On the basis of Delbrück's findings (1871:32), it has long been known that the later relative pronoun of Greek, *hós, hḗ, hó,* was also used to introduce main clauses in Homer, as in the Odyssey (4.388–389):

18. tón g' eí pōs sù dúnaio lokhēsámenos lelabésthai,
him now if somehow you you-can lying-in-wait to-catch

hós kén toi eípēisin hodòn . . .
"who" indeed to-you he-will-tell way . . .

'If somehow you can ambush him and catch him, he will tell you the way . . .'

In this passage the "relative pronoun" *hós* is used as a demonstrative. Conversely, as Delbrück pointed out, the demonstrative *ho, hē, to* is used in Homer to introduce relative clauses, as in the Iliad 1.320–321:

19.	all'	hó	ge	Talthúbión	te kaì	Eurubátēn	proséeipen,
	but	he	Ptc.	Talthybios	and	Eurybates	he-addressed

tṓ	hoi	ésan	kḗruke
they	to-him	they-were	heralds

'But he addressed Talthybios and Eurybates, who were his heralds . . .'

The varied use of such pronominal elements in Homer would of itself suggest the newness and uncertainty of the construction.

Indo-Europeanists have long attempted to account for the variation in relative-clause markers in the individual dialects (Delbrück 1900:295–406; Brugmann 1911:347–348; Meillet 1937:375–377). Brugmann, who considers **yos, yā, yod* a relative pronoun even in PIE on the basis of its reflexes in Indic, Iranian, and Greek, views it as an original demonstrative, related to Lat. *is, ea, id* 'he, she, it'. The relative pronouns in the other dialects he derives from the interrogative pronoun or the indefinite pronoun **k^{w}i-, k^{w}o-*, unless they developed from the demonstrative **to-*, as in Germanic. The variation has been widely discussed, with no solution. See especially Gonda (1954*c*:1–41) and Pierre Monteil (1963: 1–17); Monteil concludes tentatively that **yo-* was on the way to becoming a relative pronoun in PIE.

The only proper solution is syntactic, examining relative constructions in a general syntactic framework. In a consistent OV language relative clauses are preposed, often, as in contemporary Japanese, without a marker. In an SVO language they are postposed, with a marker except under special conditions, as in English.

20*a*. The man he called paid the boy.
20*b*. The man paid the boy he called.

Such relative clauses without markers are possible in modern English if the equivalent noun is object in the embedded clause. In older forms of the Germanic languages they were also possible if the equivalent noun was subject in the embedded clause.

Such patterns, with an equivalent—or common—noun represented only once in the surface, are referred to as *apò koinoû* constructions and are thoroughly discussed in the handbooks and in many special studies

(Paul, Moser, and Schröbler 1969:476–478, with bibliography). An example with equivalent nouns as subjects is found in the Gudrunlied (538.2):

21.	dô	spranc	von	dem	gesidele	her	Hagene	alsô	sprach
	then	jumped	from	the	seat	sir	Hagen	thus	spoke

'Then Sir Hagen jumped up from his seat (and) spoke as follows.'
= 'Then Sir Hagen, who spoke as follows, jumped up from his seat.'

Like relative clauses with markers we can now explain *apò koinoû* constructions on the basis of our syntactic framework. They resulted when the OV order was being changed to VO. Embedded sentences were simply adjoined without a relative-clause marker, but with equivalent-noun-phrase deletion. This explanation is supported by the time of attestation of *apò koinoû* constructions. It is more frequent in the early literature and was lost during the fifteenth century in High German. Accordingly it is lost when the language is clearly VO.

It should be noted that the construction gained a stylistic value. For this reason some writers used it more frequently than others, and some avoided it entirely. As a stylistic trait it was occasionally used for entire clauses. But this expanded use of the construction is a general poetic device, not a special syntactic construction peculiar to Germanic, as Otto Behaghel has pointed out (1923–1932:IV, 290). The extended use of the construction is mentioned here because it has been troublesome to scholars who have tried to suggest an origin for the construction. Such extensions of patterns must be as clearly identified in syntactic study as they have been in phonological and morphological studies; well-known examples are the extension of the ablaut variation in Germanic to borrowings, such as the Germanic forms of Latin *scrībere,* and in the extension of umlaut variation to many German nouns.

Relative constructions in Irish are also illuminating about syntactic developments in language. Like the other Insular Celtic languages, Irish is strictly VSO. In such a language relative constructions are postposed, with or without markers. Old Irish accordingly "has a relative particle . . . only where a preposition is required to express the relation of the antecedent to the remainder of the relative clause" (Thurneysen 1946:312; see pp. 312–325 for further discussion). Elsewhere special relative forms of the verb may be the sole indicators of a relative construction, as in the Würzburg Glosses 4ᵈ5 (Thurneysen 1946:315):

22. bid húathad creitfes
it-might-be few (that)-will-believe
'There will be few who will believe.'

This syntactic pattern is found even when the relative construction expresses a genitival relationship, as in the Würzburg Glosses 13^{d}4 (Thurneysen 1946:321):

23. don bráthir as énirt menme
to-the brother there-is weak mind
'to the brother whose mind is weak'

Attempts have been made to determine the origin of relics of relative particles in the Insular Celtic languages (Thurneysen 1946:323–325). While laudable, such attempts do not concern themselves with the central syntactic problem. For syntactic purposes it is important to observe that relative constructions are determined at least in part by the type of language in which they are found. Those Insular Celtic languages which have moved farthest from the OV structure of PIE have developed relative constructions of the kind we expect for VSO languages. In this way they illustrate the importance in syntactic studies of seeking syntactic explanations for syntactic phenomena. Etymologies of surface markers have of course their own interest. But they do not answer the central syntactic questions.

The central problems relating to the relative-clause construction in PIE have to do with a shift from an OV to a VO structure. While it was OV, PIE had preposed relative clauses without a marker. When it changed to the VO type, relative constructions came to be postposed and marked with a relative particle or pronoun. Examples from Hittite and Vedic, as well as some relative constructions of the later dialects, have given evidence for intermediate forms in this shift. The characteristic VO construction, which developed in many IE dialects in much the same way as the relative clauses in English and German, makes use of a characteristic marker whose surface form varies from dialect to dialect. Accordingly, the essential characteristics of relative constructions in many of the IE dialects are postposing of the relative clause and use of some kind of relative marker.

3.3. Attributive-Adjective Constructions.

Attributive adjectives are reduced forms of relative clauses. We may illustrate their derivation by embedding in Example 1 the Japanese sentence:

24.	inu	wa	ookii				
	dog		big-is				

25*a*.	Taroo	wa – inu	wa	ookii –	inu	o	mita
	Taro			big-is	dog		saw

By deletion of the equivalent NP this sentence becomes:

25*b*. Taroo wa ookii inu o mita
'Taro saw the big dog.'

We would expect the same derivation for attributive-adjective constructions in PIE.

Preposed position for attributive adjectives in PIE has long been assumed. Delbrück summarizes the findings for Vedic, Greek, Latin, Lithuanian, and Germanic, giving examples like the following from Vedic: *śvetā́ḥ párvatāḥ* 'white mountains' (1900:94–102). Delbrück also points out that in marked constructions adjectives may be postposed, as in *áśvaḥ śvetáḥ* 'a white horse, a gray'. Since the attributive-adjective construction has been so thoroughly investigated and documented, we do not need to discuss it in detail. We may simply note that the same characteristics as those described in the standard handbooks are found in the Anatolian languages, as in Hittite (Otten and Souček 18, § 14):

26. šuppi watar
'pure water'

The early IE languages accordingly show the expected OV construction for attributive adjectives, with adjective preposed before its noun.

3.4. Agreement Rules in Attributive-Adjective Constructions.

By the time of the dialects, nominal modifiers were inflected for various selection classes: number, case, and gender. The selection-class rules however have exceptions which indicate that the rules as applied to Classical Sanskrit, Greek, Latin, and other dialects are relatively recent. Thus even as late as Classical Latin the plural form *castra* has a collective meaning 'camp'. And certain Latin nouns such as *fas* 'right', have only one case form. Moreover, as Johannes Schmidt demonstrated in his classical study (1889), Latin masculines of the predominantly feminine first declension have a collective meaning, such as *agricola* '(class of) farmer(s)'. Accordingly the agreement rules have changed in the course of development of the early dialects.

The rules which are generally posited to govern agreement in number, case, and gender cannot have been in force until the development in late PIE of the adjective declension which we may illustrate by Latin adjectives of the first and second declension, such as *bonus, -a, -um,* 'good'. By contrast with these adjectives that are inflected for three genders, some adjectives of the third declension, such as the present-participle form, e.g., *amāns* 'loving', have no distinct forms for gender. The neuter accusative singular has of course the same form as the nominative singular, in contrast with the masculine-feminine *amantem:* the neuter nominative-accusative plural also has the "collective" *-a* ending, as in *amantia* as opposed to the masculine-feminine *amantēs.* Adjectives which are not inflected for the three genders include consonant stems, such as *vetus* 'old', *vigil* 'watchful', *memor* 'mindful'. In the nominative and accusative singular, these adjectives are marked as attributive only by their position with regard to nouns. Thus *vetus agricola* would mean 'old farmer' in contrast with *agricola vetus* 'the farmer is old'. In Hittite too some consonantal stems lack agreement markers, such as *kurur* 'hostile' and *takšul* 'peaceful', as in the following predicative example (J. Friedrich 1960: 116):

27.	kuēš	kurur	ešir
	which	hostile	they-were = 'which were hostile'

Since consonantal inflections like those of the cited stems are the oldest nominal paradigms, we may conclude that in an early stage of PIE there were no inflections for indicating agreement; in this stage of the language an attributive-adjective relationship was marked by position alone.

The steps toward development of the agreement system in late PIE and the dialects have been outlined in my paper, "On Earlier Stages of the Indo-European Nominal Inflection" (Lehmann 1958). There however I provided no motivation for the development of the system. We now can account for its development as a part of the process of the shift in PIE from OV to VO structure. For reasons that have not been thoroughly explored, VO languages, especially SVO languages, seem to require congruence markers. Outside the IE area the Bantu languages provide an excellent example. They too have apparently shifted from an OV to a VO structure (Lehmann 1972*a*:273). In the course of this shift they have developed a congruence system which is even more elaborate than that of IE. As explanation we can only suggest that postposed modifiers, or even verbs placed before objects, require agreement markers to assure simple understanding of the sentence. Thus attributive adjectives, as well as relative modifiers, are inflected in Swahili for agreement, as in the following examples from Edgar C. Polomé (1967:161):

28. mayai madogu ni mabovu
eggs small are bad
'The small eggs are bad.'

29. mayai uliyoyanunua ni mabovu
eggs you-bought are bad
'The eggs which you bought are bad.'

In Example 28, agreement is indicated by the *ma-* prefixes; in Example 29, the relative form *uliyoyanunua* has affixes indicating congruence in accordance with nouns of its class, that is, the concord-relativizing prefix *yo.* A somewhat bookish Swahili sentence may illustrate the effect of congruence markers in binding together congruent elements in the sentence:

30. watu wawili wale walivitaka vitabu vikubwa vyote
men two those wanted books big all
'Those two men wanted all the big books.'

Examples in which affixes indicate congruence can be cited from Vedic, Greek, and Latin, as well as other early dialects. The following is a simple example from an Archaic hymn, RV 2.33.9.:

31. sthirébhir áñgaiḥ pururū́pa ugró
with-firm with-limbs many-shaped mighty

babhrúḥ śukrébhiḥ pipiśe híraṇyaiḥ
brown with-bright has-adorned-himself with-gold-ornaments

'The mighty brown [Rudra] of many forms and firm limbs has adorned himself with bright gold ornaments.'

Agreement of number between nouns and verbs and between nouns and modifiers and of case and gender between nouns and modifiers is indicated in IE by means of affixes in which the markers of congruence categories have come to be conflated; but many potential distinctions are not indicated, as in the dual forms. Yet in the interests of simplicity the three categories of number, case, and gender are assumed for the underlying patterns; the defective entities are considered unmarked representations in surface forms.

Marking for number, gender, and case is determined by the heads of NPs. The head may not appear in the surface sentence, as in Example 31 above. Nonetheless the modifiers of the singular, masculine, nominative

'Rudra' are inflected for these categories, in accordance with the rule in Figure 2.

x	Mod.^{n}	N	y		
		$\begin{bmatrix} \alpha \text{ number} \\ \beta \text{ gender} \\ \gamma \text{ case} \end{bmatrix}$			
1	2	3	4		
				$\Longrightarrow$	oblig.
1	2	3	4		
	$\begin{bmatrix} \alpha \text{ number} \\ \beta \text{ gender} \\ \gamma \text{ case} \end{bmatrix}$				

The adscript *n* is to be interpreted as referring to one or more modifiers.

Figure 2. Modifier agreement rule.

Since the agreement rules have been thoroughly described, as by Delbrück (1893, 1900), they will not be enlarged on here. In Chapter 5, when the categories are treated, archaisms will be noted. Notable among these is the treatment of "neuter plurals" as collectives, a relic of the earlier inflectional system in which the ending *-a* indicated a "mass form", whether it subsequently marked a singular feminine nominative, such as Lat. *rosa* 'rose', a singular masculine nominative, such as Lat. *nauta* 'sailor', or a plural neuter nominative-accusative, such as Lat. *dona* 'gifts'. The agreement rules may be based on the ancient collective regarded as a singular, as in the Greek verb, or on semantically determined collectives, as in Germanic. When modifiers refer to nouns of different genders, they are inflected in the neuter plural, as in the following Old Saxon example (Heliand 458):

32\.

Giuuitun	im	thō	thiu	gōdun	tuuē,	Ioseph	endi	Maria
went	for-themselves	then	the	good	two	Joseph	and	Mary

bēðiu	fon	Bethleem
both	from	Bethlehem

'That excellent pair, Joseph and Mary, then went away from Bethlehem.'

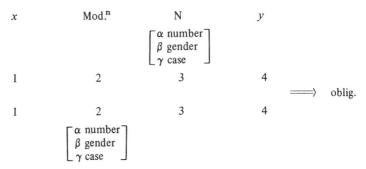

Here the neuter plural endings on *thiu, tuuē,* and *beðiu* are regulated by a rule which reflects the earlier congruence pattern (Lehmann 1957, 1958), though the neuter plural has taken over the function of the collective, which in late PIE was expressed by means of the *a* ending. In Greek, neuter plural subjects still show the earlier collective force through this agreement with singular verb forms. A precise statement of the agreement rules would accordingly be complex, though the facts are well described in the standard handbooks.

The agreement rule which regulates the proper number and person inflections on finite verb forms is stated as in Figure 3.

$$
\begin{array}{ccccc}
x & \text{NP-Nom.} & \text{V} & y & \\
 & \begin{bmatrix} \alpha \text{ person} \\ \beta \text{ number} \\ \gamma \text{ gender} \end{bmatrix} & & & \\
1 & 2 & 3 & 4 & \\
 & & & & \Longrightarrow \quad \text{oblig.} \\
x & \text{NP-Nom.} & \text{V} & y & \\
 & & \begin{bmatrix} \alpha \text{ person} \\ \beta \text{ number} \\ \gamma \text{ gender} \end{bmatrix} & & \\
1 & 2 & 3 & 4 &
\end{array}
$$

Figure 3. Verb agreement rule.

By this rule a subject, whether noun or pronoun, would regulate the person and number affixes on finite verbs; when appropriate, as in the Latin perfect passive or the Russian past, the gender of the subjects would also be involved.

Agreement in this way would be determined for nominal modifiers and for finite verb forms. For both, the inherent categorial features of the nouns and pronouns in question determine the affixes marking the agreement forms.

3.5. Attributive Genitives.

As Delbrück pointed out (1900:102–103), the position of the attributive genitive is the same as that of the attributive adjective. A striking example is given from the Old English legal language (Delbrück 1900:102):

33. ōðres mannes hūses dura
 'the door of the house of the other man'

Like the adjective construction, the attributive-genitive construction may have the modifier postposed for marked effect, as is *sómasya* in ŚB 3.9.4.15 (Delbrück 1878:43):

34. kíṃ	nas	tátaḥ	syād	íti?	prathamabhakṣá	evá	sómasya
what	us	then	it-might-be	Ptc.	first-enjoyment	Ptc.	os-soma

rā́jña	íti
of-the-prince	Ptc.

'What might then happen for us?' 'The first enjoyment of [Prince] Soma.'

The relatively frequent marked use of the genitive may be the cause for the apparently free position of the genitive in Greek and Latin. The ambivalent order may also have resulted from the change of these languages toward a VO order. But, as Delbrück indicates, the preposed order is well attested in the majority of dialects. This order is also characteristic of Hittite (J. Friedrich 1960:122). We may therefore assume it for PIE.

3.6. On the Derivation of the Genitive.

In accordance with our views on syntactic structure, the attributive genitive, like the attributive adjective, must be derived from an embedded sentence. The sentence would have a noun phrase equivalent with that in the matrix sentence and would be a predicate nominal sentence. Such independent sentences are attested in the older dialects. Delbrück gives a number of examples (1878:44–45), among them the following:

35. ŚB 3.1.3.3.	aṣṭaú	ha	vaí	putrā́	ádites
	eight	Ptc.	Ptc.	sons	of-Aditi

'Aditi had eight sons.'

36. TS 1.5.9.2.	áhar	devā́nām	ā́sīt
	day	of-gods	it-was

'Day belonged to the gods.'

As Delbrück pointed out, the copula had to be included in Example 36 because of the past tense. These sentences accordingly illustrate that the genitive was used in predicate nominative sentences to convey what Calvert Watkins has labeled its primary syntactic function: the sense "of belonging" (1967:2198). When such a sentence was embedded in another with an equivalent NP, the NP was deleted, and the typical genitive construction resulted.

Delbrück himself had proposed such a derivation for sentences like the following (1878:44):

37*a*. eṣā́	vaí	dík	pitṝṇā́m
that	Ptc.	region	of-fathers

'That is the region of the fathers.'

Delbrück's underlying sentence reads as follows:

37*b*. *eṣā́ vaí dík pitṛṇā́ṃ dík
that Ptc. region of-fathers region
'That is the region [and] the region is of the fathers.'

Delbrück supports this derivation on the basis of the position of the genitive, which by his analysis should be preposed. I agree with his brilliant analysis and account for the attributive genitive as did he.

Hittite provides further evidence for this analysis as in the following example (J. Friedrich 1960:123):

38. kuit-ma DI-šar šumēl *UL* tar(ah)huwaš
which-however legal-affair your not capability (is)
'But whatever legal affair is one in which you are not capable < of your not capability.'

"This highly favored construction of Hittite" (ibid.) corroborates the analysis of the attributive genitive proposed above.

Hittite also gives us insights into earlier stages of the use of the *s* as a genitive as well as a nominative marker. For "genitives" like *haššannaš-šaš* '(one) of his race' can be further inflected, as in the accusative *haš-šannaš-šan* '(to one) of his race' (J. Friedrich 1960:123). On the basis of this feature of Hittite and of characteristic patterns in the other early IE dialects, I have proposed that at an earlier stage the suffixed -*s* indicated an "individual" item, neither the nominative nor the genitive. The genitive use then arose from constructions like those in Example 35, in which "relationship" between the subject and the further noun was indicated by a sentence pattern expressing a possessive or "belonging" sense (Lehmann 1958; 1969, esp. p. 15). As the IE congruence system developed, -*s* genitives came to be distinct from -*s* nominatives; they also came to be formally distinct, because of the difference in accent, as illustrated still in Skt. nom. *dyáus* < /dy"∧hws/ and Skt. gen. *divás* < /dyhw"∧s/. Its morphological history accordingly supports the proposed derivation of the genitive from an embedded sentence. Its derivation is then parallel with that of attributive adjectives and relative constructions.

3.7. Compounds.

Compounds have long been held to be reduced forms of sentences. Jacobi presented this point of view forcefully in his 1897 monograph; many other discussions derive compounds similarly (Richter 1898:188; Frisk 1941). These earlier treatments seem awkward because they give the appearance of deriving compounds from fully developed forms of surface sentences. By the view of language maintained here and in other contemporary treatments of syntax, compounds are derived from underlying patterns, not from surface patterns. Accordingly many rules of surface syntax do not apply in their derivation, such as the congruence rules. Rather, in the derivation of compounds special compounding rules applying to underlying syntactic structures are included in the transformational component. To understand the compounds of a given language, then, we must indicate these rules.

The verbal compounds in a language observe the basic order patterns, as may be illustrated with Japanese synonyms, one based on borrowings from Chinese. Such a pair is *tozan* and *yamanobori* 'mountain climbing'. The element for 'mountain' follows the element *to* = 'climb' in the Chinese borrowing, where it is read *zan;* this order is in accordance with the Chinese VO structure. In Japanese on the other hand, the element for 'mountain', *yama,* precedes the element for 'climb', *nobori,* in accordance with the OV structure of Japanese. For PIE we would also expect an OV order in compounds, as we indeed find it, for example Skt. *agnídh-* 'priest' < *agni* 'fire' + *idh* 'kindle.'

A direct relationship between compounds and basic syntactic patterns is found only when the compounds are primary and productive. After a specific type of compound becomes established in a language, further compounds may be constructed on the basis of analogy, for example Gk. *híppagros* 'wild horse', in contrast with the standard productive Greek compounds in which the adjectival element precedes the modified, as in *agriókhoiros* 'wild swine' (Risch 1944–1949:287). Here we will consider the primary and productive kinds of compounds in PIE.

Two large classes are found: the synthetics, which according to Ernst Risch (1944–1949) make up approximately 60 percent of the PIE compounds, and bahuvrihis, which make up 25–30 percent. The remainder are minor types, such as synthetics in which the first element is adverbial rather than nominal, compounds consisting of adjectival elements plus nouns, and a small number of additive compounds. It is noteworthy that adjectives-plus-noun compounds, which are highly productive in Classical Sanskrit and later dialects, were not productive in PIE. Risch points out that even in Greek they were relatively late (1944–1949:272, 290–291). Besides identifying the two prominent types of compounds in PIE, we will determine their internal structure and their role in sentences.

Synthetics consist of a nominal element preceding a verbal, in their unmarked forms, as in Skt. *agnídh-* 'priest'. As in this compound, the relation of the nominal element to the verbal is that of *target.* The great preponderance of Vedic synthetics have this relationship. As discussed in § 2.1 and § 2.4 we derive such compounds from embedded sentences which consist simply of a verb and its object: Σ → Target V. The particular relationship of nominal and verbal elements was determined by the lexical properties of the verb; accordingly, the primary relationship for most PIE verbs was that of *target.* But other nominal categories could also be used with verbs.

The compounds that were formed give us therefore valuable information on the PIE lexicon. The kinds of relationships have been described in detail (Lehmann and Pflueger, forthcoming). Here they will be outlined briefly, with examples.

An example of the *receptor* relationship is found in *devahéḍana* 'angering the gods', as in:

39. RV 7.60.8. mā́ karma devahéḍanaṃ
not we-do god-angering
'We will not do anything angering the gods.'

An example of the *instrument* or *means* relationship is found in *ádrijūta* 'speeded by the stones', as in:

40. RV 3.58.8. rátho ha vām ṛtajā́ ádrijūtaḥ
chariot Ptc. your born-at-right-time speeded-by-stones

pári dyā́vāpṛthivī́ yāti sadyáḥ
about heaven-earth goes in-one-day

'Your chariot, created at the right time, speeded by stones, goes around heaven and earth in one day.'

The compound *ṛtajā* of this passage may illustrate the *time* relationship.

As an example of the *source* relationship we may cite *aṅhomúc* 'freeing from trouble', as in:

41. RV 10.63.9. bháreshv índraṃ suhávaṃ havāmahe
in-battles Indra well-called we-call-on

'ṅhomúcaṃ sukṛ́taṃ
freeing-from-trouble doing-well

'In battles we call on Indra, whom it is well to call, who frees from troubles, who does well.'

Compounds expressing this relationship are very infrequent.

To illustrate the *place* relationship we may cite *druṣád* 'sitting in a tree', as in:

42. RV 9.72.5.

vér	ná	druṣác	camvòr	ā́sadad	dháriḥ
bird	like	sitting-in-tree	bowls	he-has-sat	fallow

'Like a bird sitting in a tree the fallow one has sat down in the two bowls.'

The *manner* relationship may be illustrated with *īśānakṛ́t* 'acting like a ruler', as in:

43. RV 2.17.4.

ádhā	yó	víśvā	bhúvanābhí	majmánā
here	who	all	worlds-above	with-strength

īśānakṛ́t	právayā	abhy	ávardhata
acting-like-a-ruler	with-youthful-strength	above	he-grew

'Who grew beyond all worlds with his strength, acting like a ruler, having youthful strength.'

These compounds exhibit the various relationships of nominal constituents with verbal elements that we have noted for complete sentences in § 2.4. In this way they support the assumption of the various underlying nominal categories given there, other than the *agent.* This relationship is expressed too in some compounds, as in *tvā́-datta* 'given by you', as in:

44. RV 8.92.18.

vidmā́	hí	yás	te	adrivas	tvā́dattaḥ
we-know	Ptc.	which	your	having-the stones	given-by-you

'For we know your [wealth] given by you, you of the pressing-stones.'

Synthetics attested in the Rigveda accordingly illustrate all the nominal relationships determinable from sentences.

Synthetics were introduced into sentences in accordance with P Rule 6:NP → (Det.) N (Σ). Frequently they are comparable to relative constructions, as in the following sentence:

45. RV 6.16.19.

ā́gnír	agāmi	bhā́rato
to-Agni	he-was-approached	the-Bharatan

vṛtrahā́	purucétaṇaḥ
Vṛtra-killer	by-many-seen

'Agni, the god of the Bharatas, was approached, he who killed Vṛtra, who is seen by many.'

As I indicated in an earlier treatment of compounds, this synthetic is comparable to a passage in which the relationship is expressed by a surface sentence (Lehmann 1969:12):

46. RV 6.13.3.

sá	sátpatiḥ	śávasā	hanti	vṛtrám
he	good-master	with-strength	he-kills	Vṛtra

ágne	vípro	ví	paṇér	bharti	vā́jam
O-Agni	wise	Ptc.	of-Paṇi	he-bears	booty

'He, the powerful lord, kills Vṛtra with his strength, the wise one, O Agni, distributes the booty of Paṇi.'

The first clause of Example 46, without the further epithet and the instrumental, could have been expressed with the compound included in the second line of Example 45. Synthetics could thus be introduced into a matrix sentence like any relative construction. They could also be introduced with an unspecified noun:

47. RV 2.1.11.

tváṁ	vṛtrahā́
you	Vṛtra-killer

'You are the one who kills Vṛtra.'

Synthetics in this way are embedded either adjectivally with nouns, or as nouns.

Besides the large number of synthetics of the NV pattern, others are attested with the pattern VN. These are largely names and epithets, such as *púṣṭi-gu,* a name meaning 'one who raises cattle' (RV 8.51.1.), and *sanád-rayi* 'dispensing riches'.

48. RV 9.52.1.

pári	dyukṣáḥ	sanádrayir
Ptc.	in-heaven -living	dispensing-riches

bhárad	vā́jaṃ	no	ándhasā
bear	blessings	to-us	through-extract

'May the heavenly [soma] which dispenses riches bring us blessings through the juice.'

As in this passage, the distinction between an OV synthetic like *dyukṣá* and the marked VO pattern may not be great; but *dyukṣá* is generally adjectival, with the normal meaning 'bright, heavenly' in contrast with the more striking VO compounds. In these more striking VO compounds the N is the target of the V. These compounds are also marked and are often epithets or even proper names, in this way exemplifying their special position in PIE.

The second large group of PIE compounds, bahuvrihis, are derived in accordance with the sentence pattern expressing possession. This pattern is well known from the Latin *mihi est* construction (Bennett 1914:159–166; Brugmann 1911:511):

49. Plautus *Curculio* 189. nulli est homini perpetuom bonum
to-no it-is to-man perpetual good
'No man has perpetual blessings.'

We account for the derivation of bahuvrihis, like Lat. *magnanimus* 'great-hearted', by assuming that an equational sentence with a noun phrase as subject and a noun in the receptor category indicating possession is embedded with an equivalent noun, as in the following example ('great spirit is to man' = 'the man has great spirit'):

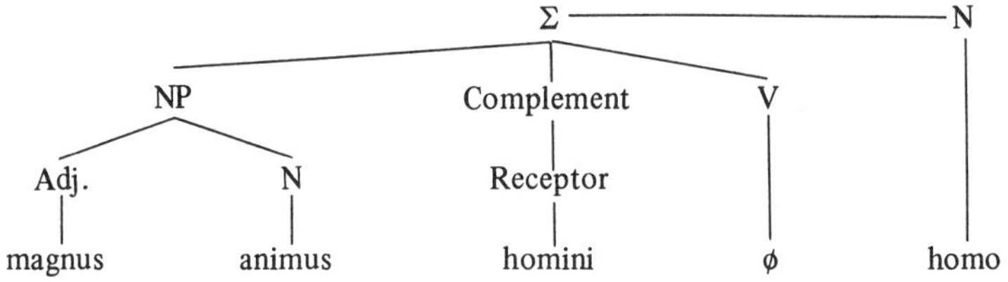

On deletion of the equivalent NP *(homini)* in the embedded sentence, a bahuvrihi compound *magnanimus* 'greathearted' is generated. As has been noted, this pattern of compounding ceased to be primary and productive when the dialects developed verbal patterns for expressing possession, such as Lat. *habeo* 'I have'.

Bahuvrihis may be adjectival in use, or nominal, as in the vocative use of *sūnari* 'having good strength' in the following passage:

50. RV 1.48.10. víśvasya hí prā́ṇanaṃ jī́vanaṁ tvé
of-all Ptc. breath life in-you
ví yád uchási sūnari
Ptc. when you-shine having-good-strength
'For the breath and life of everything is in you.
When you light up the skies, you who have good strength.'

The Greek cognate may illustrate the adjectival use:

51. Odyssey 13.19. phéron d' eu̅́nora khalkón
they-bore Ptc. powerful bronze
'They carried on board the bronze of good strength.'

Besides illustrating the uses of compounds, these Greek and Sanskrit cognates demonstrate their PIE origin; moreover, as F. B. J. Kuiper has demonstrated (1951), the lengthened *ū* of *sūnári* must have been produced at a time when the laryngeals were still present in the phonological system, for the compound is made up of *su* 'good' and **xner-* '(magical) strength'.

The bahuvrihis are accordingly similar to synthetics in being comparable to relative clauses (Speyer 1895:33), as in the following passage:

52. RV 4.2.4.

aryamáṇaṃ	váruṇam	mitrám	eṣāṃ
Aryaman	Varuṇa	Mitra	of-them

índrāviṣṇū	marúto	aśvínotá
Indra-and-Visnu	Maruts	Ashvins-and

sváśvo	agne	suráthaḥ	surā́dhā
good-horsed	O-Agni	good-charioted	good-gifted

éd	u	vaha	suhavíṣe	jánāya
Ptc.	Ptc.	bring	good-sacrificing	man

'Of those bring hither Aryaman, Varuṇa, Mitra, Indra, and Vishṇu, the Maruts and the Ashvins, O Agni, you who have fine horses, a fine chariot, and fine gifts, to the man who makes fine sacrifices.'

Although the bahuvrihis were no longer primary and productive in the later dialects, their pattern remained remarkably persistent, as we may note from the various *philo-* compounds in Greek, such as *philósophos* 'one who holds wisdom dear', *phíloinos* 'one who likes wine', and many more. Apart from the loss of the underlying syntactic pattern, the introduction of different accentual patterns removed the basis for bahuvrihis. As Risch pointed out (1944–1949:29), Greek *eupátōr* could either be a bahuvrihi 'having a good father' or a tatpurusha 'a noble father'. In the period before the position of the accent was determined by the quantity of final syllables, the bahuvrihi would have had the accent on the prior syllable, like *rā́ja-putra* 'having kings as sons', RV 2.27.7, in contrast with the tatpurusha *rāja-putrá* 'king's son', RV 10.40.3. The bahuvrihis in time, then, were far less frequent than tatpurushas, of which only a few are to be posited for late PIE.

An example is Gk. *propátōr* 'forefather'. If the disputed etymology of Latin *proprius* 'own' is accepted, **pro-p(a)trios* 'from the forefathers', there is evidence for assuming a PIE etymon; Wackernagel derives Sanskrit compounds like *prá-pada* 'tip of foot' from PIE (1905:256–257). Yet the small number of such compounds in the early dialects indicates that they were formed in the late stage of PIE (Risch 1944–1949:290–291).

Dvandvas, such as *índrāviṣṇu* of Example 52 and a few other patterns, like the teens, were not highly productive in PIE, if they are to be assumed at all. Their lack of productiveness may reflect poorly developed coordination constructions in PIE (Lehmann 1969:5).

Besides the expansion of tatpurushas and dvandvas in the dialects, we must note also the use of expanded root forms. Thematic forms of noun stems and derived forms of verbal roots are used, as in Skt. *deva-kṛta* 'made by the gods'. Such extended constituents become more and more prominent and eventually are characteristic elements of compounds, as the connecting vowel *-o-* in Greek and in early Germanic; Gk. *Apollódōros* 'gift of Apollo' (an *n-* stem) and Goth. *guma-kunds* 'of male sex' (also an *n-* stem). Yet the relationships between the constituents remain unchanged by such morphological innovations. The large number of tatpurushas in the dialects reflects the prominence of embedded-modifier constructions, as the earlier synthetics and bahuvrihis reflected the embedding of sentences, often to empty noun nodes. As noted above, they accordingly have given us valuable information about PIE sentence types and their internal relationships.

3.8. Determiners in Nominal Phrases.

Nouns are generally unaccompanied by modifiers, as characteristic passages from an Archaic hymn of the Rigveda and from an Old Hittite text may indicate. Demonstratives are infrequent; nouns which might be considered definite have no accompanying determinative marker unless they are to be stressed. The demonstrative then precedes, as in the following Vedic passage. The relationship between such demonstratives and accompanying nouns has been assumed to be appositional; it may be preferable to label the relationship a loose one, as of pronoun or noun plus noun, rather than adjective or article plus noun. In Homer too the "article" is generally an anaphoric pronoun, differing from demonstratives by its lack of deictic meaning referring to location (Munro 1891:224). Nominal phrases as found in Classical Greek or in later dialects are subsequent developments; the relationship between syntactic elements related by congruence, such as adjectives, or even by case, such as genitives, can often be taken as similar to an appositional relationship (Meillet 1937: 360).

To illustrate nominal phrases, two extended passages are cited here.

53. RV 1.167.7.

prá	táṃ	vivakmi	vákmyo	yá	eṣām
Ptc.	this	I-proclaim	to-be-praised	which	of-them

marútām	mahimā́	satyó	ásti
of-Maruts	majesty	true	it-is

sácā	yád	īm̥	vŕ̥ṣamaṇā	ahaṃyú
in-company	which (since)	Pron.	manly-minded	proud

sthirā́	cij	jánīr	váhate	subhāgáḥ
firm	even	women	she-drives	having-good-blessings

'I proclaim this, which of them is to be praised,
of the Maruts, [their] majesty, [which] is true,
which is that the manly minded [Rodasī], the proud,
also firm, drives along [other] women, well-favored.'

In this passage the nominal phrase which may seem to consist of a demonstrative preceding a noun, *eṣām marútām,* is divided by the end of the line; accordingly *eṣām* must be interpreted as pronominal rather than adjectival. The three "adjectives" describing Rodasī must also be taken independently, as must the epithet for *jánīr* (see also Delbrück 1888: 28–29).

The following Hittite passage from a ritual illustrates a similar asyndetic relationship between the elements of nominal phrases (Otten and Souček 1969:20, § 22–25):

54.

harkanzi-	ma	-an	^{d}Hantašepeš	anduhšaš	harša[(r)]	-a	^{giš}ŠUKUR $^{hi.a}$
they-hold-	but	-it	Hantašepa-gods	of-men	heads	-and	lances

-i̯a	šakuwa-šmet	išhaškanta	wēššanda	-ma	išharwantuš
-and	eyes-their	bloodied	they-are-clothed	-but	blood-red

TÚG$^{hi.a}$uš	putalii̯antešš	-a
garments	lightly-clad	-and

'But the Hantašepa-gods hold heads of men as well as lances. Their eyes are bloody. But they are clothed in blood-red garments and are lightly clad.'

In this sentence the nouns for 'heads' and 'lances' supplement 'it'. Moreover, while the meaning of the last word is uncertain, its relationship to the preceding elements is imprecise, for it is a nominative plural, not an accusative like *išharwantuš.*

Virtually any line of Homer might be cited to illustrate the absence of close relationships between the members of nominal phrases.

55. Odyssey 1.185.

nē̂us	dé	moi	hē̂d'	héstēken	ep'	agroû	nósphi	póleos,
ship	Ptc.	me	yonder	stands	beside	field	far-from	city

en	liméni	Rheíthrōi	hupò	Nḗíōi	hulḗenti
in	port	Rheithron	under	Neion	wooded

'My ship is berthed yonder in the country away from the city,
in a harbor called Rheithron below Neion, which is wooded.'

The nouns have no determiners even when, like *nēus,* they are definite; and the modifiers with *liméni* and *Neíoi* seem to be loosely related epithets rather than closely linked descriptive adjectives.

The conclusions about the lack of closely related nominal phrases may be supported by the status of compounds in PIE. The compounds consisting of descriptive adjectives plus noun are later; the most productive are reduced verbal rather than nominal constructions. And the bahuvrihis, which indicate a descriptive relationship between the first element and the second, support the conclusion that the relationship is relatively general; *rājá-putra,* for example, means 'having sons who are kings' rather than 'having royal sons'; *gó-vapus* means 'having a shape like a cow', said of rainclouds, for which the epithet denotes the fructifying quality rather than the physical shape.

Accordingly, closely related nominal expressions are to be assumed only for the dialects, not for PIE. Definiteness was not indicated for nouns. The primary relationship between nominal elements, whether nouns or adjectives, was appositional.

The syntactic patterns assumed for late PIE may be illustrated by narrative passages from the early dialects. The following passage tells of King Hariśchandra, who has been childless but has a son after promising Varuna that he will sacrifice any son to him. After the birth of the son, however, the king asks Varuna to put off the time of the sacrifice, until finally the son escapes to the forest; a few lines suffice to illustrate the simple syntactic patterns.

56. AB 7.14.

athainam	uvāca	varuṇaṁ	rājānam	upadhāva	putro
then-him	he-told	Varuna	king	you-go-to	son
Acc. sg.	Perf. 3 sg.	Acc. sg.	Acc. sg.	Imper. 2 sg.	Nom. sg.

me	jāyatāṁ	tena	tvā	yajā
to-me	let-him-be-born	with-him	you	I-worship
	Imper. 3 sg.	Inst. sg.	Acc. sg.	Mid. Pres.

iti.	tatheti.	sa	varuṇaṁ
end-quotation	indeed–end quotation	'he'	Varuna
	(<tathā iti)	3 sg. Nom.	

rājānam	upasasāra	putro	me	jāyatāṁ	tena
king	went-to	son	to-me	let-him-be-born	with-him
	Perf. 3 sg.				

tvā	yajā	iti.	tatheti.
you	I-worship	end-quotation	indeed–end-quotation

tasya	ha	putro	jajñe	rohito	nāma.
his, of-him	now	son	he-was-born	Rohita	name
Gen. sg. m.	Ptc.		Mid. Perf. 3 sg.		

taṁ	hovācājani	te	vai	putro
him	Ptc.–he-told–he-was born	to-you	indeed	son
Acc. sg.	Aor. Pass. 3 sg.		Ptc.	

yajasva	māneneti.	sa
you-worship	me–with-him–end-quotation	'he'
Mid. Imper. 2 sg.	Acc. sg.–Inst. sg.	

hovāca	yadā	vai	paśur	nirdaśo
Ptc.–he-told	when	indeed	animal	above-ten
	Conj.	Ptc.	Nom. sg. m.	Nom. sg. m.

bhavatyatha	sa	medhyo	bhavati.	nirdaśo
he-becomes–then	he	strong	he-becomes	above-ten
Pres. 3 sg.–Ptc.		Nom. sg. m.		

'nvastvatha	tvā	yajā	iti.
Ptc.–let-him-be–then	you	I-worship	end-quotation
Imper. 2 sg.	Acc. sg.		

tatheti.	sa	ha	nirdaśa	āsa
indeed-end-quotation	he	now	above-ten	he-was
				Perf. 3 sg.

Then he [the Rishi Narada] told him [Hariśchandra]: "Go to King Varuna. [Tell him]: 'Let a son be born to me. With him I will worship you [= I will sacrifice him to you].'"

"Fine," [he said].

He went to King Varuna [saying]: "Let a son be born to me. I will sacrifice him to you."

"Fine," [he said]

Now his son was born. Rohita [was his] name.

[Varuna] spoke to him. "A son has indeed been born to you. Sacrifice him to me."

He said thereupon: "When an animal gets to be ten [days old], then he becomes strong [= fit for sacrifice]. Let him be ten days old; then I will worship you."

"Fine," he said.

He now became ten.

As this passage illustrates, nouns have few modifiers. Even the sequence: *tasya ha putro,* which might be interpreted as a nominal phrase corresponding to 'his son', consists of distinct components, and these should be taken as meaning: "Of him a son [was born]." As in the poetic passage cited above, nouns and pronouns are individual items in the sentence and when accompanied by modifiers have only a loose relationship with them, as to epithets.

3.9. Apposition.

Because of the relationship between nouns and modifiers, and also because subjects of verbs were only explicit expressions for the subjective elements in verb forms, Meillet considered apposition a basic characteristic of Indo-European syntax (1937:360). As in the previous passage (Example 56), subjects were included only when a specific meaning was to be expressed, such as *putra* 'son'. The element *sa* may still be taken as an introductory particle, a sentence connective, much as *iti* of *tathā iti,* etc., is a sentence-final particle. And the only contiguous nouns in the same case, *varuṇaṁ rājānam,* are clearly appositional.

Though apparently simple, apposition has not been satisfactorily handled in grammars or in grammatical theory. Bloomfield defines it as "when paratactically joined forms are grammatically, but not in meaning, equivalent" (1933:186). By this definition any compound nominal phrases (Jack and Jill), verbal phrases, or even coordinate clauses would be appositional. The relationship which Meillet claimed for PIE subjects was labeled by Bloomfield *semiabsolute* (1933:185). Besides the differing views concerning apposition in standard works of the past, we must also take into account the recent use of *appositional* as corresponding to *descriptive,* particularly with regard to relative clauses. Here a distinction is made between *appositional* and *attributive* (see also Delbrück 1900:3); an appositional relationship between two or more words is not indicated by any formal expression, whereas an attributive relationship generally is. Thus the relationships in the following line of the Odyssey are attributive:

57.	1.5.	arnúmenos	hḗn	te	psukhḕn	kaì	nóston	hetaírōn
		striving-for	his	Ptc.	life	and	return	of-companions

The relationship between *hḗn* and *psukhḕn* is indicated by the concordance in endings; that between *nóston* and *hetaírōn* by the genitive. On the other hand the relationship between the two vocatives in the following line is appositional, because there is no mark indicating the relationship:

58.	1.10.	tôn	hamóthen	ge,	theá,	thúgater	Diós,
		of-these	from-some-point	Ptc.	goddess	daughter	of-Zeus

eipè kaì hēmîn
you-tell also to-us

'Tell us of these things, beginning at any point you like, goddess, daughter of Zeus.'

Both vocatives can be taken independently, as can any appositional elements.

Meillet's interpretation of subjects in PIE as appositional may be supported by sentences in which a noun subject is included with a second singular verb:

59. RV 6.16.10. ní hótā satsi barhíṣi
down priest you-sit on-straw
'You sit down [as] priest on the sacrificial straw.'

If the nominative form *hótā* is included in this way with a second singular verb, rather than a vocative *hotar,* any noun may be a subject even with a third singular verb.

Further evidence for distinguishing between an attributive and an appositional relationship may be taken from modifiers to vocatives which are in the nominative, such as the following Rigvedic attributive in contrast with the appositional relationship in Example 58:

60. RV 10.61.14. śrudhí no hotar ṛtásya hótādhrúk
you-hear us O-priest of-truth a-priest-not-harmful
'Hear us, O priest, [who art] a well-wishing priest of truth.'

The attributive modifier of the vocative here is accented and in the nominative, unlike appositive vocatives (see also Delbrück 1900:197); as the translation indicates, this construction corresponds to a descriptive relative clause, in contrast with an asyndetic appositive.

It may also be noted at this point that asyndetic constructions which are not appositive are frequently attested, especially in Indic (Delbrück 1900:181–194):

61. RV 4.37.2. té vo hṛdé mánase santu yajñá
these you in-heart in-mind they-should-be sacrifices
'These sacrifices should be in accordance with your heart, your mind.'

Coordinate as well as appositive constructions could thus be without a specific coordinating marker; as Delbrück pointed out, however, in the later dialects conjunctions were generally used rather than asyndetic constructions (1900:194).

Comparable to appositional constructions are titles, for, like appositions, the two or more nouns involved refer to one person. In OV languages titles are postposed in contrast with the preposing in VO languages; compare Japanese *Tanaka-san* with *Mr. Middlefield.* The title 'king' with *Varuna* is accordingly postposed in Example 56 above. Similarly, in the Odyssey, when *ánaks* is used as a title:

62. 9.412. allà sú g' eúkheo patrì Poseidáōni ánakti
but you Ptc. you-pray to-father to-Poseidon to-king
'But pray to our father, King Poseidon.'

Even in the early texts, however, titles often precede names, in keeping with the change toward a VO structure.

Appositions normally follow, when nouns and noun groups are contiguous, as in the frequent descriptive epithets of Homer:

63. Odyssey 1.80. Tòn d' ēmeíbet' épeita theá, glaukō̂pis Athḗnē
him Ptc. she-answered then goddess owl-eyed Athene
'Him then answered the goddess, owl-eyed Athene.'

To indicate a marked relationship, however, they may precede (Schwyzer 1950:615). But the early PIE position is clear from the cognates: Skt. *dyaus pitā,* Gk. *Zeû páter,* Lat. *Jūpiter.* This position is found in the first sentence of the following passage reproduced here from Delbrück (1878: 63) to provide a further illustration of the relatively simple nominal constructions of early Vedic, and presumably PIE, prose (ŚB 1.6.3.1–12):

64.

1. tváṣṭur ha vaí putrás triśírṣā ṣaḍakṣá āsa.
of-Tvaṣṭar Ptc. Ptc. son three-headed six-eyed he-was
'Tvaṣṭar had a son who was three-headed and six-eyed.'

2. tásya tríṇy evá múkhāny āsuḥ.
of-him three Ptc. heads they-were
'He had three heads.'

3. tád yád evámrūpa ā́sa tásmād viśvárūpo nā́ma.
that because such-shape he-was therefore all-shape name
'Because he was so shaped, Viśvarūpa was his name.'

4. tásya somapā́nam evaíkaṁ múkham āsa, surāpā́ṇam
of-him soma-drinking Ptc.-one mouth it-was liquor-drinking
ékam, anyásmā áśanāyaíkam.
one for-other for-eating-one
'One mouth of his was soma-drinking, one was sura-drinking, one was for other nourishment.'

5. tám índro didveṣa
him Indra he-hated
'Indra hated him.'

6. tásya tā́ni śī́rṣā́ṇi prá cicheda.
of-him those heads forth he-cut
'He cut off those heads of his.'

7. sá yát somapā́nam ā́sa tátaḥ kapíñjalaḥ sám abhavat.
now what soma-drinking it-was from-it hazel-hen together it-became
'Now that one which was soma-drinking, from it the hazel-hen arose.'

8. tásmāt sá babhruká iva, bábhrur iva hí sómo rā́jā.
from-that it brownish like brown like for Soma king
'Therefore it is brownish, because King Soma is brownish.'

9. átha yát surāpā́ṇam ā́sa tátaḥ kalavíṅkaḥ sám abhavat.
now what sura-drinking it-was from-it sparrow together it-became
'Now that one which was sura-drinking, from it the sparrow arose.'

10. tásmāt sò 'bhimādyatká iva vadaty, abhimā́dyann iva hí
from-that he half-drunk like he-speaks half-drunk like for
súrāṃ pītvā́ vádati.
liquor having-drunk he-speaks
'Therefore it sings like someone who is partly drunk, because when one has liquor he speaks like one who is half-drunk.'

11. átha yád anyásmā áśanāyā́sa tátas tittíriḥ sám abhavat.
now what for-other for-eating-it-was from-that grouse together it-became.
'Now that one which was for other eating, from it the grouse arose.'

12. tásmāt sá viśvárūpatama iva.
from-that it very-all-colored like
'Therefore it is many-colored.'

This text, accented and presumably older than the text of Example 56, is also syntactically simple. The attributive modifiers contained in it are preposed, for example the relative constructions of Sentences 3, 7, 9, and 11, and the demonstrative modifier *tā́ni* of Sentence 6. The attributive genitive *tváṣṭur* of Sentence 1 is also preposed, but its position may be due to stylistic marking, as Delbrück proposes. The compounds *somapā́na* and *surāpā́ṇa* are synthetics, with OV order. This text then illustrates some of the conclusions discussed above concerning PIE syntax. An even older Hittite text will be included in § 4.7.; it too may serve to illustrate the statements presented above concerning nominal modifiers.

3.10. Conclusion.

To summarize then, the evidence of the early dialects, notably Hittite and Vedic, indicates that PIE relative constructions were preposed before the noun modified, at an early period without a relative particle. Similarly, attributive adjectival and genitival constructions were placed before the noun modified. As late PIE moved towards a VO pattern, relative particles were introduced. The earliest pattern is preserved in Hittite, where a relative marker in the preposed clause indicates its role as a modifier of an element of the matrix clause. Such constructions are also found in Vedic, though its marker is from the PIE stem *yo-* rather than *kwi-*, the etymon of the Hittite relative marker. As the VO pattern came to predominate, relative constructions, attributive adjectives, and genitives were placed after the noun modified, until this pattern of arrangement became nearly consistent in the dialects which are SVO and consistent in the VSO dialects, like Insular Celtic.

The earlier OV pattern was long preserved in nominal compounds derived from clauses. Eventually these too followed the VO pattern, as in NE *pickpocket* versus Vedic *goṣā́* 'cow-gain > gaining cattle'. Adjective-noun compounds, e.g. NE *blackbird*, like attributive adjectives before nouns in English, still follow an OV pattern of arrangement in many dialects; the history of these constructions, whether conservative or innovating, is a problem for research in the individual dialects, not in PIE. Determiners, which are not introduced from embedded clauses, preceded nouns in PIE and in the dialects. Their order, like that of modifying constructions, is in keeping with that of the P rules.

4. Verbal Modifiers

4.1. On Elements Introduced through the Q Component.

4.1.1. Introduction. The grammar proposed in Chapter 1 generates elements, like interrogation and negation, which relate to the entire sentence, by means of the Q constituent of the rule $\Sigma \rightarrow$ Q Prop. Although such elements have been discussed in earlier theoretical works, they have not been completely and unambiguously identified. An earlier statement, with some bibliographical review was given by Otto Jespersen (1924: 301–337). Theoretical statements like those of Jespersen, which are based largely on logical analysis with reference to European languages, will have to be augmented by investigations of the elements concerned in a broad span of languages (Hope 1972, Lehmann 1973*a*) and by closer analysis of well-known languages (Calbert 1971; Pflueger, Saad, and Lehmann, forthcoming). But already some elements have been hierarchically related as well as clearly identified. For the surface expression in many consistent VSO languages and (S)OV languages reflects with remarkable exactness the hierarchical structure of Q elements in surface features associated with the verb.

Before examining the verbal phrase of PIE we will review briefly the central Q features which we expect to find in languages. We will also note syntactic features which are introduced in the P constituent and, like Q features, often attached to verbs. And since PIE was OV in structure, we will examine briefly the verbal system of characteristic OV languages; for we may expect these to contribute to our understanding of the verbal system of PIE.

4.1.2. Some Characteristics of OV Verbal Systems. As we have noted in Chapter 1, verbal inflection of OV languages is accomplished by means of suffixation. Moreover, OV languages are generally agglutinative (Lehmann 1973*a*). To understand the PIE verbal system it is also highly important to be aware of the OV characteristic that a verb form may have a minimal suffix, as well as a group of suffixes conveying a complex verbal meaning. We illustrate this characteristic by means of examples from Turkish.

In Turkish a form for stating generally valid facts is expressed with a suffix, (VOWEL)r, followed by deictic suffixes indicating person and number. This form contrasts with one which indicates a momentary action. The forms of these two inflections, which are also called Present I and Present II, made from the root *gel-* (infinitive *gelmek* 'come') are as follows:

	General Action	Momentary Action
1 sg.	gelirim 'I come'	geliyorum 'I am coming'
2 sg.	gelirsin	geliyorsun
3 sg.	gelir	geliyor
1 pl.	geliriz	geliyoruz
2 pl.	gelirsiniz	geliyorsunuz
3 pl.	gelirler	geliyorlar

Besides the agglutinative characteristics illustrated by these forms, Turkish exhibits another frequent characteristic of OV languages: vowel harmony. In its eight-vowel system a suffix like *im* selects one of the four high vowels in accordance with the preceding vowel; a suffix like *ler* selects either the front variant *e* or the back *a*. Some elements, like the *yor* of the suffix indicating momentary action, however, are themselves not affected by vowel harmony. The eight-vowel system is as follows:

i	ü	ı	u
e	ö	a	o

In the illustrations of further verb forms only the first singular and the third singular will be given.

The interrogative (affix *mi, mu*) of the momentary inflection:

1 sg.	geliyormuyum	'Am I coming?'
3 sg.	geliyormu	

The negative (affix *mi*):

1 sg.	gelmiyorum	'I am not coming.'
3 sg.	gelmiyor	

The interrogative of the negative:

1 sg.	gelmiyormuyum 'Am I not coming?'
3 sg.	gelmiyormu

The optative (affix *e*) of *gelmek,* for the first person singular:

Simple Optative	Interrogative	Negative
geleyim 'I may come.'	geleyimmi	gelmeyim

The necessitative (affix *meli*) of *gelmek* for the first person singular:

Simple Necessitative	Interrogative	Negative
gelmeliyim 'I must come.'	gelmelimiyim	gelmemeliyim

These selected forms illustrate the structure of an OV verb system. Suffixes are appended one to another to convey compound meanings. But the compound suffixes are not mandatory. Rather, a simple form may consist only of a stem, such as *gelir-,* and a person suffix, such as *-im.* A similar form has survived in the Vedic injunctive.

Injunctive forms consist only of the verbal stem plus a suffic indicating person. Illustrations by means of forms which occur in Vedic texts are given for the root *sthā-* 'stand' in its present and aorist stem:

	Present	Aorist
1 sg.	——	sthām
2 sg.	tiṣṭhaḥ	sthāḥ (ḥ < s)
3 sg.	tiṣṭhat	sthāt

For further details see Karl Hoffmann, who lists the occurrences of injunctives and discusses their meaning in one of the most impressive publications among recent works on IE (1967).

As Panini recognized, the injunctive is not a distinct inflection comparable with the present indicative, optative, imperative, and so on of Vedic. Rather, injunctive forms are survivals of the PIE verb system at a time when its mode of formation resembled that of systems like that of Turkish.

Recent analysis has provided further insights into the earlier system. The verb endings in the inflections of the dialects and of late PIE are composites, as Indo-Europeanists have held for more than a century. After the authoritative statement by Rudolf Thurneysen (1885), it has been generally agreed that the primary endings *mi, si, ti* are composed of the personal endings *m, s, t* found in the Vedic injunctives, plus a suffix *i* (see Watkins 1969:45–46 for details). The discovery of Hittite, with its further such suffixes, and our greater understanding of PIE phonology, which resulted largely from the laryngeal theory, provided additional credence for the reconstruction of the earlier forms of IE verbal endings. I illustrate these by means of the first-person singular endings of the middle in Indo-Iranian; the data are taken from Warren Cowgill (1968:24–31).

On the basis of the cited forms, the Proto-Indo-Iranian endings for the first singular may be reconstructed as follows:

	Athematic	Thematic	Vedic Athematic	Thematic
Aorist indicative (secondary)	*-i	*-ai	náṃśi	vóce
Present indicative (primary)	*-ai	*-ai	yuñjé	bháre
Subjunctive	*-āi	*-āi	stávai	pṛcchai
Optative	*-īya	*-aiya	bhakṣiyá	voceya

By comparing endings in other dialects and by internal analysis of the Indo-Iranian endings, the PIE form of the optative ending may be reconstructed with the suffixes:

*-yeʔ-	+	x	+	o
optative suffix		first-person suffix		middle suffix

The subjunctive ending is also a composite of three suffixes, followed by the primary suffix *i/y:*

o	+	x		o	+	i(y)
subjunctive suffix		first-person suffix		middle suffix		primary suffix

Such reconstructions, which are based on the work of many Indo-Europeanists who have examined the forms solely on the basis of morphological evidence in the dialects, illustrate that the endings found in late PIE and the dialects are reflexes of sequences of suffixes similar to those in Turkish and in other OV languages.

In the early PIE sequence of verbal suffixes we distinguish suffixes for the deictic category of person and for number. We also distinguish suffixes for the Q categories. These suffixes and the inflections in which they are used have been given traditional labels in IE grammars, such as middle, optative, and subjunctive. It is one of the obligations of a syntactic analysis of PIE to describe the functions of the suffixes so labeled in accordance with a long and idiosyncratic tradition and to determine the categories in accordance with general linguistic theory. Before we do so, however, we will note an important difference between the verb system of OV languages like early PIE and that of languages like Greek, Sanskrit, and the other dialects, for which we posit compound endings.

In the verbal system of OV languages, each affix is to be regarded as an independent segment which may or may not be employed in a given sentence. It would therefore be misleading to equate Vedic *-eyam,* the equivalent in the active of Vedic *-īya,* with Turkish *-eyim,* even though the meaning of a specific form like Turkish *geleyim* may be equivalent to that of a specific Vedic form like *gácheyam.* For *-īya* and *-eyam* are composite units. Turkish *-eyim,* on the other hand, is an aggregate of suffixes to which further suffixes may be added, as illustrated above with negative and interrogative forms of the Turkish optative. The Japanese forms given in Chapter 1 may also be compared as illustrations of the agglutinative structure of verbal affixes in an OV language.

Moreover, it would also be misleading to equate the meaning of the Vedic optative suffix with that of the Turkish equivalent. For the Vedic optative endings are composites with compound meanings that contrast as composites with other endings of the Vedic verb, such as the subjunctive, imperative, and indicative. On the other hand, each of the Turkish suffixes adds a distinct meaning to the verb form, as we may illustrate with an example of the Turkish potential *-bil-* (which is suffixed to the gerund form *-e-* of a root):

1.	Insan	bunu	bilmiyebilir
	person	this	know-not-potential-suffix

The sentence means: 'It is possible that a person doesn't know this' (Jansky 1954:128). If the suffixes formed a composite unit with a compound meaning like the Vedic endings, we might expect the meaning 'It is not possible that a person should know this.' For, in the composite endings of PIE, one element affects other elements as well as the stem. The composite structure and the compound meanings of IE verb endings have had a profound effect on the syntax of late PIE and the dialects. For, in contrast with Turkish and many other languages, one element—person—has come to dominate other elements and also the entire clause, including complements. Before we note the effects of this dominance of person in the late PIE verb, we will review the major Q elements.

4.1.3. On the Identification of Q Elements. A major problem in the identification of Q elements results from their variety of expression in language. This surface expression may be made in the inflectional system of a language, in the derivational system, in the lexical system, or by means of suprasegmental morphemes. The variety of expression has led to problems in analysis and terminology, as we may note from discussions of aspect.

When we consider the opposition between imperfective and perfective action, we find that Russian is a language in which the contrast is indicated by means of derivational processes in the verbal system, as in:

imperfective	smotret′	'see'
perfective	posmotret′	'look'

In English the contrast between these two categories is expressed lexically, as the glosses 'see' and 'look' may indicate. In Homeric Greek the contrast was indicated by means of inflection, with the present indicating imperfective aspect and the aorist indicating perfective aspect.

As another example we may cite the feature Caus., which in Arabic is indicated by inflectional processes in the verbal system. As the following examples may indicate, one of the causative conjugations also carries the feature Vol. Using the symbols F, M, L for the first, middle, and last consonants of the typical trisyllabic root, we may illustrate the inflectional modifications as follows:

FaM$\overset{i}{\underset{u}{a}}$La (simple form), e.g., hasuna 'be good'

FaMMaLa (volitional, causative), e.g., darrasa 'teach, instruct'

ʔaFMaLa (unintentional agency), e.g., ʔajlasa 'cause to sit down'

In English, on the other hand, the causative feature is expressed in a few nonproductive derivational pairs, such as *set* versus *sit, lay* versus *lie.* But generally it is expressed by means of phrases, such as those in *He made her sit down; He had the eggs put in the basket.*

Discussions of the features concerned and of the means of expressing them abound in earlier work on language as well as in recent studies. Moreover, some of the features concerned have attracted the interest of logicians and have led to intensive attention to modal logic. This is not the place to comment on the current state of modal logic, which by one definition "has to do with the structure of statements which are in grammatical moods other than the indicative" (Snyder 1971:2). This definition is obviously based on the perspective of IE languages. Clearly a great deal of work will be necessary on the "modal" elements of language, by linguists as well as logicians. Instead of commenting directly on such work, at this point I am merely interested in coming to terms with some of the earlier linguistic discussions.

The Q features labeled Perf. and Imperf. are among those most thoroughly studied by linguists. When such features are expressed in the inflectional system, they have been referred to as *aspect*. When, on the other hand, they are expressed lexically, they have been referred to as *mode of action, Aktionsart*. The complexities of the features, coupled with the varying possibilities of expression, make their treatment one of the most difficult problems in the study of language, even without such terminological complications, which are based on surface phenomena. For, if we regard only the simplest portion of the problem, that is, the means of expression, we find that even a language like Russian with well-developed means for indicating aspect, also makes the distinction lexically, as in the contrast between:

Imperfective	govorit′	'say'
Perfective	skazat′	'tell'

Moreover, any verbal prefix affects the aspectual meaning in Russian and in earlier languages with systematic means of expression for aspect, such as Homeric Greek and Gothic. Discussions of the problems involved have been not only voluminous but also frequently at variance with one another.

For improved understanding of aspect and other Q elements, we must deal with them as underlying elements rather than with their surface means of expression. The work in modal logic is promising, because logic is essentially concerned with underlying elements. As one important insight, modal logicians have recognized that deictic categories like tense differ from other modalities, that, in the words of D. Paul Snyder, "time reference of statements . . . seems not to be a modal matter at all" (1971: 7). For Snyder, "modal matters" include "alethic modality" (possibility, necessity, entailment, compatibility), "deontic modality" (obligation, permission), "epistemic modality" (knowledge, belief), and "intentional modality" (wishes, hopes, desires, intentions). These are only some of the Q features, notably those expressed by the "moods" of IE languages.

The recent attention to modalities in linguistic works has suffered from excessive preoccupation with English, as indicated by the relating of modalities to English function words: *be, have, cause to, put,* and so on. It has also suffered from the awkwardness resulting when these are regarded as individual sentences in a P marker. For besides requiring many intricate reduction processes, such as equivalent-NP deletion, the P markers must then equate the modality elements with the sentence structures of a given language. The treatment of modality features, or Q elements, will be greatly advanced by their study in a wide range of languages. It will profit further from the study of their analysis in earlier linguists' works, such as that of Sibawayyi. While such materials will be referred to here, the chief basis for further illumination of the Q features in PIE will come from an analysis of their roles in successive periods of the various early IE languages.

Before examining the individual Q features we may note briefly the inflectional forms for them in Vedic Sanskrit. In part to illustrate the richness of its inflectional system, the forms are limited to those of one root, *yaj-* 'make an offering, sacrifice', in one work, the Taittirīya Brāhmaṇa; they are taken from Ananthanarayana (1970*a*).

The modality in which the speaker is concerned with expressing a fact (declarative; epistemic) is marked by the indicative, *yajati.* The unmarked form is the injunctive, *yajanta.* For interrogative and negative modality, syntactic devices other than inflection are used.

For reflexive modality the middle is used, *yajate.* The moods other than the indicative express deontic, alethic, and intentional modalities. The imperative indicates the necessitative, *yaja,* supplemented in the first and third persons by the subjunctive, *yajāti.* The optative expresses the volitional, *yajet.* Further, a secondary conjugation has been developed in Sanskrit to express the intentional modality, the desiderative, *iyakṣasi.*

Aspects are expressed by the perfect, *īje,* to indicate perfective modality, as opposed to the imperfective indicated by the present system. The aorist, *ayāt,* conveys the further meaning of momentary, perfective aspect.

Inflections for the tenses may be mentioned here for the sake of completeness, though as mentioned above these are not included under modalities: imperfect *ayajat* and future *yakṣyasi.*

For additional modalities the forms are taken from William D. Whitney (1885): causative *yājayati,* intensive *yāyaj-.*

Among the other Indo-European dialects the inflectional forms for indicating modalities are fewer, as is well known. Greek is closest to Sanskrit in this respect. In the other dialects many of the modalities are expressed by means of lexical items, as are interrogation and negation even in Vedic, or by derivation, as is aspect in Slavic. The use of such devices is found also in the Prakrits, that is, that stage of Indic which is chronologically parallel with the forms we have from many of the other IE dialects. For early stages of PIE, however, inflectional elements were the primary elements expressing modality, as we note in the following sections.

4.1.4. The Declarative (Dec.), Interrogative (Int.), and Negative (Neg.) Qualifiers. When using the Q element Dec., the speaker is primarily concerned with expressing a fact, without wishing "to exert an influence on the will of his hearer directly through his utterance" (Jespersen 1924: 302). Its surface indication is frequently suprasegmental, as in English, with the intonation contour /(2) 3 1 #/ in contrast with the nonfactual /(2) 3 3 ||/.

2. ²He is ³sleeping¹ # vs. ²He is ³sleeping³ ||

In some languages, however, such as the VSO Squamish with *č* and the OV Lisu with *a̪*, Dec. is indicated by means of a segmental element (Kuipers 1967:157, Hope 1972:158–161):

3.	Squamish	č-n ʔi'tut	vs.	ʔi'tut-an			
		Dec. I-sleep		sleep-I			
		'I indeed sleep.'		'Shall I sleep?'			
4.	Lisu	ása dye-a̪	vs.	ása dye mà-u̪	⇒		
		Asa go-Dec.		Asa go not-Dec.			
		'Asa is going.'		ása dye mà ϕ	⇒	ása mà dye	
						'Asa didn't go.'	

Since PIE was an OV language, we would expect it to have a final suffix expressing Dec. This is the value we posit for the *-i* of the so-called primary endings.

Ever since Thurneysen's brilliant paper on the imperative (1885:172–180), scholars concerned with the earlier forms of verbal endings in PIE have assumed that *-i* must be identified as a distinct affix. The analysis is clearest when we compare the so-called primary present indicative endings of Vedic with those of the injunctive.

	Injunctive	Indicative
2 sg.	bharas	bharasi
3 sg.	bharat	bharati

The injunctive has long been identified as a form unmarked for mood and marked only for stem and person. It may thus be compared with the simplest form of OV languages. By contrast the present indicative indicates "mood." We associate this additional feature with the suffix *-i*, and assume for it declarative meaning.

Yet it is also clear that, by the time of Vedic Sanskrit and, we assume, late PIE, the injunctive no longer contrasted directly with the present indicative. We must therefore conclude that the declarative qualifier was expressed by other means in the sentence. We assume that the means of expression was an intonation pattern. For, in normal unmarked simple sentences, finite unaccented verbs stood finally in their clause, as did the predicative elements of nominal sentences; Delbrück's repeatedly used example may be cited once again to illustrate the typical pattern:

5.	víśaḥ	kṣatríyāya	balím	haranti
	villagers	to-prince	tribute	pay
	'The villagers pay tribute to the prince.'			

Since the verb *haranti* was unaccented, i.e., had no high pitch, we may posit for the normal sentence an intonation pattern in which the final elements in the sentence were accompanied by low pitch.

We support this assumption by noting that a distinctive suprasegmental was used in Vedic to distinguish a contrasting feature, *interrogation* or *request* (Wackernagel 1896:296–300). This marker, called *pluti* by native grammarians, consisted of extra length, as in *ágnā3i* 'O fire' (3 indicates extra length). But a more direct contrast with the intonation of simple sentences may be exemplified by the accentuation of subordinate clauses. These have accented verbs, as in the following line from the Rigveda:

6.	RV 8.48.2.	antáś	ca	prā́gā	áditir	bhavāsi
		inside	if	you-have-entered	Aditi	you-will-be
		'If you have entered inside, you will be Aditi.'				

As the pitch accent on *ágā* indicates, verbs in subordinate clauses maintained high pitch, in contrast with verbs of independent clauses like *bhavāsi.* We may conclude that this high pitch was an element in an intonation pattern which indicated incompleteness, somewhat like the 232 | pattern of contemporary English.

Evidence from other dialects supports our conclusion that, in late PIE, Dec. was indicated by means of an intonation pattern with a drop in accentuation at the end of the clause. In Germanic verse, verbs of unmarked declarative sentences tend to occupy unaccented positions in the line, notably the final position (Lehmann 1956:74). Although the surface expression of accentuation patterns in Germanic is stress, rather than the pitch of Vedic and PIE, the coincidence of accentuation pattern supports our conclusions concerning PIE intonation.

The Q feature interrogation (Int.) was apparently also indicated by means of intonation, for some questions in our early texts have no surface segmental indication distinguishing them from statements, for example, Plautus *Aulularia* 213:

7. aetatem meam scis
   age my you-know
   'Do you know my age?'

Only the context indicates to us that this utterance was a question; we may assume that the spoken form included means of expressing Int., and in view of expressions in the later dialects we can only conclude that these means were an intonation pattern.

Questions have generally been classified into two groups: those framed to obtain clarification *(Verdeutlichungsfragen),* and those framed to obtain confirmation (*Bestätigungsfragen*—Delbrück 1900:259–271; see Jespersen 1924:302–305 for the labels proposed for the two kinds of questions). For both kinds we posit the feature Int. This feature accompanies statements in which a speaker sets out to elicit information from the hearer. It may be indicated by an intonation pattern, as noted above, or by an affix or a particle, or by characteristic patterns of order, as in German *Ist er da?* 'Is he here?' When Int. is so expressed, the surface marker commonly occupies second position among Q elements, if the entire clause is questioned. The Turkish sentences given above provide examples. If Dec. is not indicated segmentally, the surface expression for Int. stands closest to the end of a clause. In OV languages it would occupy final position, as does *ka* in Japanese and *mi* in Turkish. Such means of expression for Int. are found in IE languages, though not in the dialects which are attested earliest.

A notable example is Lat. *-ne,* which, according to Minton Warren "occurs about 1100 times in Plautus and over 40 times in Terence" (1881: 50). Besides expressions like *egone* 'Me?', sentences like the following occur (Plautus *Asinaria* 884):

8. Parasite: Aúdin quid ait? Artemona: Aúdio.
   you-heard-Int. what he-says I-hear
   'Did you hear what he is saying?' 'Yes.'

Other evidence for a postposed particle for expressing Int. is found in Avestan, in which *-na* is suffixed to some interrogatives, as in *kas-nā* 'who (then)?'; and in Germanic, where *na* is found finally in some questions in Old High German. Old Church Slavic is more consistent in the use of such a particle than are these dialects, as in *chošteši li* 'Do you wish to?' This particle is also used in contemporary Russian. In view of the lack of such particles in the earliest dialects, we may have to assume that they were introduced after PIE, as a result of influence from OV languages (see Schmitt-Brandt 1971:242).

Yet it is remarkable that the particle used to express Int. in Latin, Avestan, and Germanic is homophonous with the particle for expressing negation. Indo-Europeanists have been greatly concerned with determining the origin of this particle, whether it was related to the negative particle **ne* or to the Vedic particle of comparison *na* (Delbrück 1897: 537–540; 1900:263). While we are only secondarily concerned with the origin of surface markers, it is noteworthy that the OV languages Turkish, with *mi,* and Quechua, with *ču,* use homophonous elements for the interrogative and the negative. It is not unlikely therefore that PIE *ne* of questions is the same particle as that used for the negative. As the interrogative particle, however, it has been lost in most dialects. Its loss is one of the indications that late PIE was not a consistent OV language. Rather than a postposed particle, intonation was used to express the Q component Int., as well as particles that were placed early in clauses, often initially. These will be examined below.

Indications of negation (Neg.) in the early dialects are also like the means of expression in VO languages. Neg., by which the speaker negates the verbal means of expression, commonly occupies third position in the hierarchy of Q elements. In Japanese, as illustrated above, it precedes the element for Int., e.g., *yomanai ka* 'Does he not read?' In Classical Hebrew the expression for Neg. follows that for Int. For PIE, however, we can only posit the particles *ne* and *mē,* neither of which is normally postposed after verbs; see however Example 70 below. Neg., as well as Int., is accordingly expressed by surface elements that indicate VO structure for late PIE. Unlike the means of expression for qualifiers that remain to be discussed, neither Neg. nor Int. was incorporated in the inflectional endings which are found in the dialects.

4.1.5. Reflexivization (Refl.) and Reciprocity (Recip.). By Refl. the action expressed by a verb is made to refer to the subject of that verb, e.g., *He saw himself.* A further category, Recip., may be combined with reflexivization when two or more persons are involved; by Recip. the action of one person is made to reflect on another, e.g., *They saw each other.* In SVO languages both categories are commonly expressed by means of pronouns, as in English. In OV languages, however, and in VSO languages, they are commonly expressed by means of verbal affixes.

Quechua provides an excellent example, as in the following forms (Bills, Vallejo, and Troike 1969:73, 150), in which *ku* indicates Refl.; *na,* Recip.:

9. tapukusan
   ask Refl. Continuative (Cont.) 3 sg.
   'He is asking himself.'

10. qunakusayku
    give Recip. Refl. Cont. 1 pl. exclusive
    'We are giving [it] to each other.'

The order of these affixes is of interest. In Quechua the affix for Refl. occupies Position 9 of the thirteen "modal-suffix" positions identified by Bills, Vallejo, and Troike (1969:333–334). All of these precede Neg. and Int. as well as Dec., which Bills et al. label "the factual suffix." Similarly, in VSO languages, the affix expressing Refl. follows the means for expressing Int. and Neg., as in the Classical Hebrew sentence:

11. lo: hit̄labbe:š̌
    Neg. Refl. dress
    'He did not dress himself.'

We account for the survival of the affix expressing Refl. and Recip. in PIE by assuming that, as the language became less consistently OV, the final Q expressions on V were placed preverbally or indicated suprasegmentally. The affix expressing Refl. and Recip., the suffix for the so-called middle, was however maintained until Refl. and Recip. came to be expressed in accordance with the patterns of SVO languages (Lehmann 1973*b*).

Examination of expression for the middle in the early dialects illuminates the method of indicating Q constituents in earlier stages of PIE, as we noted above in § 4.1.2. The suffix for the middle, *o,* was placed after the person suffix, but before the suffix expressing Dec., *i.* It is curious that this device was adopted again in Hittite, where *-ri* and *-t(i)* are facultative affixes of the mediopassive. Whether we should account for these characteristic Hittite suffixes as a continuation of the OV patterning of PIE or as an independent development resulting from the influence of OV languages in and near Anatolia is a problem for Hittite scholars. Whatever the explanation for them, the Hittite forms have supported the analysis of endings proposed earlier by Thurneysen—an analysis in keeping with the method of formation well known in OV languages.

As we indicated earlier in this chapter, not all elements are required with every finite verbal form. Thus Quechua may have simple verb forms consisting of verbal root and personal ending:

12.

hamu -	nku
come	they

'They (will) come.'

13.

hamu -	sa -	nku
come	Cont.	they

'They are coming.'

Verb forms may also be further extended:

14.

hamu -	sa -	nku -	ču
come	Cont.	they	Neg.

'They are not coming.'

15.

yača -	či	na -	ku -	λa -	sa -	nku
know	Caus.	Recip.	Refl.	Delimitative	Cont.	they

'They are only teaching each other.'

If at some time in the course of development of a language the means of expression for some of the Q categories are placed before the verb, as were those for Int. and Neg. in late PIE, the remaining categories may be expressed with frozen elements. The combination of these with verbal roots may then constitute a fixed paradigm, such as we find in Sanskrit (Whitney 1896:208–212). From the "schemes of normal endings" presented here we may note those for the third-person singular, active and middle:

Primary		Secondary		Perfect		Imperative		Subjunctive		Optative	
Act.	Mid.	Act.	Mid.	Act.	Mid.	Act.	Mid.	Act.	Mid.	Act.	Mid.
ti	te	t	ta	a	e	tu	tā́m	at(i)	ate	yā́t	ītá
									ātai	et	eta

The compound morphemes of Ṣanskrit and the other dialects, which are referred to in IE studies as *endings,* incorporated a limited set of markers for features. Besides person and number, these represented voice (active as opposed to middle), mood (imperative, optative, subjunctive), aspect (perfect, present, aorist), and subsequently tense. This development of compound morphemes, rather than successions of relatively independent affixes as in Quechua, led to considerable changes in the IE syntactic system, as we note below, especially in § 4.2. But on the basis of intensive analysis, the earlier affixes can be identified from relatively transparent forms of the early dialects (Brugmann 1913; 1916; Meillet 1937; Watkins 1969; Cowgill 1968). The categories indicated by these elements will be reviewed in the following sections.

4.1.6. The IE Moods: Necessitative (Nec.) and Voluntative (Vol.). Nec. indicates that the person involved in the action is required to carry it out. Examples may be given with Turkish *meli/malı* forms:

16. yapmalı
    '(he, she, it) must do'

17. oturmalısınız
    'you must sit down'

The PIE subjunctive may resemble in meaning an obligative (Obl.). Both of these modalities are included in modal logic under alethic modality. Yet each feature may be expressed separately in a language, as in Quechua, where Obl. is indicated by a periphrastic construction (Bills, Vallejo, and Troike 1969:139) and Nec., or the imperative, by an inflection (ibid.: 13 et passim). In spite of such possible differences, the imperative and subjunctive are here introduced through Nec.

Apart from unmarked forms in the second person, the imperative was expressed by means of a *-u* affix, as may be illustrated by Skt. *bharatu, bharantu.* The subjunctive was expressed by means of an affixed *e/o,* as in the first person **-o-x-o-y* as opposed to the (primary) indicative ending **-x-o-y* (Cowgill 1968:27; § 4.1.2). The first affix of the subjunctive form indicates the mood; the second, the person; the third, the middle voice; and the last represents Dec. The subjunctive merged with the imperative in Indic; the merger supports the assumption of a similar meaning. In other dialects it underwent other developments, partly as a result of the subsequent structure of the verbal system, partly as a result of phonological developments, such as the loss of laryngeals. These developments also affected the mood which expressed the volitional (Vol.).

By Vol. the subject expresses a wish. The affix in PIE was *-yeʔ-*, as in the Indic athematic optative first singular ending **-iya,* from **-iʔ-x-o* < **-yeʔ-x-o* and the thematic **-aiya* < **-o-yʔ-x-o.* The developments by which the optative merged with other verb forms or was lost as a distinct inflection will be indicated below.

As we have noted above, wishes have been included under *intentional* modality, along with desires, hopes, and intentions. Expressions for desire are found in some languages, as in the Japanese desiderative, e.g., *yomitai* 'he wants to read.' Sanskrit too has an inflection for the desiderative, as in the form *iyakṣasi* noted above. The marker and the uses of the desiderative are similar to those for the future, as in Skt. *yakṣyasi.* The evidence is unclear for PIE, in which these affixes may have been sporadic. We may therefore view expressions for desire as a part of the derivational system in PIE and their subsequent developments in the dialects as features of the individual dialects rather than of the parent language.

4.1.7. Aspects. If we use the term *aspect* for semantic features, disregarding their manner of expression in a given language, we may posit two basic categories: Imperf. and Perf. (or -Perf. and +Perf.). Use of Perf. indicates that the action is assumed to be completed. As a consequence, Imperf. commonly indicates incomplete action; yet it is more precise to state that, with an Imperf. expression, there is no implication that the action is completed. As Wolfgang Dressler noted in his capable monograph (1968:43), imperfective forms are predominant in negative sentences.

The contrast in aspect is accompanied by other connotations, which have been extensively discussed. Thus Perf. also carries the connotation of punctual action, or even totality *(ganzheitlich).* And Imperf. carries the connotation of linear, continuative, or durative action and lack of totality *(nicht ganzheitlich).*

Moreover, Giacomo Devoto has pointed out the quantitative connotation of aspect (1958:396–398). It is this connotation which Dressler has explored in his monograph on plurality. For continuative aspect may be associated with distributive or iterative meaning; it may also be related to intensive aspect, which in turn may imply emphatic aspect.

Support for the assumption of such interrelationships may be provided by noting the IE *-ske* suffix and its varied uses. In Hittite it is primarily iterative (J. Friedrich 1960:74–75, 140–141); though, as Friedrich illustrates with well-chosen examples, it may also have distributive or repetitive meaning. By Kammenhuber's analysis it is a durative-distributive (1969:220). In Latin it came to have a durative-ingressive meaning, and subsequently indicated inchoative action (Leumann 1965:298). In Greek the suffix did not acquire the prominence it had in Latin; a notable development, however, is its use to indicate iterative preterites in Ionic (Schwyzer 1939:706–712). With this use we may compare its development as an aorist suffix in Armenian (Meillet 1936:115). Aspect accordingly provides difficult problems for IE studies, in part because the inflections of the verb systems in the various dialects came to indicate tense distinctions rather than aspect, but largely because of the broad implications of the categories themselves.

For PIE we posit a separate inflection for perfective aspect—the form which has developed into the perfect in Sanskrit and Greek and into various preterite forms in other dialects. The perfect was characterized in PIE by special endings in the singular (*-xe, -the, -e,* as opposed to *-m, -s, -t*) and by *o* grade of the root. Besides their basic perfective meaning, forms inflected in the perfect indicated a state resulting from previous or completed action, as in the often cited example—Gk. *oĩda,* Goth. *wait,* Skt. *veda* 'I know'—in contrast with the imperfective meaning of the present inflection, as in:

18. RV 2.35.2. kuvíd asya védat
certainly it he-will-understand
'Gewiß wird er es verstehen.' (Geldner 1951-1957:I, 321)

Since the perfect stood in direct contrast with the imperfective present, the basic aspectual contrast in PIE was between perfective and imperfective.

Perfective aspect was in turn distinguished for –momentary versus +momentary aspect. As the cited Vedic example (18) indicates, and as is suggested by the characterization *stative* for the perfect, its perfective aspect was –momentary. By contrast, momentary aspect was indicated by means of the so-called aorist. This was characterized by zero grade of the root and secondary endings. The contrasts may be illustrated by the three following examples from the Rigveda:

19. RV 6.24.9. sthā́ ū ṣu ūrdhvá (aorist)
stand at-cnce straight
'Stand up straight at once.'

20. RV 10.27.14. tasthaú mātā́ (perfect)
has-stood-up mother
'The mother is standing.'
'Die Mutter steht still.' (Geldner (1951-1957:III, 167)

21. RV 8.19.10.
yásya tvám ūrdhvó adhvarā́ya tíṣṭhasi (present)
whose you straight for-religious-celebration you-are-standing
'For whose religious celebration you are standing erect.'
'Zu dessen heiliger Handlung du aufrecht darstehst.' (Geldner 1951-1957: II, 320)

As the further context indicates, in Example 21 the present form implies continued support for the celebrant; in Example 20, by contrast, the perfect indicates a completed action, without an implication of momentary activity. Example 19 simply implies a momentary, completed action.

We posit this aspectual relationship for PIE, with a hierarchy as follows:

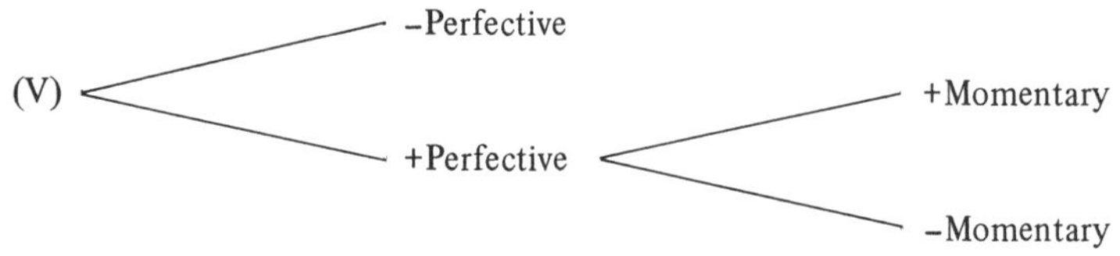

Indications for aspect were made partly by suffixation, as for the perfect with its suffix *-e* and personal endings, partly by form of the stem, as for the aorist as well as the perfect. Details will be discussed in § 4.4. below for these and other aspects of PIE.

Tense was not indicated in the early IE verb system, but it came to be the prominent characteristic in the early dialects. As the use of the prefix *e-* may indicate, the prominence of tense must have developed in subgroups of late IE. Prefixation of the augment vowel also indicates that at this time there was a tendency away from an OV structure. The shift from an aspect system to a tense system is accordingly one of the developments that must be examined individually for sets of dialects like Armenian, Greek, and Indo-Iranian, or for Germanic and Italic. Although the changes then are topics for the history of the dialects rather than the parent language, they will be dealt with in outline below.

4.1.8. The Causative (Caus.) and the Passive (Pass.). Causation was expressed by suffixes in the early dialects, and presumably in late PIE. Yet the predominant suffix, *-éyo-*, must be late because of its vocalism and because of its form in Baltic and Slavic (Brugmann 1904*a*:535). Further, this meaning of *-éyo-* attached to *o* grade roots may have developed from an iterative-frequentative, as in Gk. *phoréō* 'I carry back and forth' in contrast with *phobéō* 'I came to flee' (Delbrück 1897:118–119). As Brugmann states (1904*a*:536), the causative meaning is particularly prominent in Indic, Germanic, and Slavic.

Caus. was also indicated by an *-n-* affix, as is particularly notable in Hittite. Vedic forms also provide evidence for this meaning, such as *invati* 'cause to go' beside *eti* 'go'. The exact function of these two causative suffixes remains to be determined, if indeed there is adequate data in our surviving texts. It may be that one was inherently volitional, like the Arabic Form II, e.g., *darrasa* 'instruct', and the other nonvolitional, like Arabic Form IV, e.g., *ʔajlasa* 'make sit down'.

Among other problems to investigate is the relationship of each to the so-called Vedic passive, a present inflection with *-yá-* suffix. This form expresses an intransitive, stative meaning, especially in early stages of Sanskrit. Since "passives" are formed from causatives in *-éyo-* (Whitney 1885:238), the essential meaning of the *-éyo-* causatives may be nonvoluntative.

Besides the possible further illumination of the IE verb system resulting from additional study of the causative formations, we may note from their restricted forms the similarity of the early IE verb system to that of OV languages. It is well known that causatives in *-éyo-*, like other derived forms, "belonged only to the present stem" (Brugmann 1904*a*:535). This restriction indicates to us that such suffixes were added to the basic root of the verb and that their formation was similar to that of the aorist and perfect, much as "modal affixes" in an OV language like Quechua are comparable to one another.

Only when the IE verb system developed a set of standard inflections and fixed endings were derived forms like those in *-éyo-* treated like simple stems. This is the situation well known from Classical Greek, Latin, Germanic, and the other late dialects, including Classical Sanskrit. By the last half of the first millennium B.C., the verbal system of all the dialects had developed considerably away from that of early PIE (Wackernagel 1926:170). We can understand the earlier system only by reconstruction from Vedic, Hittite, and Homeric Greek, from relic patterns in other dialects, and from comparison with verbal systems in other languages of OV structure.

4.1.9. Congruence and Deixis Categories. Indications for congruence and for deixis differ considerably from those of Q categories. As one important difference, expressions for such categories are often lacking in verb systems, especially with respect to OV languages; Japanese for example has no inflectional indications of either person or number. Among the important differences when congruence and deixis are expressed is the lack of hierarchy with relation to the expressions of Q categories. Among the Q categories, as we have noted, expressions for Int. and Neg. are placed closer to the sentence boundary than are expressions for moods and aspects. The position of expressions for congruence and deixis is independent of that for any Q categories. This independence has obscured the analysis of some endings, as we will note below.

In PIE the deixis categories referred to as first, second, and third person were expressed in verb forms, as were the congruence categories singular, dual, and plural. Since the basic functions of these are well known and relatively uncomplicated, they will not be discussed further here. The subsequent role of person in the verb came to affect its entire system and to bring about one of the characteristic features of IE languages, as we will note in the following section.

4.2. The Subjective Quality of the Verb in IE.

Among characteristics of IE, in contrast with other languages, is the sharp distinction between the noun and the verb. Meillet states emphatically that the distinction is more precise in IE than in other languages (1937:187). As a further important characteristic, the IE verb is characterized by a feature which Ernst Lewy has labeled *subjective* (1942:24). This designation refers to the inclusion in the finite verbal forms of an indication for the actor or subject. Thus, though they lack indications of mood and tense, the injunctive forms in Vedic include indications of the person involved in the action.

Many languages, on the other hand, do not include expression of person in finite verb forms. For example, a Japanese verb form such as *yomu* 'read' may be used when the subject is 'I, you, he, she, it, we, they' or nouns. The same is true of other finite forms such as *yonda* 'read (past)'. The Japanese system accordingly lacks indication of the subjective feature in its simple forms. Another contrast with the IE verb system may be illustrated by Basque, in which the verb is characterized by differing intransitive and transitive forms which are accompanied by different inflected forms of the subject. As the dominant characteristic of the Basque verb, Lewy sees the "passive feature *(Fassung)*" of the transitive. A further contrasting system is illustrated by Samoyede, in which Lewy sees as an essential characteristic the possessive feature of the transitive verb; for the transitive expression corresponding to 'I cut' is like that of the nominal possessive construction 'my boat', literally therefore, 'my cutting'. As these examples may illustrate, the requirement that the acting subject be expressed in the verb form differentiates the IE verb system characteristically from that of many other languages.

The incorporation of the expression for subject has also had an important influence on the IE verbal system and on its categories. For the included subject came to dominate not only the verb and its categories, but also the entire clause; in this way it has also determined the form and meaning of embedded elements. This domination has modified especially the meaning of verbal forms like the subjunctive and optative, as well as nonfinite forms, as we will see below.

Before examining these effects, we may note that verbal systems are capable of undergoing fundamental modifications. Modern Hindi, for example, has a system more like that of Basque and Dravidian than like that of Vedic. And Hungarian has given up some characteristics of the Finno-Ugric system, apparently under influence of the neighboring IE languages, notably German. PIE itself includes indications that the verbal system reconstructed from the dialects was fundamentally modified at one point in its history. For a large number of "impersonal" verbs point to an earlier system in which the actor, or subject, is not expressed; for any given verb form, the subject then may have been as varied as for the Japanese verb. Thus the Latin verb *paenitet* means 'there is woe for . . .' rather than 'he, she, it undergoes woe, is sorry'. For more precise specification a pronoun is necessary, for example, *paenitet me* 'I am sorry'. Similarly the impersonal passives common in older Latin have no reference to person, as in line 273 from Plautus's *Pseudolus:*

22.	Quid	agitur	Calidore?	Amatur	atque	egetur	acriter;
	What	is-carried-out	Calidorus	is-loved	and	is-missed	vehemently

'How are things, Calidorus?' 'I'm in love, and in great agony.'

On the basis of such verbs, which are particularly prominent in reporting natural events, e.g., *pluit* 'is raining', we may conclude that at an earlier time the IE verb was not subjective.

In the course of time the incorporated subject dominated not only the meaning of the root but also that of the Q element, as we may illustrate with virtually any verb form. The Vedic optative first plural *vánāmahai* accordingly means 'we want to' plus '(we) win', that is 'we want to win', By contrast the desiderative element in Japanese may merely dominate a further segment of the verb form, as in the form *seraretashi* of the formal written style. The simple desiderative, as in *shitashi,* may be translated 'I want to do'. The desiderative suffix may be added to the passive, of which the simple form *serareru* may be translated 'be done'. The passive also may have a potential meaning; because such a meaning suggests "politeness," the passive may be used to refer to the action of the person addressed. Where the desiderative is made of the passive, as in *seraretashi,* the form is translated 'I want you to do'. The desiderative accordingly dominates only the "passive" affix, not the entire verb form. A similar example of restricted dominance was given above for Turkish. In late PIE such a restricted field of dominance was found in only a few forms; in the dialects these were lost, or modified in accordance with the subjective principle.

As the following examples indicate, the moods in PIE are controlled by the person indicated in the finite form (Delbrück 1900:425–427):

23. RV 5.54.15.

idáṃ	sú	me	maruto	haryatā	váco
this	well	for-me	O-Maruts	you-must-accept	word

yásya	tárema	tárasā	śatáṃ	hímāḥ
whose	we-may-pass	through-strength	100	winters

'Receive favorably this my word, O Maruts, through whose strength we would like to survive a hundred years.'

24. RV 9.101.9.

ā́	bhara . . .	rayíṃ	yéna	vánāmahai
hither	you-must-bear . . .	riches	by-which	we-want-to-win

'Bring riches here, through which we wish to conquer.'

Examples of the dominance of the incorporated person marker over participles are also common, such as:

25. RV 4.2.3.

antár	īyase	aruṣā́	yujānó
between	thou-goest	two-roans	yoking

'You travel among [them] after yoking your two roans.'

Nonfinite verb forms could be used in this way to maintain the subject of the dominant verb.

As a consequence of dominance by the subjective component of the principal verb, the inflected verbs of embedded clauses lost their independent qualifier meanings; the qualifier affixes then indicated subordination. This effect is clearest with regard to the optative and the subjunctive, which in the course of time were used largely in embedded clauses and lost the meaning found for them in independent clauses of the earliest texts (see Macdonell 1916:362–363).

Further effects will be noted in greater detail below, such as the well-known "sequence of tenses" in the classical languages and modifications of person in embedded clauses, e.g.:

26. I told him that he should come.
From: I told him: (You) come!

At this point I have been primarily concerned with indicating the subject's dominance over individual verb forms and its consequences for the development of the verb systems in late PIE and the dialects. In view of these modifications we must determine the meaning of the PIE inflected forms from their uses in simple sentences, as we will do in the following section.

4.3. Modified Forms of the PIE Simple Sentence.

4.3.1. Declarative Sentences. As we have seen above, the simplest form of the sentence in late PIE was characterized by normal word order and by an intonation pattern with final drop. Such a sentence could consist of a verb alone, as in the frequently cited expressions for natural phenomena (Brugmann 1904*a*:624–626):

27. Skt. vāti (cf. RV 4.40.3)
'Blows' = 'The wind is blowing.'

Other intransitive verbs could also make up a complete sentence, as in the Hittite *Muršilis Sprachlähmung* (Götze and Pedersen 1934:4, § 3) with sentence connective *nu:*

28. nu nahhun
'And I got scared.'

As Meillet and others have indicated, in PIE such sentences were complete and did not require a separate subject. When a "subject" was included, it is to be regarded as appositional to the subjective element of the verb form, as in Meillet's example:

29. mūgit taurus
he-bellows bull
'The bull is bellowing.'

When transitive verbs were used in sentences, an object was required. Next to sentences consisting of verb alone, object plus verb made up the simplest form of the sentence. The object could stand in any one of the oblique cases, as exemplified in Chapter 2. An example of a sentence with an accusative object is from *Muršilis Sprachlähmung* (Götze and Pedersen 1934:6, § 15):

30. nu GUD puhugarin únuu̯er
and bull scape- they-adorned
'And they adorned a scape-bull.'

If in addition a subject was specified, the sentence observed the order SOV, as in the next line (Götze and Pedersen 1934:6, § 16):

31. nu- šan ᴰUTUˢᴵ ŠU-an daiš
Ptc.-Ptc. (my) sun = I hand put
'And I placed my hand on it.'

Such simple sentences could have many surface varieties, among them coordinate expressions, as in the following sentence from a Strophic poem of the Rigveda. The object consists of two coordinate genitives; the verb *kir* is inflected in the intensive subjunctive.

32. RV 4.39.1. divás pṛthivyā́ utá carkirāma
sky earth and we-praise
'We want to praise the sky and the earth.'

Whatever the varieties, the normal unmarked form of the PIE sentence has the order (S)OV.

With marked order the position of these sentence constituents is changed. A fine example may be taken from the Hittite Laws; in a sequence that has SOV order when the S refers to a specific kind of culprit, the order is OSV when S refers to an indefinite actor (J. Friedrich 1959:68, § 25):

33. takku SIG_4 kuiški taiezzi
if bricks someone he-steals
'If someone steals bricks . . .'

Or the verb may stand in first position, as in:

34. RV 4.48.1. vihí hótrā
you-enjoy poured-offerings
'Enjoy the libations!'

In such sentences the verb is often an imperative, as in Example 34.

Imperatives and vocatives may also make up a complete sentence or a complete clause, as is indicated by their accentuation in the Rigveda when they are embedded or when each is taken as a separate clause:

35. RV 4.9.1. ágne mṛḷá mahā́ṅ asi
O-Agni you-be-gracious great thou-art
'Be gracious, Agni. You are great.'

Like other verb forms, imperatives may be accompanied by objects.

Besides the sentences consisting of a verb, with or without an object and an explicit subject, sentences could be expanded by means of optional noun phrases. These noun phrases could stand in any of the oblique cases, according to the sense of the sentence. Their position was determined by stylistic reasons. Because such expansions are similar to one another regardless of the case, only a few examples will be given here (J. Friedrich 1959:68, § 25):

36. takku šamanaz $NA_4^{HI.A}$ kuiški taiezzi
if from-foundation stones someone he-steals
'If someone steals stones from a foundation . . .'

37. RV 4.16.5. ubhé ā́ paprau ródasī mahitvā́
both up he-filled worlds with-great-size
'(Indra) filled up both worlds with his great size.'

The Hittite example contains an ablative in addition to the object and subject; the Vedic example contains an instrumental. Examples with datives, locatives, and genitives might also be included here; they would merely provide further evidence of the variety of adverbial elements that could be included in simple sentences by the addition of noun phrases in oblique cases.

4.3.1.*a*. Nominal Sentences. Equational sentences, in which a substantive is equated with another substantive, an adjective, or a particle, make up a second type of sentence in PIE. In previous treatments they have been called nominal sentences, and accordingly the term is maintained here.

Examples are as follows:

38. Old Persian (Kent 1953:116). adam Dārayavauš
I Darius
'I am Darius.'

39. RV 7.12.3. tvám̩ váruṇa
you Varuna
'You are Varuna.'

40. Hittite (J. Friedrich 1960:117). attaš aššuš
father good
'The father is good.'

41. RV 4.28.5. evā́ satyám maghavānā
thus true benefactors
'Thus is the truth, O benefactors.'

As these examples illustrate, a verb is not required in such sentences. The sentence consists simply of a topic in first position plus a description or predicate in second.

The basic form of nominal sentences has, however, been a matter of dispute. Some Indo-Europeanists propose that the absence of a verb in nominal sentences is a result of ellipsis and assume an underlying verb ˀ*es*- 'be' (Benveniste 1950). They support this assumption by pointing to the requirement of such a verb if the nominal sentence is in the past tense:

42. Hittite (J. Friedrich 1960:118). *ABU.IA* genzuu̯alaš ešta
my-father merciful he-was
'My father was merciful.'

Yet, as we have noted, tense was not a feature of the verbal system of PIE; sentences like Example 42 are accordingly post-Indo-European. Time of the state or action could have been indicated earlier by particles. Accordingly I follow Meillet (1906–1908) in the view that nominal sentences did not require a verb but that a verb might be included for emphasis.

This conclusion may be supported by noting that the qualifiers which were found in PIE could be used in nominal sentences without a verb. As an example we may cite a Hittite sentence which is negative and imperative (J. Friedrich 1960:117):

43. 1-aš 1-edani menahhanda lē idāluš
one to-another towards not evil
'One should not be evil toward another one.'

Yet, if a passage was to be explicit, a form of the root ˀ*es* could be used, as in the following:

44. RV 4.30.1. nákir indra tvád úttaro ná jyā́yāṅ asti
no-one O-Indra from-you higher not greater he-is
'No one is higher than you, Indra, nor greater.'

In the course of time a nominal sentence required a verb; this development is in accordance with the subjective characteristic of PIE and the endings which came to replace the individual qualifier markers of early PIE. The various dialects no longer had a distinct equational sentence type. Verbs might of course be omitted by ellipsis. And, remarkably, in Slavic, nominal sentences were reintroduced, as Meillet has demonstrated (1906–1908). The reintroduction is probably a result of influence from OV languages, such as the Finno-Ugric. This phenomenon illustrates that syntactic constructions and syntactic characteristics must be carefully studied before they can be ascribed to inheritance. In North Germanic too an OV characteristic was reintroduced, with the loss of prefixes towards the end of the first millennium A.D. (Lehmann 1970*a*). Yet in spite of these subsequent OV influences, nominal sentences must be assumed for PIE.

4.3.1.*b*. Sentences Expanded by Means of Particles. In addition to expansions by means of additional nouns in nonrequired cases, as illustrated above in Examples 36 and 37, sentences could be expanded by means of particles.

Three subsets of particles came to be particularly important. One of these is the set of preverbs, such as *ā* in Example 37. Another is the set of sentence connectives, such as Hitt. *nu*. The third is the set of qualifier expressions, e.g., PIE *mē* '(must) not'. An additional subset, conjunctions introducing clauses, will be discussed below in the section on compound clauses.

Preverbs are distinctively characterized by being closely associated with verbs and modifying their meaning. In their normal position they stand directly before verbs (Watkins 1964), as in the following line from an Archaic hymn:

45. RV 8.48.8.

mā́	no	aryó	anukāmám	párā	dāḥ
not	us	of-foe	desire	away	you-give

'Do not desert us in accordance with the desire of our enemy.'

As in this example, the preverb is accented in independent clauses (Macdonell 1916:468–469); but in subordinate clauses it is unaccented, as is *saṃ* below:

46. RV 8.48.1.

víśve	yáṃ	devā́	utá	mártiāso
all	which	gods	and	mortals

mádhu	bruvánto	abhí	saṃ	cáranti
honey	saying	about	together	they-come

'About which all gods and mortals, calling it honey, assemble.'

In marked order, on the other hand, the preverb stands at the beginning of the clause:

47. RV 8.48.2.

ánu	rāyá	ṛdhyāḥ
towards	wealth	you-thrive

'Prosper us with wealth.'

Such constructions are also prominent in Homeric Greek and in Hittite, as in the following passage from the Hittite Laws (J. Friedrich 1959:76, § 56):

48.

takku	annaš	TÚG-*ZU*	IBILA-ši	edi	nāi	nu-za-kan
if	mother	garment-his	son-her	away	she-directs	Ptc.-Refl.-Ptc.

DUMU^{MEŠ} -*ŠU*	parā	šūizzi
son-her	forward	she-pushes

'If a mother throws out the garment of her son, then she expels her son.'

Preverbs in this way make up a distinctive syntactic combination with their verbal roots. As the translations given above indicate, for example that of Skt. *párā dāḥ* (Example 45), these combinations had specific meanings differing from those of the root. Moreover, they also developed distinct syntactic properties, as in the transitive combination (Example 47), when *anu* is used with the root *ṛdh-,* which normally has an intransitive meaning.

In the course of time these combinations were conflated to single words, as in Classical Greek and Latin and in the other late dialects. This development took place over a long period of time, as is evident from combinations like Gothic:

49. ga-u-laubjats
'Do you two believe?'

in which the preverb is separated from the verb by the interrogative particle. The IE pattern has also left reflexes in Modern German, as in *Vór-mund* 'guardian', OHG *fóramundo,* in which the preverbal element was accented in accordance with compound-noun patterning. In *verliéren* 'lose', on the other hand, the preverb is unaccented. By its vowel it indicates the Germanic and IE situation in which its etymon, maintained also in Hitt. *parā* (Example 48), Skt. *prá,* Gk. *pró,* and so on, was a separate word in Germanic until the time when a stress accent was fixed on the first syllable of words. And the German "separable-prefix" construction, as in:

50. Er liest vor. 'He is lecturing.'

maintains the pattern in which the preverb had its own accent.

The PIE combination, in which each of the elements of the preverb-verb syntagm was independent, though the combination functioned as a unit, required the classification of preverbs as a distinct class of particles and of sentences in which such combinations occurred as a distinct subclass. (See also Delbrück 1888:44–51, 432–471; 1897:103–109.) The subsequent history of these elements, when the preverb came to be attached to verbs in some combinations and developed independently to adverbs and to prepositions, varies from dialect to dialect and must be separately described for each.

While the syntactic patterning of preverbs is well understood, the role of sentence connectives is not. Delbrück had pointed out that particles like Skt. *sá, nú,* and *tú* were used as connectives in clauses (1888:215–216, 514–519). Moreover, a connective *nū* frequently introduces sentences. When Hittite was discovered, it was noted that cognates of these particles, *nu, ta, šu,* were consistently used to introduce sentences (J. Friedrich 1960:155–161). Although E. H. Sturtevant brought this use dramatically to the attention of Indo-Europeanists by proposing that the demonstrative pronoun, as in Skt. *sás, sā́, tád,* was a reflex of these particles combined with anaphoric pronouns, the syntactic significance for PIE of the sentence connectives was not widely discussed until Albrecht Götze and Myles Dillon linked the Hittite syntactic patterning with the use of sentence-initial particles in Celtic (Sturtevant 1942:26, Dillon 1947:15–24). Yet the syntactic patterning of such elements has not been precisely described, in part because we do not yet know how sentence connectives function in the various language types.

Sentence connectives are prominent in the VSO language Squamish (Kuipers 1967:154–187, 169). If sentence connectives are to be expected in VSO languages, we might look for a similar syntactic pattern in the VSO Insular Celtic languages, where they indeed occur. If typological features are to be expected in a specific language type, the sentence connectives and their patterning in the Anatolian and possibly even in the Indic languages may then have been borrowings. Accordingly an interpretation of the use of sentence connectives faces many problems. For the understanding of PIE syntax, the use of sentence connectives will have to be investigated in each of the dialects. See also the urging of Erich Neu (1970:61) concerning the need of investigations.

Carol Raman has carried out such a study for Hittite. She has concluded that in clauses with *nu* the same noun is topic as in the main or earlier clause. This function may be illustrated in a passage from *Ein althethitisches Gewitterritual* (Neu 1970:10, 6). After the introduction of the subject, with a modifying clause, three verbs without a specified subject are introduced by *nu* (or *nu* + *e* 'they'), as follows: "The UBĀRU people and whichever lord happens to be sitting before the king . . ."

51. ne šara tienzi nu appa tienzi ne aranda
up they-step back they-step they-remain-standing
"they get up, they step back and remain standing."

This function of *nu* may have developed because the topic noun is commonly deleted from the matrix clause and kept in the embedded clause, as here. An English chronicler would phrase the above sentence: "The UBĀRU people and the lord who happens to be sitting before the king get up, step back, and remain standing." For the understanding of this pattern in Hittite syntax we may note that *nu* in this use becomes much more frequent in the later texts (J. Friedrich 1960:157).

Johannes Friedrich also points out (1960:157–158) that *nu* is not used in certain clause and sentence patterns, for example, at the beginning of a new section, in commands and exclamations after negative commands, in emphatic sentences, in parenthetical supplementary clauses, and in the somewhat similar clauses indicating state *(Zustandssätze).* In all of these patterns there is characteristically a shift in the topic; accordingly the absence of *nu* would support Raman's conclusion. Furthermore, it is tempting to see in the expanding use of *nu* in later Hittite an influence from neighboring VSO languages, such as the Semitic.

If we account for the use of *nu* in this way, we still need to consider the comparable use of *ta* and, less frequently, *šu* in the older language (J. Friedrich 1960:161). These are the particles that seem to be cognate with Indic *ta* and *sa* and thus led Sturtevant to propose his etymology of the demonstrative **so, sā, tod.* There is no doubt about the occurrence of these Hittite sentence connectives; but both are far less frequent than is *nu* in the later texts. Since however the particles are used similarly in both Hittite and Vedic, we may well assume etyma for them in PIE and the use of sentence connectives in some of its sentences. But such use was probably similar to that noted by Raman for Hittite; sentence connectives accordingly were found in only a small number of sentences. Such sentences are not to be characterized as a specific subclass; the sentence connective in PIE should rather be classed with conjunctions.

We are then left with the problem of accounting for introductory particles like *nū́* in Vedic (Delbrück 1888:514–515) and the sentence connectives that Dillon and Götze noted in Old Irish (Dillon 1947). Vedic *nū́* simply introduces clauses, with the meaning 'now'. From such a use the Hittite pattern might well have been expanded, and that of Old Irish *no* as well (Watkins 1962:113–114; 1963:10–17). As noted above, "empty preverbs" to which enclitic pronouns are suffixed may well be characteristic of VSO languages. Such an assumption may be supported by a remarkable parallelism in the use of the Squamish "clitics/namʔ/ 'go' and /mʔi/ 'come'" and forms of Hitt. *pāi-* 'go' and *uu̯a-* 'come' (Kuipers 1967: 207; J. Friedrich 1960:159); in both Squamish and Hittite these verbs stand initially, functioning like particles in that other particles may be affixed to them. The occurrence of sentence connectives is then a problem for general grammar as well as for the grammar of PIE.

The particles which signal Q characteristics, like the interrogative and negative, must however be regarded as indicating specific clause types. These clause types will be discussed individually in the following sections.

4.3.2. Interrogatives. As noted above, § 4.1.3, interrogative sentences could be distinguished by intonation alone, as in Example 7, or by the use of an interrogative particle or other interrogative words, as in Example 8. The device of order was apparently not used to indicate questions in PIE. But both other devices were used in each of the types, clarification questions and confirmation questions (see Delbrück 1900:259-288).

Clarification questions generally have the interrogative pronoun or particle in initial position, as in the following Hittite example (J. Friedrich 1960:147):

52. kuit apāt
what that
'What's the purpose of that?'

Initial position is the general pattern in the dialects; but in marked patterns the interrogative word could stand elsewhere, as in the following Strophic passage:

53. RV 4.5.8. pravā́cyaṃ vácasaḥ kím me asyá
to-be-reported of-word what to-me of-it
'What of this word is to be reported to me?'

This may also be the reason for the position of the interrogative in the following example (J. Friedrich 1960:147):

54. nu namma kuit
Ptc. still what
'What is there in addition?'

More than one interrogative word could also be used in clarification questions, as in the following question (see also Delbrück 1893:511; 1900:256-260):

55. Odyssey 1.170. tís póthen eis andrôn?
who whence are-you of-men
'Who among men are you, and where are you from?' (= 'Who is your father?')

This pattern, found also in Polish (Wachowicz 1974) is not possible in many IE dialects, including English. In general, clarification questions have one interrogative word and this is initial in its clause, as also in:

56. Odyssey 1.158. ê kaí moi nemesḗseai
? now with-me you-will-be-angry
'Will you be angry with me?'

Confirmation questions also have an initial or near-initial interrogative, unless they are without an overt means of expression, as in the following Hittite example (J. Friedrich 1960:146):

57. ŠEŠ-IA-za malāši
brother-my-Ptc. Refl. you-consent
'Are you agreed, brother?'

As noted above, § 4.1.4, specific particles are found in the various dialects, such as *nu* in Sanskrit, *nú* or *ē̂* in Greek, *ne, nonne,* and *num* in Latin, *u* in Gothic, *li* in Slavic, and so on.

58.	John 9:35.	sù	pisteúeis	eis	tòn	huiòn	toû theoû
	Gothic.	þu	ga-u-laubeis	du		sunau	gudis?
		you	be-?-lieve		on-the	son	of-god

'Do you believe on the Son of God?'

It has often been pointed out that these particles are located initially or in near-initial position as a result of a transportation rule (Streitberg 1920:161). The rule was proposed by Wackernagel in an influential article (1892:333–434); it will be discussed below in § 4.5.

In the later dialects, interrogative particles are associated with presuppositions. Greek *ou* presupposes a positive answer, as do *nonne* in Latin and *niu* in Gothic. Presumably this is also the force of the initial "negative" particle in Hittite (J. Friedrich 1960:146):

59. *UL*-u̯ar-an-kan tuētaza memii̯anaz kuennir
"not" quotes-him-away from-you from-word they-killed
'Didn't they kill him at your word?'

On the other hand, Gk. *mḗ* plus *ē̂* presupposes a negative answer, as do Lat. *num* and Goth. *ibai.*

60.	Odyssey 9.405.	ē̂	mḗ tís	seu	mêla	brotôn	aékontos	elaúnei
		?	no one	your	sheep	of-mortals	unwilling	he-drives

'It is scarcely true that some one of mortals is driving off your sheep against your will?'

Since the particles differ from dialect to dialect, it is difficult to argue that interrogative particles with specific presuppositions should be ascribed to PIE. The pattern may have been inherited, however, and the surface forms changed; for as Hittite *natta* (generally written as Akkadian *UL*) and Greek *ou* illustrate, such particles were commonly changed or new particles were introduced.

In addition to the simple questions illustrated above, PIE very likely had disjunctive questions. Delbrück gives examples with *pluti* (1900: 268); in Greek the particle *ê/ēé* was used, either between the two queries or initially in both.

61. Iliad 10.534. pseúsomai ê étumon eréō?
I-lie or truth I-tell
'Should I lie or should I tell the truth?'

In a nominal sentence, only the predicate nouns are essential, as in:

62. Odyssey 1.226. eilapínē ēè gámos
revel or wedding-feast
'Is it a drinking party or a wedding feast?'

In such disjunctive sentences the function of the particle has been argued. It has been interpreted as an interrogative particle. But for Delbrück it was simply a disjunctive conjunction (1900:268–269), and the interrogative itself was signaled by intonation. If so, the Greek examples cited here would be similar to Sanskrit disjunctive questions. Since Hittite disjunctive questions are also indicated by a disjunctive particle rather than by an interrogative particle, Delbrück's conclusion seems the correct one.

Apart from the final interrogative particles attested in Latin, Slavic, and Germanic, the indications for questions are characteristic of those in VO languages. In addition to these particles, only the particle movement rules suggest that a final interrogative particle may have been present in PIE, in keeping with other OV patterns. By the time of the dialects, however, the patterns for interrogation were comparable to those of most current IE dialects and consisted either of a characteristic intonation pattern or of interrogative words.

4.3.3. Sentence Negation. The archaic IE dialects, such as Vedic with *mấ* and *na,* distinguish between two sentence particles for the negative; on the basis of their forms in other dialects, such as Gk. *mḗ* and Lat. *ne,* these are reconstructed **mḗ* and **ne.* Hittite has a lateral in the first, *lē,* in accordance with the sporadic change of nasals to *l,* as in *lāman* 'name'; Greek has *ou, ouk* of unknown origin rather than **ne.* Despite the difference in surface form, in both dialects the functions of the negative pair correspond closely with those in Sanskrit. The change in form provides another illustration that syntactic patterns may be maintained although changes are introduced in surface expressions.

In some dialects, such as Tocharian B, Germanic, and Latin, the distinction between the two particles has been lost. Tocharian B has only *mā,* but in Tocharian A *mar* corresponds to PIE **mē* and *mā* to **ne.*

Elements may also be combined with the negative particles, for "strengthening," in the words of Jespersen (1924:335), as in Hitt. *natta,* Skt. *nēd,* Lat. *nōn,* and so on. On the basis of an extended form with *-i* in several dialects, Lat. *nei, nī,* Lithuanian (Lith.) *neĩ,* Slavic (Slav.) *ni,* Delbrück (1897:524–529) assumes **nei* for PIE. PIE would then have had three negative particles: **mē, *ne,* and **nei,* an emphatic form of **ne; *nei* however must have been only a variant of **ne.*

In negative prohibitions **mē* was used, **ne (nei)* elsewhere. In the Rigveda, the verb used with *mā́* was an injunctive:

63. RV 3.33.8. étad váco jaritar mā́pi mr̥ṣṭhāḥ
this word O-singer (do)-not-away you-forget
'Do not forget this word, singer!'

Besides its use with the other moods, *ná* could also be used with the injunctive; the injunctive then expressed a general statement (Hoffmann 1967:99–100):

64. RV 3.3.1. átha dhármāṇi sanátā ná dūduṣat
thus laws from-old not he-forgets
'Thus he (Agni) never forgets the laws.'

Other dialects support the basis of the assumed distribution of the negative particles in PIE, even though they have verb forms other than the injunctive with reflexes of **mē.*

Although the functions of the negative particles are clear, the position of the particles in the PIE sentence must be determined. In the dialects the negative particles are commonly placed before the verb (Delbrück 1897:521; Jensen 1959:188 for Armenian; J. Friedrich 1960:145), as in the following Tocharian A sentence (Krause 1955:38):

65. ñatsey-ac mā kumnäṣ
distress-to not he-comes
'He won't fall into distress.'

Preverbal placement is apparently archaic; it survives in Latin verbs like *nōlo* < *ne vōlo,* in Goth. *nist,* generally in Lithuanian, and in some Slavic forms. But in later texts of most dialects the negative particle stands at or near the beginning of the sentence, a placement pattern also found frequently in the archaic dialects:

66. RV 4.31.9. nahí ṣmā te śatám caná rā́dho váranta āmúraḥ
not-for at-all your 100 and-not giving they-check enemies
'For they do not check your giving at all, not even a hundred enemies.'

Since the placement pattern varies in this way, we assume that placement in either of the two positions results from a late placement rule and that earlier the negative particle was postverbal, as may be expected in an OV language. K. J. Dover (1960:14) assumes such a placement rule for Greek, noting that it is observed more rigorously in the earlier texts.

Postverbal negatives are attested in Latin, as in the following negative question in Plautus's *Curculio* 423:

67. nostin?
'Do you not recognize [it]?'

To this question Lyco replies:

68. Quidni noverim?
'Why shouldn't I recognize it?'

Thus the negative particle is postposed after interrogatives as well as verbs, as also in *Truculentus* 723, where the response is simply:

69. Quidni?
'Why not?'

Since it is precisely the emphatic *nī* < **ne* + **i* which is used in these passages, I would like to propose that the "strengthening" element is that used to indicate declarative meaning (§ 4.1.4). The two elements would have contracted when **ne* was postverbal and was followed in turn by the declarative **-i.*

There is additional evidence for postverbal position of the negative. In Hittite, both negative particles can stand finally. Johannes Friedrich interprets such a use as emphatic (1960:146); this interpretation supports the proposed origin for **nei:*

70.

namma-ma-kan	KUR	^{URU}Hapalla	kuenta-i̯a	*UL*
for-however-down	country	Hapalla	you-smote-and	not

epta-i̯a-at	*UL* (= natta)
you-took-and-it	not

'For you didn't however conquer the country Hapalla, and you didn't capture it.'

Schwyzer also gives examples of the negative particles in final position in Greek (1950:596–597); again the use is for emphasis.

Normally, however, in Greek and in the other dialects, the negative particles are placed preverbally; if negation were not expressed postverbally in OV languages, the small amount of evidence for it in the IE dialects would scarcely seem adequate to propose such a position for PIE. Because of this small amount of evidence, it may be that negation was indicated by a postverbal marker only in some negative patterns.

The various dialects have introduced further new negative patterns. Correlative patterns came to be expressed with special negatives, such as Gk. *oúte* and Lat. *neque,* rather than the repeated simple negative as in the Hittite sentence (Example 70) above. The privative syllable **ne, *n,* which was confined to nominal compounds in PIE, came to be used more extensively; it was also used with participles, and eventually it could be prefixed to any word, leading to the situation in the dialects where there is no distinction between word negation and sentence negation.

In the dialects sentence-negative particles were typically placed early in the sentence, though after interrogatives, as the second question from the Odyssey (Example 72) illustrates:

71. Odyssey 3.249. poû Menélaos éēn?
where Menelaos he-was
'Where was Menelaos?'

72. Odyssey 3.251. ê ouk Árgeos êen Akhaiikoû
? not Argos he-was Achaean
'Was he not in Achaean Argos?'

This is the normal position for negative particles in the dialects. When subjects were included in sentences, negative particles were placed after them:

73. Odyssey 3.313. Kài sú, phílos, mḗ dēthà dómōn ápo têl' alálēso,
and you friend not long houses from far you-travel
'Then don't, O friend, travel long far from your home.'

Negative particles could also be placed before the words to be negated:

74. Odyssey 4.64. epeì oú ke kakoì toioúsde tékoien
for not indeed lowly such they-might-beget
'For lowly men surely wouldn't beget such [sons].'

In time placement was regulated by the specific rules in each dialect.

4.3.4. The Reflexive and the Reciprocal. As indicated above, § 4.1.5, the categories for reflexivity and reciprocity are commonly expressed with verbal affixes in OV and also in VSO languages. Only in SVO languages can we expect to find pronominal forms for use in expressing these categories. The recognition that these are Q categories expressed in this way permits us to account for the IE middle inflection and for the development of pronominal means of expression as dialects came to be SVO in structure.

The functions of the middle were recognized by the Indian grammarians, and are well reviewed by Delbrück (1897:412–432). These functions are also found in Greek and in Hittite (Neu 1968:92–116). As an example of reflexive meaning, Johannes Friedrich cites *unuttat* 'she adorned herself'; as an example of reciprocal meaning, *šarrandat* 'they parted from one another' (1960:135). Since Hittite in this way corroborated the uses in the other dialects, there can be no question of the basic uses of the middle in PIE. As noted above, it was expressed by an *-o-* affix. In Hittite, further middle suffixes were commonly added after the middle endings inherited from PIE: *-ri, -ru, -di, -t* (Sturtevant 1951:145-148). These are characteristics that we would expect of OV languages.

Basically it is the function of the middle to indicate that the verbal meaning, whether action or state, is to be interpreted with reference to the subject. Delbrück gives excellent illustrations (1897:412–432), as with forms of the Sanskrit root *yaj-* 'sacrifice':

75. RV 4.24.5. ā́d íd dha néma indriyáṃ yajanta
then indeed Ptc. some Indra's-power they-sacrifice
'Then some sacrifice to the power of Indra for their own benefit.'

Active forms indicate that an action, such as a sacrifice, is being carried out with no special reference to the subject; middle forms indicate that the action has some reference to the subject. Depending on the context, this could be reflexive:

76. RV 1.134.3. vāyúr yuñkte róhitā . . . ráthe
Vayu he-yoked the-two-tawny-ones . . . to-chariot
'Vayu yoked the tawny pair to his chariot.'

The meaning in other contexts is reciprocal:

77. RV 10.88.17. yátrā vádete ávaraḥ páraśca
where they-speak lower upper-and
'Where the upper and lower speak to one another.'

In such examples, the function of the middle is like that of reflexive and reciprocal forms in a language like Turkish.

Some roots in PIE came to be used generally or exclusively with middle endings, e.g., Skt. *ā́ste* 'he sits', Gk. *hḗstai* 'he sits', in contrast with forms of PIE *sed-*, which characteristically has active endings, as in Skt. *sádati*.

78. RV 7.11.1. ny àgne hótā prathamáḥ sadehá
down Agni priest first sit-here
'Sit down here, Agni, first as priest.'

Agni clearly is not asked to sit for his own benefit. But in another hymn of Book 7, priests who wish to get benefits from Indra are described as sitting at the soma sacrifice like bees or flies on honey:

79. RV 7.32.2. mádhau ná mákṣa ā́sate
on-honey like flies, bees they-sit
'They sit [for their own benefit] like bees on honey.'

Roots which came to be inflected consistently in the middle, such as PIE **key-* 'lie', but with "active" meaning, are referred to as deponents, notably in Latin and Celtic grammar, but also in Hittite (J. Friedrich 1960: 135). As the handbooks inform us, the middle meaning of deponents and of roots inflected only in the middle was eventually lost; Skt. *śéte* and Gk. *keîtai* scarcely mean 'he is lying down for his own benefit', but simply 'he is lying down'. Similarly, Lat. *sequor* means 'I follow'. The force of the middle came to be lost as the marker was no longer distinct; this development led to other innovations than that of deponents and of active meanings.

A development in all the dialects was the rise of reflexive and reciprocal pronouns. In PIE, as in many OV languages, there was no reflexive or reciprocal pronoun. In the dialects an adjective **sew(e)-*, meaning 'own', was taken over as a reflexive adjective; it was also adapted as the basis for the reflexive pronoun. The lack of a reflexive pronoun in Sanskrit and the variation in forms from dialect to dialect leave no doubt about the late development of these forms. Statements in the handbooks ascribing a reflexive pronoun to PIE (Brugmann 1904*a*:409) must be revised. The late origin of the reflexive pronoun may also be demonstrated by noting its defective set of forms in the dialects, even in a contemporary dialect like German. A full paradigm never was developed. In the third person a single form, *sich,* is used without distinction in number or gender. In the first and second person, forms of the personal pronoun are used; on the basis of parallelism with these, a genitive *seiner* was developed for *sich.* The reflexives in the various dialects could be cited similarly to illustrate that reflexive pronouns and reciprocal pronouns are recent in the IE languages.

The shift from a special verb form, such as we would expect in an OV language, to reflexive pronouns and adjectives is also illustrated by an observation Delbrück made about changes in Sanskrit (1897:413). When *sva-* 'own, one's own' came to be used, the accompanying verb form might simply be in the active:

80. RV 1.46.9. svā́ṃ vavríṃ kúha dhitsathaḥ
own body where you-desire-to-place
'Where do you intend to deposit your own bodily form?'

For this line Karl Geldner has an interesting note (1951–1957:I, 57), suggesting that the verb may be active but have a middle sense; the line would then ask the Aśvins: 'Where do you intend to put on your natural bodily form?'

Another indication of innovations to indicate reflexivity is the use in Homer of the adjective *philós,* often to be translated 'dear', to convey a reflexive meaning (Benveniste 1969:335–353):

81. Odyssey 12.331. phílas hó ti kheîras híkoito
own what ever hands it-comes-to
'whatever might come into their hands'

This use of *phílas* also reminds us of the shift in syntactic order which necessitated the introduction of new elements. As we have noted above, an innovation was also introduced in the word for 'not', *ou, ouk;* a third notable innovation is found for the conjunction 'and', *kai.* It has not been determined whether these elements are native neologisms or whether they were borrowed. They are powerful indicators however of a shift in syntactic devices.

As a part of the syntactic shift, the passive was developed as a category contrasting with the active. The process has been well described. For some verbal roots the reflexive sense is close to a passive; a root like Skt. *muc-* 'release' would, as Delbrück illustrates (1897:432–435), scarcely be distinguishable as a reflexive, 'gain a release with reference to oneself', or as a passive, 'be released'.

82. RV 1.31.4. śvātréṇa yát pitrór múcyase páry
with-strength when parents you-free-yourself (were-freed) about
'As soon as you were freed from your parents with force.'

See also Neu 1968:109–116. The history of the development of the passive category must be pursued in each of the dialects. It must be recognized as distinct from the middle when an agent comes to be included regularly in its clause.

The middle itself was gradually replaced by constructions made up of verbal forms combined with reflexives and reciprocals, and by intransitives. Its basic meaning in PIE may have been weakened even in the earliest texts, as Neu has illustrated in his fine study. A Hittite sentence, such as the following with declarative marker *-i* and a direct object, may have been interpreted with little of the middle force:

83.	Neu 1968:55.	nan-kan	hattešna	GAM-anta	hattari
		Ptc.-it-Ptc. (down)	in-pit	downward	he-stabs

'And he stabs it downward into the pit. (And he butchers the piglet in the pit [for his own benefit].)'

Middle forms were also accompanied by interrogative and negative qualifiers, but, since these functioned as they did with active forms, no examples will be given here.

4.3.5. Necessitative and Obligative. Forms with necessitative modality indicate that the action should or must be carried out. The meaning is straightforward and transparent in positive sentences; in the negative, however, and in questions and dependent clauses, the meaning is less straightforward and accordingly more difficult to interpret. Of forms indicating necessitative modality, those in the positive of the imperative are the simplest to interpret. Imperative forms in the third singular are also most clearly distinguished from forms indicating declarative and reflexive modality, as in Sanskrit:

	Present Indicative (Declarative)	Middle (Reflexive-Reciprocal)	Imperative
3 sg.	bharati	bharate	bharatu
3 pl.	bharanti	bharante	bharantu

In these endings, accordingly, there was a direct contrast between the *-u* of the imperative and the *-i* of the present indicative, as well as the *-o(+ i > -e)* of the middle.

In the other persons the surface forms are not parallel. The second singular of the imperative was distinguished by the bare root, as in Lat. *fer, fac, dic, duc;* by the stem, as in Skt. *bhara,* Gk. *phére;* or by the suffix *-dhi;* the second plural was distinguished by the suffix *–te.* Subsequently the imperative came to be restricted in most dialects to second singular and plural forms. But, in Vedic and in Hittite, forms indicating necessitative meanings are found for all persons and numbers. In Vedic the forms are subjunctive.

Indo-Europeanists have differed in their views on the meaning of the subjunctive in PIE, as on that of the optative. The differences may be due to the development of these moods in the various dialects. Any attempt to equate the uses of the subjunctive and optative in Sanskrit or Greek with the uses of their earlier forms in PIE will lead to serious misinterpretations. For both moods came to be used largely in subordinate clauses. In PIE, however, subordination was indicated by other constructions (§ 4.8). The meanings of the earlier forms of the subjunctive and the optative must therefore be determined from their uses in simple sentences of the early dialects.

Before examining these meanings with the aid of examples from Vedic Sanskrit and Homeric Greek, we may exemplify the effect of the subjective quality of the PIE verb. The dominance of the subject affected the entire sentence, as may be illustrated by means of a Vedic example of the subjunctive in a *yad-* clause:

84. RV 7.27.1.

índraṃ	náro	nemádhitā		havante
Indra	men	opposing-one-another		they-call-on
yát	pā́ryā	yunájate	dhíyas	tā́ḥ
so-that	decisive	he-accept	prayers	those

'Men call on Indra in battle so that he will accept their prayers as decisive.'

In this example and in many other passages, the verb form and the pronoun or person of *yunájate* have been modified in accordance with the well-known rules of complementation in the early dialects. But the subjunctive retains its basic PIE meaning. For if instead of the subordinate clause introduced by *yad* the poem had continued with a direct quotation, this would have been obligative, comparable to:

'Men call on Indra in battle, saying:
"You must accept our prayers as decisive."'

In time the obligative meaning of the subjunctive came to be subsidiary to its function of indicating subordination.

The obligative meaning of the subjunctive has been maintained especially in the first person:

85. Odyssey 8.133.

Deûte,	phíloi,	tòn	kseînon	erṓmetha
hither	friends	the	stranger	we-must-ask

'But come, friends, let us ask the stranger.'

This use, often called hortatory, is apparent also in the following disjunctive question:

86. TS 6.5.4.1.

táṃ	vy	àcikitsaj	juhávānī3	mā́	hauṣā́3m	iti
him	Ptc.	he-pondered	I-offer (Subj.)	not	I-offer	Ptc.

'With reference to him he pondered: "Should I perform an offering or should I not?"'

It is significant that here and in similar passages in Greek, the negative **mē* is used, for this is the negative expression found in hortatory statements (§ 4.3.3).

87. Odyssey 3.55.

Klûthi,	Poseídaon	gaiḗokhe,	mēdè	megḗrēis
listen (Imper.)	Poseidon	Earth-holder	and-not	you-grudge (Subj.)

'Listen, Poseidon Earth-holder, and do not be unwilling.'

The use of the same negative for imperative and subjunctive, and the sequence of the two mood forms, as in this passage, argues strongly in favor of assuming a comparable meaning.

This meaning is also found in questions:

88. Iliad 1.150.

pōs	tís	toi	próphrōn	épesin
why	anyone	you, or Encl.	willing	with-words

peíthētai	Akhaiôn
he-should-be-persuaded (trust in) (Subj.)	of-Greeks

'Why should anyone of the Greeks willingly believe your words? (In what way is it necessary that anyone . . .)'

The hortatory meaning may be clearest in the second person, as in the following passage in which the subjunctive follows an imperative:

89. RV 7.67.4.

ā́	vāṃ	vahantu	sthávirāso	ā́śvāḥ
hither	you-two	they-drive	powerful	horses

píbātho	asmé	súṣutā	mádhūni
you-two-should-drink	with-us	nicely-produced	juices

'Let the powerful horses bring you two here. The two of you must drink with us the nicely extracted soma juices.'

The imperative *vahantu* indicates a clear request, in keeping with its basic necessitative meaning. But the subjunctive also involves entailment; after the Aśvins have arrived, they are required to join in drinking the soma. There is no doubt that a hortatory use also existed in the third person:

90. RV 8.43.22.

imáṃ	naḥ	śṛṇavad	dhávam
this	our	he-must-hear	call

'He must listen to this our call.'

These examples then indicate a close relationship between the subjunctive and the imperative.

Subjunctive forms have also been compared with injunctives; but, as

Hoffmann has demonstrated (1967:249–253), a note of purpose or will accompanies subjunctives, while injunctive forms in the first singular of an aorist stem express an action of the immediate future. The three subjunctives in the following passage illustrate this use:

91. RV 4.33.5.

jyeṣṭhá	āha	camasā́	duā́	karéti (karā + iti)
oldest	he-said	beakers	two	I-must-make-Ptc. I-will-make

káni̇̄yān	trī́n	kṛṇavāméty	āha
younger	three	we-must-make-Ptc. we-will-make	he-said

kaniṣṭhá	āha	catúras	karéti
youngest	he-said	four	I-must-make-Ptc. I-will-make

'The oldest said: "I must make two beakers."
The younger said: "let us make three."
The youngest said: "I will make four."'

As the next stanza of the hymn indicates, the Ribhus actually made four beakers; accordingly, the subjunctive first singular *karā* of the third line means something like: 'I think we must make four.' The basic obligative meaning is accordingly apparent also in the first-person subjunctives.

From this use a future meaning could readily develop, as the translation of the third line above may indicate. Yet the use of the subjunctive after a past tense indicates that purpose is involved, not merely a future action (Hoffmann 1967:244–245):

92. RV 1.32.5.

áhan	vṛtrám . . .
he-slew	Vṛtra . . .

áhiḥ	śayata	upapṛ́k	pṛthivyáḥ
serpent	he-must-lie	related-to	earth

'[Indra] slew Vṛtra; . . . the serpent must lie flat on the earth.'

While interpreting *upapṛk* as closer in meaning to the root *pṛc-* 'fill, fructify', Hoffmann points out the necessitative meaning of the subjunctive, as does Geldner, in his note if not in his translation (1951–1959:I, 37). This passage may also serve to indicate how the subjunctive came to be used in subordinate clauses. In this use, which is prominent in the dialects, it is generally accompanied by a conjunction (Macdonell 1916: 355–360 gives ample examples, as do other grammars).

The obligative meaning that we propose for the subjunctive for PIE is apparent with middle as well as active verb forms. It is also found with interrogatives and with negatives (Macdonell 1916:354–355):

93. RV 2.29.3. kím ū nú vaḥ kṛṇavāma
what Ptc. Ptc. you we-must-do
'What should we do for you?'

94. RV 6.28.3. ná tā́ naśanti
not they they-should-vanish
'They must not disappear.'

The subjunctive and the imperative must then be reconstructed as forms having distinct meanings, as they are distinguished by means of distinct affixes: *e/o* for the subjunctive, *u* and other affixes for the imperative. In accordance with this analysis, the declarative suffix might be expected with some subjunctive forms. And, as is well known, the subjunctive may take primary or secondary endings (see Hoffmann 1967: 268, n. 4; 276; 278, n. 22; Brugmann 1916:524–526). It is noteworthy that the primary endings are particularly prominent in the middle in Indic (Brugmann 1916:533, 643), possibly because the reflexive-reciprocal meaning lends itself to an obligative use:

95. RV 10.108.9. svásāraṃ tvā kṛṇavai
sister you I-will-make
'I will treat you as my sister [for my own benefit].'

Possibly because the subjunctive endings were so close in form to the indicative, the subjunctive was lost as a separate category in the dialects. Its endings were maintained only where they came to be especially prominent, as in Italic and Celtic (Brugmann 1916:539–542) and possibly in Germanic (Lehmann 1943*b*). In many dialects the characteristically dependent verb forms which developed were based on PIE optative forms as well as on subjunctives, for the optative forms were more clearly distinguished.

The subjunctive survived with obligative, necessitative meaning notably in the first person of the Sanskrit imperative and also of the Hittite. In Hittite the endings were reshaped, especially by the attachment of *-u* to the first singular: Act. *-(a)llu,* Mid. *-haharu.* In a similar way the declarative *-i* was attached in Sanskrit to the first singular, *-āni,* and to the second singular, *-dhi,* maintained as a simple dental in Hittite (Sturtevant 1951:142), as in *it* 'go'. The Hittite first singular, *-l(u),* may therefore be equated with Skt. *-n(i),* with *l* corresponding to *n,* as in Hitt. *lā-man,* Skt. *nāman* 'name'. In Sanskrit and Hittite, then, a merged conjugation developed which corresponded to PIE necessitative forms. In the other dialects the imperative alone was maintained; obligative meaning was expressed largely by means of compound sentences.

4.3.6. Voluntative. Especially in early Vedic, wishes were expressed with optative forms, particularly in the first person:

96. RV 7.71.1. vāṃ huvema
you-two we-want-to-call
'We want to call you two [Aśvins].'

97. RV 1.92.8. úṣas tám aśyāṃ yaśásam . . . rayím
O-dawn that I-want-to-obtain glorious . . . wealth
'Dawn, I would like to obtain that glorious wealth.'

98. Odyssey 13.42. amúmona d' oíkoi ákoitin
noble Ptc. at-home wife
nostḗsas heúroimi sùn arteméessi phíloisin
having-returned I-would-like-to-find with safe friends
'On my return I hope to find my noble wife and friends safe at home.'

Wishes such as these are very similar to expressions of likelihood. Especially in Greek, the optative generally expressed possibility or likelihood, even in first-person forms:

99. Odyssey 8.216. prôtós k' ándra báloimi oisteúsas
first Ptc. man I-would-hit having-shot-arrow
'I would be first to shoot and hit a man.'

Because these two meanings are found in the earliest texts of those dialects that alone have maintained the optative as a distinct formal and semantic category, the central meaning of the optative has been disputed.

Delbrück has contributed most to the view that the basic meaning of the optative was voluntative (1871:13); he was strongly opposed by William W. Goodwin (1893:373–389), who viewed the optative as "a weak future form" (1893:388). Yet both the potential and the "weak future" uses are found in subordinate clauses, or, as in Example 99, with a particle indicating potentiality: *ke.* These meanings may then be assumed to be secondary to the voluntative meaning, which is found in independent sentences, as illustrated above.

The development may be illustrated by the following passage:

100. RV 8.44.23.

yád agne syā́m ahám tvám
if O-Agni I-am (Opt.) I you

tvám vā ghā syā́ ahám
you Ptc. Ptc. you-are (Opt.) I

syúṣ ṭe satyā́ ihā́śíṣaḥ
they-would-be your true now-prayers

'If, Agni, I were you, and you were I, your prayers would now be carried out.'

Without *yád* the sentence would mean: 'Agni, I wish I were you . . .' With *yád* it is potential, as for the most part in early Greek. For the potential use, with subordinate force, largely replaced the volitional meaning in Homer. The potential meaning is also evident in passages like the following in Vedic; only the accent on the optative gives formal evidence of subordination:

101. RV 7.71.2.

yuyutám asmád ánirām ámīvām
you-two-ward-off from-us listlessness disease

dívā náktam mādhvī trā́sīthām naḥ
by-day during-night honeyed you-two-protect (Opt.) us

'Ward off from us listlessness and disease, day and night, lovers of honey, you should protect us.'

The potential meaning of the optative is found in the statement of Eurymachus telling Telemachus that the gods will decide who will be king in Ithaca:

102. Odyssey 1.402.

ktḗmata d' autòs ékhois kaì dṓmasin
possessions Ptc. self you-have (Opt.) and in-house

hoîsin anássois
in-own you-rule (Opt.)

'But you yourself may keep your possessions and you may rule over your own house.'

But the volitional sense is clear in the first optative of the two in the following examples:

103. Odyssey 1.47.

hō̃s apóloito kaì állos, hótis toiaûtá ge rhézoi
thus he-perishes (Opt.) also other whoever such Ptc. he-does (Opt.)
'So may anyone else perish who may do such things.'

104. RV 8.23.19. imáṃ ghā vīró amṛ́taṃ dūtáṃ kṛṇvīta mártyaḥ
this Ptc. man immortal messenger he-makes (Opt.) mortal
'A mortal man should make this immortal his messenger.'

Because of its voluntative use in simple sentences of Vedic, as well as in Greek, I assume that Delbrück's analysis was correct, and I take the earlier form of the optative to be the major means of expression for the voluntative in PIE. This view receives support from the survival of optative forms in Lithuanian with imperative sense (Stang 1966:421–422).

Indo-Europeanists have wondered why the optative has secondary endings, inasmuch as primary endings came to predominate in the subjunctive. I assume that these simply reflect the age of the optative; it must have been a distinct inflection when the secondary endings were still standard. Moreover, since the optative did not express certainty, there was no basis for adding to the optative secondary endings the declarative affix *i*. This assumption that the optative is an archaic form has semantic support. It is the only inflection which may manifest the situation illustrated above (Example 1): that the affixes may be independent of one another. Thus the optative form of Example 103 may be interpreted: 'I wish he would perish.' Delbrück made this point clear in the first of his syntactic investigations (1871:13). It would be intriguing to speculate on the reasons for a first-person subject with the affix -*yeˀ*-. Here the point will only be made that this characteristic of the optative demonstrates its archaic character, as does the restricted use of secondary endings.

This conclusion leads to the question of why there is no evidence for the optative in Hittite. For an answer we may look to the characteristic suffix of the optative. In its full form this was -*yeˀ*-. On loss of -ˀ-, with compensatory lengthening, the suffix became -*yē*- when accented and -*ī*- when unaccented. Moreover, after the thematic vowel -*o*-, it became -*i*-. Reflexes of the three forms of the suffix are apparent in Skt. *yā, ī, e*, and in Gk. *iē, ī, oi*, with further changes. In Hittite the -ˀ- would not have contracted with the preceding vowel, and accordingly -*ye*- and -*i*- would have been the expected reflexes, possibly with further reduction (J. Friedrich 1960:27). Apparently these reflexes were inadequate to maintain a distinct paradigm. Hittite merged the forms for the necessitative and voluntative, maintaining only one mood other than the indicative, the so-called imperative. This preserved even more strongly the first-person forms than did the Sanskrit imperative, as well as the various meanings of the merging categories. In Hittite the imperative had voluntative and hortatory as well as necessitative force (J. Friedrich 1960: 139). When desired, the potential was indicated by particles, as also in Greek; moreover, particles such as *yadi* 'if', indicating subordination, are more frequent with the optative in the Brahmanas than in the Veda.

In questions the optative indicates potentiality, as in the following three lines, which have a subjunctive, an optative, and an injunctive in succession:

105. RV 7.86.2.

kadā́	nú	antár	váruṇe	bhuvāni
when	Ptc.	within	Varuna	I-am (Subj.)

kím	me	havyám	áhṛṇāno	juṣeta
what	my	libation	without-anger	he-enjoys (Opt.)

kadā́	mṛḷīkáṃ	sumánā	abhí	khyam
when	mercy	having-good-spirits	about	I-see (Inj.)

'When should I come to be in close touch with Varuna?
What libation of mine would he enjoy free from anger?
When will I in good spirits perceive his mercy?'

It may be hazardous to make much of such contrasts; the subjunctive however indicates a specific point in time; the optative, a potential; and the injunctive, an event to be fulfilled whenever Varuna has mercy on the suppliant.

This passage may indicate the modifications of modal meanings in questions: the subjunctive indicates that the speaker is doubtful about an event; the optative, that the event is potential. These uses compare with those of the optative (and also the subjunctive) in dependent sentences, as in the following negative relative clause, embedded in a clause expressing a wish:

106. RV 8.48.10.

ṛdūdáreṇa	sákhiā	saceya
wholesome	friend	I-associate (Opt.)

yó	mā	ná	ríṣyed
who	me	not	he-injures (Opt.)

'I wish to associate with a wholesome friend, who would not injure me [when he is drunk].'

Since this became the primary use of the optative, in the dialects the potential meaning is most prominent. Both the meaning and the subordinate use are results of the kind of complementation found in dialects (see § 4.7).

These patterns result from the indication of subject in the late PIE verb and the increasing prominence of a system of tense. The tense system, like the aspect system indicated by the form of roots with attached affixes in PIE, is derived from categories in the proposition. These two categories will be discussed in the following section with other aspectual expressions.

4.4. Tense, Aspect, and Related Categories.

In PIE, tense and the time of the action were not indicated by means of verbal affixes. Indications of the time of the action were given by means of particles or adverbs or were implicit in the aspects of the verb forms. Sanskrit and Greek have preserved patterns in which particles indicate the time of action of the verb, as Brugmann (1904*a*:571–572) and Wackernagel (1926:47, 156–162) have pointed out. For example, the present middle of *sac* 'accompany' is used with *purā́* in the following Strophic passage to indicate past time:

107. RV 7.88.5.

kvà	tyā́ni	nau	sakhyā́	babhūvuḥ
whereto	these	for-us	friendships	they-have-become

sácāvahe	yád	avṛkám	purā́	cit
we-accompany-each-other	for	without-enmity	earlier	Ptc.

'Where have these our friendships vanished?
For in the past we have been associating with each other without enmity.'

In these and other examples, such as the frequently cited line from the Iliad, the past time of the action is indicated by a particle, usually a cognate of *purā́* and *pró*:

108. Iliad 1.70.

hòs	ḗidē	tá	t'	eónta	tá	t'	essómena	pró	t' eónta
who	knew	those	Ptc.	being	those	Ptc.	will-be	before	Ptc. being

'Who knew the things happening now, those that will happen and those that have happened.'

Such evidence and the system of verbal forms indicate that tense was not a grammatical category in PIE.

4.4.1. Aspect: Imperfective versus Perfective, Momentary versus Durative. Rather than tense, verb forms indicated aspect, that is, state of the action or process expressed by the verb. As pointed out above (§ 4.1.7), this characteristic of the PIE verb system may be determined most clearly in injunctive forms of Vedic; for the difference in verbal stem and endings indicates the difference in state of the action. We assume a basic contrast between imperfective and perfective aspect, and a further contrast between momentary and durative aspect.

The contrast between imperfective and perfective aspect was indicated either by means of affixes or by characteristic forms of the verbal root. The imperfective forms developed into the present forms in the dialects; the perfective developed into the perfect of late PIE, Sanskrit, and Greek. Because of this realignment of the verbal system, the earlier forms and their meanings have been debated at length, especially after the discovery of Hittite. For the Hittite *mi-* conjugation corresponds to the present of Sanskrit and other dialects; and the *hi-* conjugation corresponds to the perfect. Yet the correspondences of the Hittite verb system are not exact, either with the forms in the non-Anatolian dialects or with the conjectured aspectual meanings. For Hittite, like the other dialects, failed to maintain completely the system proposed here for PIE.

Evidence that the earlier form of the perfect was a "perfective present" has long been supported by means of forms like Skt. *veda,* Gk. *oîda,* Goth. *wait,* Middle English (ME) *wot* 'I know'; for as the shapes of these forms indicate, and as their cognate, Lat. *vīdi* 'I have seen', confirms, the Sanskrit, Greek, and Germanic forms are perfects of the extended root *weyd-* 'see'. When the change from an aspectual to a tense system took place, these perfect forms of *weyd-* and such other forms as the preterite-presents of Germanic underwent a lexical rather than a grammatical shift (Lehmann 1943*a*:25). In Hittite, similar shifts took place when the *mi-* and *hi-* conjugations came to be parallel in indicating tense rather than aspect.

Yet the earlier distinction of meaning is still apparent in Hittite verbs which are inflected both in the *mi-* conjugation and the *hi-* conjugation (J. Friedrich 1960:106–108). One of these is *šunna-,* from the adjective *šu* 'full' (Kronasser 1966:563–564). Forms are found in the Hittite Laws, a *hi-* conjugation, third singular present *šunnai* (J. Friedrich 1959:46, § 96, 97), and a *mi-* conjugation, third singular present *šunizzi* (J. Friedrich 1959:74, § 51). The form *šunnai* refers to a single act of filling a receptacle with grain. The *mi-* present, by contrast, is translated 'sows', presumably from "filling" a field with grain; this meaning suggests that it refers to a continued action and is imperfective. Although the Hittite verb system requires far more study before we can claim to understand it in the various periods of Hittite, such details as agreement of the use of *šunna-* with perfective meaning and perfective forms provide welcome support for the widely held view that the IE perfect developed from a perfective present (see also Wackernagel 1926:150, based on Appolonius, second century A.D., and 166–168).

According to Louis Renou (1925:7, passim) the PIE perfect indicates a fulfilled state, in contrast with the present, which indicates a process that is under way. Wackernagel (1926:166–168) cites various groups of verbs which have a present meaning in Homer when inflected in the perfect: verbs indicating sounds, such as *bébrūkhe* 'he bellows'; action of the sense organs, such as *ópōpa* 'I see'; emotions, such as *gégēthe* 'he rejoices'; gestures, *sésēre* 'he grins'; and others fitting still other meaning classes, such as *tethēlṓs* 'blooming' (see also Munro 1891:31–32). As a common feature of the verbs, Wackernagel sees the intensity or repetition of an action. Yet each of the classes fits the characteristic meaning of the perfect proposed by Renou: 'bellow, see, rejoice, grin, bloom' indicate states resulting from previous activity. Since Wackernagel finds similar meanings in other dialects, he considers this basic meaning of the perfect inherited from PIE. It is noteworthy that many of the Hittite *hi*-conjugation verbs correspond in meaning: *halzāi*- 'shout'; *au*- 'see'; *uak*- 'bite'. The root *ak*- 'die' is also inflected in the *hi*- conjugation; compare Gk. *téthnēke* 'he is dead'. The Hittite *hi*- conjugation accordingly provides semantic support for the assumption that it developed from a PIE inflection that indicated a state in the present resulting from previous action.

Hittite also provides formal support for assuming that the PIE *h*- inflection was a distinct paradigm indicating stative meaning. The characteristic perfect affix was *-e*. This affix corresponded to other affixes like the *-o-* of the middle. Moreover, the perfect had characteristic person affixes in contrast with those of the imperative present:

The Two Sets of Person Affixes

	m- Inflection (Secondary)	*h*- Inflection		*h* + Perfect
1 sg.	m	x		xa
2 sg.	s	th	+ e >	tha
3 sg.	t	ϕ		e

To these endings the declarative *-i* could be affixed, as noted above for *m s t*. The combined affixes yielded the endings *mi, si, ti,* found in Hittite as well as Sanskrit and other dialects.

The second set of person affixes plus the perfect affix *e*, but without a final declarative affix, gave rise to the endings of the perfect forms in Greek and other dialects:

Person Affixes with *i, e(a), e(a) + i, o*

	Primary	Perfect		Greek	Hittite *hi-*	Middle (Secondary)
1 sg.	mi	*xa	>	a	*hai > hi	xo
2 sg.	si	*tha	>	tha	*thai > ti	so
3 sg.	ti	*e	>	e	*ai > i	to

Before examining further implications of these forms for PIE, we may observe that the *a* of the first and second singular *xa* and *tha* was modified from *e* because of contiguity with *a* colored laryngeals; *-a* then replaced *-e* in the third singular in pre-Hittite. The Hittite *hi-* conjugation endings have the declarative affix *i* added to these endings. This derivation for Hittite *hi, ti, i* was proposed by Bernhard Rosencranz (1953), and expanded by Neu (1968:125–131).

Although the *m s t* person affixes came to be generalized and as a result are viewed as the predominant characteristics for person in the IE verbal systems, it is important to observe that *x* rather than *m* was used in the first singular middle. The *x th ϕ* affixes must not then be interpreted as characteristic of the perfect or as restricted to the perfect; the middle endings in the Hittite *hi-* conjugation have the *x th ϕ* person affixes, while the middle endings of the other dialects show a combination of these with the *m s t* affixes. In both Sanskrit and Greek, the second singular secondary endings are based on *-th;* the Sanskrit first singular endings are also based on the first-person affix *x*.

Middle Endings

	Hittite *hi-*	Sanskrit		Greek	
		Primary	Secondary	Primary	Secondary
1 sg.	hari/hahari	e	i	mai	mēn
2 sg.	ta/tati	se	thās	(s)ai	(s)o/thēs
3 sg.	a/ari	te	ta	tai	to

While this chart illustrates the wide use of the *x th ϕ* affixes, it also makes clear the modifications which the verbal endings underwent. The spread of the *m s t* person affixes is illustrated by the Greek primary endings; details for Greek and other dialects are available in the handbooks and are not pertinent to the basic argument presented here. The forms listed here are cited to illustrate the formal relationships between the PIE perfect and the middle, on the one hand, and the uses of the person affixes *m s t* and *x th ϕ*, on the other. The endings in this chart are found after the stage of the language when the middle with *-o-* and the perfect with *-e-* were competing forms, each with a characteristic meaning.

This situation of PIE is reflected in the Hittite lack of a distinction in the middle between *mi-* verbs and *hi-* verbs. In the Hittite present active there is a contrast in form and meaning as also in PIE; but the distinction is minimal in the preterite active and throughout the middle. Hittite accordingly has a verbal system similar to that proposed here for PIE, in that the middle contrasts on the one hand with the *hi-* conjugation and on the other hand with the *mi-* conjugation. In the other Indo-European dialects the systematization has proceeded further; the middle contrasts basically with the active, notably in Greek and Sanskrit. Subsequently other contrasts become more prominent, such as that of the passive versus the active. These subsequent contrasts are well known and well described and are of pertinence here only for the insights they provide on the increasing modifications away from the verb system of PIE.

The greater similarity between the Hittite system and that of PIE does not provide an argument in favor of the Indo-Hittite hypothesis; it merely reflects the greater antiquity of Hittite. Moreover, like the other IE dialects, Hittite underwent a progressive development away from the PIE system, notably in the tendency to merge the *mi-* and *hi-* conjugations. The tense distinction then came to predominate in later Hittite, as it also did in later Greek, Latin, Germanic, and other dialects.

The verbal system of early Hittite supports accordingly the conclusions based on analysis of the forms in other early dialects concerning a distinct perfect inflection with a characteristic *e-* affix in the indicative. In the other moods, the endings are those expected (Whitney 1896:292-295, Brugmann 1913:494).

The meaning of the perfect in PIE must be proposed on the basis of the thoroughly explored Vedic and Homeric texts, though the other dialects confirm the stative, resultative meaning, as in the Germanic preterite-presents. Support is also provided by the long-observed alignment between middle and perfect forms, such as the Greek perfect *dédorka* 'I see' and the middle *dérkomai* 'I see' (Wackernagel 1926:168). This alignment must be interpreted on the basis of the resultative implications of the two forms. The middle, as noted above, indicates that the result of action expressed by the verb has an impact for the subject ('I see with some impact on my further action'; also 'I see myself').

109. Iliad 16.10.

dakruóessa	dé	min	poti	dérketai	óphr' anélētai
weeping	but	her	towards	she-looks (Mid.)	so-that she-will-pick-up (Mid.)

'Weeping [the girl] looks at her [mother] so that she will pick her up.'

Many examples of the perfect in Homer and the Vedic could be cited to indicate that an action has taken place with a specific result:

110. Iliad 22.94–95.

édu	dé	té	min	khólos	ainós
it-entered	Ptc.	Ptc.	him	anger	terrible

smerdaléon	dè	dédorken
fiercely	Ptc.	it-gazes (Perf.)

'And terrible anger entered it [the snake], and it gazes fiercely.'

Since both the perfect and the middle in this way have implications based on the result of an action, their forms show a natural relationship. But, apart from their relationship in sharing resultative meaning, they should not be more closely aligned, as if the perfect were a preterite to a middle present. On the contrary, the two inflections are parallel derivations from verbal roots.

The subsequent alignment of the aorist and the perfect also developed from similarities in meaning. As is commonly assumed in IE studies, an aorist should not be posited for PIE as a separate verbal category comparable to the aorists of Sanskrit and Greek. The aorist forms in these dialects have simply developed from PIE roots with punctual meaning. A characteristic shape of the root is in zero grade, as of *wid-* for the extended root *weyd-*. Suffixed only with secondary endings, the verb forms built on such roots had punctual, perfective meaning. In this way they contrasted with the forms of the perfect, which were *-punctual* or *-momentary.* The contrast may readily be noted in many occurrences in Homer, such as the perfect in Iliad 1.85 and the aorist in 1.148.

111. Iliad 1.85.

eipè	theoprópion,	hóti	oĩstha
you-say	revelation	which	you-have-seen (Perf.)

'Tell us the revelation which you know.'

112. Iliad 1.148.

tòn	d'	ár	hupódra	idȭn
him	Ptc.	Ptc.	from-beneath-the-eyebrows	glancing (Aor.)

proséphē	pódas	ōkùs	Akhilleús
he-addressed	feet	swift	Achilles

'With a scowl swift-footed Achilles addressed him.'

Since the distinction between the perfect and the aorist is so thoroughly established, further examples will not be given here. Moreover, examples are unnecessary to demonstrate that, like the perfect, the aorist came to be used to indicate past time when the shift from an aspectually based to a tense-based verbal system was carried out in the various dialects.

The independent status of the aorist was most clearly developed in those dialects in which the augment was used: Indo-Iranian, Armenian, and Greek. Slavic to be sure has an aorist; but it contains no perfect. The aorist in Slavic refers to events in the past; more than "40% of the attested OCS [Old Church Slavic] aorists are imperfective" (Lunt:1955: 136, based on Dostál). The aorist accordingly was maintained as a category comparable with that in PIE in only a small number of dialects.

Since in these dialects the augment must have had an effect on the meaning of the aorist, our most secure evidence for determining the meaning of the aorist in PIE will be taken from augmentless forms, like that in Example 112, or injunctives in the Vedas.

Aorist injunctives have as one of their prominent meanings a "resultative statement of confirmation" (Hoffmann 1967:214–235). A passage like the following confirms a situation which has resulted from previous action:

113.	RV 6.19.2.	índram	evá	dhiṣáṇā	sātáye	dhāt
		Indra	indeed	Dhiṣaṇa	for-gain	he-placed
		'Dhiṣaṇa (has) designated Indra for gain.'				

The resultative use of the aorist is found also in Greek (Wackernagel 1926:182–184). It illustrates how the aorist could have been amalgamated with the perfect, especially when used with the augment. For the "actual past" the augmented aorist is used in the Rigveda (Hoffmann 1967:219); between this use, that of the perfect in Latin, and that of the preterite in Germanic there was little difference. In each of these dialects the inherited aspectually distinguished forms were adapted for a tense system.

Presumably the resultative meaning led to the coincidence of *s*- formations with the aorist characterized by zero grade of the root. For the suffixed verbs with *s* that have survived outside the aorist have a resultative sense, such as Skt. *dvéṣṭi* 'he hates' (the nonsuffixed root is found in Gk. *dei-*, as in *deídō* 'I fear'); Avestan *yāstē*, Lith. *juóste* 'he girds' (versus Skt. *yuváti* 'he ties on'); Skt. *úkṣati* 'he grows up'; Goth. *wahsjan* 'grow' (versus Lat. *augēre* 'increase'). The *s*- suffix apparently came to be used with some roots as a marker for the aorist (Brugmann 1913: 390–392). As Delbrück concluded at the end of his examination of the various aorist forms in Sanskrit (Delbrück 1876:88), all the aorist forms were used similarly in Vedic. The surface affix *s* and its variants simply came to indicate the aorist category, in addition to the zero-grade form of roots. While the aspect system remained in force the aorist contrasted with the perfect primarily through its momentary meaning; and both the aorist and the perfect contrasted with the present through their perfective meaning.

The close association between the aorist and the perfect, as well as the structure of the PIE verb system, may still be demonstrated by means of the aorists in the Rigveda, which are based on perfect stems, as Hoffmann puts it (1967:64–65). Examples are *paptas* and *vocas,* as in the following passages:

114.	RV 10.95.15.	púrūravo	mā́	mṛthā	mā́ prá	papto
		Purūravas	not	you-die	not Ptc.	you-run-away
		'Pururavas, you shall not die; you must not run away.'				

115.	RV 6.52.14.	mā́	vo	vácāṅsi	paricákṣyāṇi	vocaṃ
		not	to-you	words	disregarded	I-speak (Aor.)
		'May I not speak to you words that are disregarded.'				

These forms demonstrate that aorists could have been based on presents in *x th* *ɸ* as well as on the imperfective presents in *m s t.* They also permit us to understand why the aorist did not develop as a separate category in Hittite and why it maintained itself in Indo-Iranian and Greek. In Hittite the perfective developed a separate conjugation parallel with the imperfective *mi-* conjugation. Each had a preterite. Each also had an imperative, which was used in preventive sentences; there was accordingly no need for a separate aorist, especially in preventive sentences—one of its important uses in Vedic. Like Indo-Iranian, Greek maintained an aspectual basis for its verb system. Tense was indicated largely by particles, notably the augment. The various aspectual forms were accordingly maintained in both of these dialects. Eventually however the category of tense—which in Sanskrit and Greek was secondary to that of aspect, as indicated by the separate imperfect in the present system as well as the augmented forms in the aorist and Greek perfect systems—came to predominate over the aspect system. The interplay between aspect and tense, which was manifested differently in each of the dialects, is one of the intriguing topics to pursue in their individual histories.

4.4.2. Secondary Aspects. Similar to the imperfective aspects are indications of continuity. Expressions for continuative, iterative, distributive, and intensive aspect can be proposed for PIE. These expressions however are not as prominent as those for perfective and imperfective aspect, and accordingly they are here labeled secondary.

Dressler, noting Devoto's relating these aspects to quantitative expressions examined them under the topic *plurality* (1968:43). Viewing these aspects in this way does much to clarify their position in language and their treatment in grammar. Plurality of verbal action, as in Hitt. *akkušk-* 'drink repeatedly' versus *eku-* 'drink', must be viewed in the same way as plurality expressed by nouns, as in Hitt. *watar* 'water' (sg.), *widār* (pl.). Plurality may well be interpreted as a semantic feature. This feature can be applied to verbs as well as nouns.

Combined with imperfective aspect, plurality yields continuative aspect. With perfective aspect, it yields iterative or distributive aspect. When used with emphasis it indicates an intensive. Such an analysis provides an understanding of affixes which seem to have a diversity of meanings and even widely different developments in the Indo-European dialects. The most notable of these is the *-sk-* affix.

The *-sk-* affix (*-ch-* in Sanskrit) was identified by Delbrück as the marker of one of four characteristic present classes (1897:59–64). His characterization of its meaning as "terminative," however, was not accurate and led him even in his brief discussion to difficulties of interpretation. One of the *-sk-* formations that must be posited for PIE is that of the root *g^{w}em-* 'come, go—move'; forms are found in Greek as well as Sanskrit. Among passages cited by Delbrück (1897:60–61) is the following:

116. RV 10.155.3. téna gacha parastarám
with-that go farther-off
'With that go away in the distance.'

This imperative, used to a witch, can scarcely be interpreted as terminative. The same is true of the use of the equivalent imperative in Greek, even though Zeus is commanding the dream to go to the ships of the Achaeans:

117. Iliad 2.8. básk' íthi
go there
'Go away.'

Rather than terminative aspect, the Sanskrit and Greek presents in *-sk-* indicate continuative aspect, a meaning which developed from the earlier meaning still apparent in the Greek iteratives in *-skon.*

Delbrück discusses these iteratives at greater length than the presents (1897:62–64). His analysis of their meaning is remarkably accurate and is corroborated by the subsequently discovered Hittite iterative-durative in *-šk-* (J. Friedrich 1960:74–75). The iteratives in *-šk-* are of further interest because of the clarification they provide for the reconstruction of the PIE verb system. It is remarkable that they take secondary endings. Delbrück considers it a matter of chance that no present form *pháskō* was attested beside *éphaskon*/*phásken* 'said'. Furthermore, he concludes from the Latin *-sk-* form of *es* 'be', *escit,* that Gk. *éskon* must once have had a present beside it. It is important however to account for the forms that are attested. The restriction of secondary endings cannot be accidental, whether the forms are accompanied by an augment, as in *éphaskon,* or not, as in *phásken.* These iteratives are simply reflexes of PIE roots affixed with *-sk-* which maintained the earlier system when the secondary endings were the basic person markers. In the course of time the *-sk-* forms were incorporated into the verb systems of the various dialects and came to express meanings which differed from the original iterative. Analysis of these is a matter of concern for the individual dialects and has been thoroughly discussed (Schwyzer 1939:706–712; Leumann 1963:341, 1965:298).

To understand the situation in PIE we must make use of the earliest evidence, such as that in Greek, notably Ionic Greek, and in Hittite. Used with an imperfective root, such as PIE *g^w^em-* 'come, go, proceed', *-sk-* indicated continuative action; used with a perfective root, such as PIE *ṛ-*, it indicated iterative, distributive action, as in Hittite *ar-* 'reach', *arnu-* 'move to' and the following Strophic passage:

118.	RV 4.16.3.	vṛ́ṣā	yát	sékaṃ	vivipānó	árcāt
		bull	when	drink	swallowing	he-may-sing

'When Indra may join in the song [from time to time], gulping in the soma.'

A further example of an *-sk-* form from this intriguing root is found in the Odyssey:

119.	14.23.	autòs	d'	amphì	pódessin	heoîs	aráriske	pédila
		he	Ptc.	about	feet	his	he-was-fitting	sandals

'But he was fitting sandals on his feet.'

The PIE root *ṛ* (< *γer-*) meaning 'reach, move' came to have wide application in its suffixed form *r-sk-,* as in Vedic to 'rays of light, peaks of thunder, bursts of song, grinding of the soma'; but basically it indicated a plurality of individual actions of the meaning of the simplex.

Such a meaning also could be interpreted as an intensive (Brugmann 1904*a*:493–494, passim), as in Hittite *azzikk-* 'feast' beside *ed-* 'eat'. Intensive meaning was also expressed by means of reduplication, as in the Sanskrit secondary conjugation (Whitney 1896:362–372). In other dialects there was no distinct inflection for intensive action. We may assume that in PIE it was expressed by means of a plurality affix, whether reduplication or the *-sk-* suffix.

4.4.3. The Causative. In a causative construction the subject of the verb brings it about that someone else carries out the action of the verb. Causatives may thus be accompanied by more than one noun, or by none if the aim of the action is understood; causatives must be analyzed in accordance with these patterns. In Japanese, for example, causatives may have no accompanying noun, or a noun indicating the aim of the action, or a noun indicating the subject of the action and another noun to indicate the aim (see Yamagiwa 1942:121).

120.	Kodomo	ni	wa	maiban	ha	o	migakasenasai
	children	by	Ptc.	nightly	teeth	Obj. Ptc.	cause-to-brush

'Make children brush their teeth every night.'

Such causatives have given rise to an analysis by which the causative is accounted for through raising to a sentence with a pro-verb, in a derivation which may be expressed as follows:

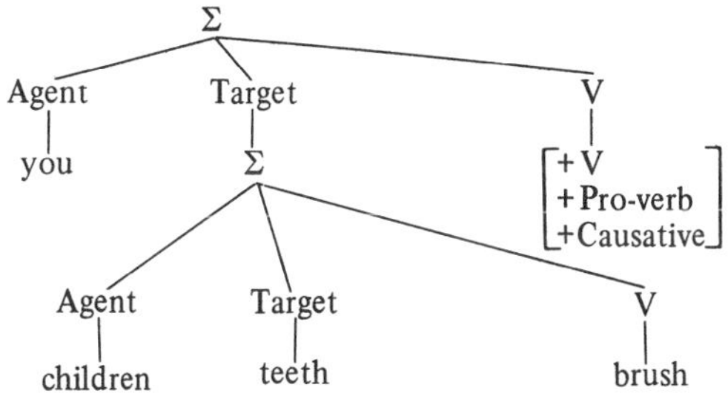

When the causative has a surface marker, this is affixed to the verb of the lower sentence, as is Japanese *-se-* to *migaka-*. The agent of the lower sentence is often expressed by means of an instrumental or an instrumental phrase, like *kodomo ni.* As in the English sentence below, however, the causative force may be expressed lexically, and the agent may have no special indication other than order.

121. Teach the children their lessons.

In such sentences the verb of the lower sentence is transitive *(The chil-*

dren learn their lessons) in contrast with sentences having intransitive verbs *(The children sleep).*

In PIE, causatives were largely derived from intransitive verbs. The causative affix was *-n-*, which was infixed between a root and its affix, as in PIE *γer-, γr-ew-, γr-n-ew-*. An example of this root with causative affix is found in the following sentence:

122. RV 1.174.2. ṛṇór apó
stir-up waters
'Stir up the waters.'

The causative force of the affix is especially prominent in Hittite, as in the form *arnu-* 'move to', from *ar-* 'reach':

123. J. Friedrich 1959:20, 19*a*. É̱ir-šet-pat arnuzi
house-his-Ptc. he-moves-to
'He brings [him] to his own house.'

The previous example illustrates the dominant pattern for causatives in PIE, whether with the *-n-* affix or with the subsequently more widespread affix *-eyo-* attached to a root in *o* grade.

124. RV 5.5.10. tátra havyā́ni gā̆maya
thither offerings cause-to-go
'Make the offerings go there.'

When the verb of the lower sentence is transitive, the agent in the surface sentence is expressed in the accusative.

125. RV 2.37.6. uśán devā́ñ uśatáḥ pāyaya havíḥ
desirous gods desirous cause-to-drink offering
'Desirous one, make the desirous gods drink the offering.'

Subsequently, in the Brahmanas, the agent of the causative is expressed in the instrumental. It is this construction that is often considered the causative proper, as in the Japanese sentence given above (Example 120). If an expressed agent is required in causative constructions, early PIE cannot be said to have included a causative in its verb system. The *-n-* infix forms and the *-eyo-* forms may rather be labeled factitive. In Hittite this factitive use of the *-n-* infix is particularly prominent; for the suffix *-nu-* is used to make factitives from adjectives and nouns, e.g., *tepnu-* 'diminish' from *tepu-* 'little' (J. Friedrich 1960:74). Such verbs are similar to transitives, in Hittite as well as the other dialects. See Delbrück's fine comparison of Skt. *ṛṇóti* 'set in motion' as opposed to *íyarti* 'move' (1897:21–22, 41) as well as his discussion of the *-n-* formations in general (1897:40–59). Saussure's view of the various *-n-* formations as resulting from one PIE class is now generally recognized (Schwyzer 1939:690–701), though with a slightly different morphological analysis (Lehmann 1952:24, Strunck 1967:25). We assume that the basic meaning of the *-n-* forms was factitive and that the causative became prominent only in late PIE and the early dialects.

It is to the absence of a causative proper that we ascribe the lack of a passive in PIE. A passive is a construction in which the agent of a causative is treated as subject. Inasmuch as such agents were not found in PIE, there was no basis for a passive. The forms labeled "passive" (Whitney 1896:275–277) are without agents in the early language and accordingly are basically intransitives, even in the late portions of the Rigveda, such as the wedding hymn:

126. RV 10.85.13. aghā́su hanyante gā́vó
among-Aghas are-killed cows

'rjunyoḥ páry uhyate
among-the-two-Arjunas to she-is-led-home.'

'Among the Aghas cows are killed;
Among the two Arjunas she is brought home.'

The so-called aorist passive of the Vedas is also without an agent and must be viewed as a resultative even when used with an instrumental, as in the following line:

127. RV 5.1.1. ábodhy agníḥ samídhā jánānām
is-aware Agni by-kindling-wood of-men
'Agni is awake because of the kindling wood of men.'

This statement is not a passive in the strict sense, as may be noted from Geldner's translation (1951–1957:II, 1): "Agni ist durch das Brennholz der Menschen wach geworden in Erwartung der Uṣas." But through the use of instrumentals in such constructions, passives could develop, as may be even clearer in the following passage:

128. RV 3.61.6. ṛtā́varī divó arkaír abodhi
order-loving of-sky through-songs is-awake
'The order-loving [goddess] of heaven is awake because of songs.'
'The order-loving [goddess] of heaven was awakened by the songs.'

When agents as well as instruments come to be used in such constructions and in causative constructions, the passive must be included among the categories of the verbal systems. Its development has been discussed by various scholars and from various points of view (Schwyzer 1942, Gonda 1951*a*, Hartmann 1954).

Since we do not assume either a passive or a causative verbal category for early PIE, the place of the forms in *-n-* and of the "passives" discussed above must be noted. I assume that these forms are lexically derived. PIE was rich in affixes to carry out derivation. The affixes could be adopted as means of expression in the inflectional system, as was the *s* in the aorist and other affixes in individual dialects (*k* in Greek, *v* in Latin, *dh* in Germanic, and so on; Lehmann 1942:125–132; 1943*a*:19-26; see also Brugmann 1913:178–392). But, until they were incorporated in the inflectional system, they must be described as a part of the lexicon, much as are the nominal affixes and indicators of deictic relationships.

Affixes to indicate number and person are accounted for under lexical items, as are gender in participles and other nominal elements. These congruence and deictic categories will accordingly be discussed in Chapters 5 and 6.

4.5. Transportation Processes.

These processes, in the early dialects and in PIE, are notable especially for particles, pronouns, and verbs. Wackernagel has written the classical essay on the topic (1892); see also Dover (1960) for the situation in Greek. According to Wackernagel's fundamental conclusion, generally known as Wackernagel's law, the elements in question were unaccented and were typically placed in second position in the clause. Dover, labeling these elements *q* and elements like nouns *M* (1960:14), assumed for Greek the following arrangements: *MqM, MMq;* and, with more than one *q*, a preferred arrangement *Mq(q . . .) M(M . . .).* Since verbs characteristically stood in final position in the clause, as we have noted above, Wackernagel's law is the result of a transportation process, by which unaccented verbs were frequently placed in second position in the clause; other unaccented elements too were generally placed in this position. Wackernagel's hesitant suggestion (1892:427) that PIE had the same verb positions as does modern German must be rejected. Rather, it is to be assumed that verbs and other elements labeled *q* by Dover were sentence-final and subsequently shifted to an earlier position in the sentence.

In dealing with PIE it is one of the major problems to determine the elements that are transported to second position. Dover has proposed for his class *q* numerous subclasses of particles and pronouns, including also the verb *eînai* 'be' in its copulative sense (1960:12–14). He contrasts these elements with those of a group labeled *p*, which "never, or only in certain specifiable circumstances, end a clause." Among the *p* elements are conjunctions like *allá* 'but', *mḗ* 'lest', relatives, articles, and prepositions. Prepositions, as Delbrück pointed out, were postpositives in the early dialects; and accordingly these *p* elements would have been *q* in PIE. The articles and relatives were not found in PIE; neither were many of the conjunctions. And as Watkins indicated (1962), the conjunction-like elements that must be assumed for PIE are to be viewed as sentence connectives, not conjunctions like those in Classical Greek and Latin. Among Dover's other elements we are left with "the simple negative," which according to him "is not easy to classify," but which he did "not treat . . . as *p*" (1960:14). This examination of Dover's *p* class and the studies of Wackernagel lead us to conclude that at an earlier stage of the language the class of *q* elements was more comprehensive than it was in Greek, including also elements which corresponded to some of those labeled *p* for Greek by Dover.

Hittite provides evidence for including the negative particle among the *q* elements, as do other dialects; examples have been given above, § 4.3.3. As in the examples cited there, sentence negation is typically indicated postverbally in OV languages, as are indicators for the interrogative. Another remarkable agreement of PIE with OV languages is the use of the same particle for indicating interrogation and negation. For just as *-ne* is used in Latin as a final interrogative indicator (and the transported Gk. *ou*, Hitt. *U-UL*, etc.), so are Turkish *-mi* and Quechua *ču*, which is labeled a nonfactual suffix by Bills, Vallejo, and Troike (1969: 333). We may conclude therefore that, when PIE was strongly OV, interrogative and negative affixes were placed postverbally in the sentence. Further, when the order was being changed to VO, particles indicating these modalities were placed earlier in the sentence, often preverbally.

The shift in placement is particularly clear with relation to the negative. For indicators of it were placed before enclitic pronouns in the early dialects, in a pattern which has become more and more prominent, as is evident from languages like English, with contemporary forms *none, nothing, nowhere,* etc. The negated pronouns are more transparent in earlier forms of the language, as in Vedic *nákis,* Gk. *oú tis, mḗ tis,* Lat. *nēmo,* OHG *nioman* 'no one', and so on. The negative element *ne* was not used in compounding in PIE (Brugmann 1904*a*:310); *n* had this function. The presence of negated "pronouns" in the early dialects, with the pronominal element differing from dialect to dialect, e.g., *kis* in Vedic, **hemō, homo* in Latin, *man* in Germanic, indicates that the negative movement was effected dialectally and not in the protolanguage. This conclusion is highly important for our understanding of the transportation processes in the late period of PIE and the early dialects.

The subsequent placement rules for the interrogative and the negative are a matter of concern for each of the dialects and will not be treated here. As Delbrück has pointed out (1897:521–524), the negative was placed particularly before verbs and before indefinite pronouns; some conflations, like Goth. *nist* < *ni ist* 'is not' and Lat. *nōlo* < *ne volo* 'I don't wish', indicate that these verbs are characteristically those to which Wackernagel's law applied. Like the negative indefinite pronouns, the interrogative indicators in sentences vary from dialect to dialect and must be described for each dialect (Delbrück 1900:260–267). And from this variation in form, as well as the postposed position of interrogative particles like Vedic *nú*, Goth. *u*, and Russian *li*, we may assume that the dialect patterns for the interrogative came to differ considerably from those of PIE.

Moreover, there is evidence for proposing that other particles were placed postverbally in PIE (Delbrück 1897:497–519). Delbrück has classified these in a special group, which he labels *particles.* They have been maintained postpositively primarily in frozen expressions: *ē* in Gk. *egṓnē*, *ge* in *égōge* 'I' (Schwyzer 1939:606). But they are also frequent in Vedic and early Greek; Delbrück (1897:498–511) discusses at length the use of Skt. *gha*, Gk. *ge*, and Skt. *sma*, Gk. *mén*, after pronouns, nouns, particles, and verbs, as in the following sentence:

129. RV 6.44.18. índra sūrī́n kṛṇuhí smā no ardhám
O-Indra lords-of-offering make Ptc. our half, part
'Indra, take up the cause of our sacrificial lords.'

As here, these particles stand after the element they emphasize.

The particle which has maintained postposed position most widely in the dialects is the conjunctive, Skt. *ca*, Gk. *te*, Lat. *que*, Goth. *-u(h)* (Delbrück 1897:512–516). The disjunctive is also maintained in this use in Vedic *vā*, Gk. *ēwé* < Homeric *ḗ* and Lat. *ve* (Leumann 1965:521):

130. Ennius Annals 250. prudenter qui dicta loquive tacereve posset
prudently who sayings speak-or be-silent-or he-could
'Whoever could prudently report hearsay or be silent about it.'

In discussing these particles it is again important to note the syntactic use and to consider secondarily the surface forms. For Hittite with its postposed particles may illustrate a more archaic pattern than do the other dialects (J. Friedrich 1960:147–155), as in the following sentence:

131. Madduwattaš 2.64. nu-u̯ar-an šannatti-i̯a lē munnāši-i̯a-u̯ar-an lē
Ptc.-Ptc.-him conceal-and not hide-and-Ptc.-him not
'Neither conceal him nor hide him.'

The postposed negatives of this line, *lē* . . . *lē,* and the postverbal conjunctives, *i̯a* . . . *i̯a,* may then be taken to exemplify the postverbal position of qualifier expressions which we assume for PIE.

If these particles followed the typical order for OV languages, we would assume verbal sequences in PIE consisting of the root followed by affixes for qualifier categories like reflexivity, by aspect affixes, and by expressions for negation, interrogation, and the declarative, as in the examples cited in § 1.4.4. When VO order was introduced, expressions for interrogation and negation were shifted to a preverbal position. Interrogative particles and pronouns came to stand initially for the most part; negative particles were preposed to indefinites and to verbs and were often placed initially (Delbrück 1897:521–524). The postverbal expressions that were not transported, that is, the indicators of aspect, subsequently tense, reflexivity, mood, and the congruence categories, became fixed in the concretions known as verb endings. After these endings were fixed, the transportation processes applied largely to unaccented elements, except for stylistic purposes, which do not concern us here. The transportation processes in the dialects accordingly differed considerably from those in PIE. For example, Skt. *ha,* which commonly stood at the end of a clause after a finite verb, is later used in the unaccented second position (Speyer 1886:312–313; see also Macdonell 1916:340–341). We may assume then that particles which in the dialects are placed preverbally may earlier have been postverbal.

By this assumption we may account for the augment *e* in Indo-Iranian, Greek, and Armenian. It may be the affix for the perfect, shifted to preverbal position and subsequently fixed to verbal forms. In support of this origin for the augment we may note that it is maintained in those dialects which also maintained *mē*, also in compounded words like Skt. *mā́kis,* Gk. *mḗtis* 'no one'. Since Hittite has preserved evidence that *lē,* the equivalent of *mē,* could stand finally (J. Friedrich 1960:146), its subsequent position before verbs as well as other elements provides credence for assuming that the augment *e* was a transported form of the perfect affix.

In other dialects, notably Slavic but also Baltic, Germanic, and Italic, transposed elements were combined with verbs to mark aspectual rather than temporal relationships (Delbrück 1897:146–170). The process of combination then varied from dialect to dialect (Brugmann 1904*a*:288, 484–486), as did the transportation rules. The unaccented pronouns, which in early PIE may have been the chief syntactic elements to stand in second position, continued to be placed in this position. But interrogatives, negatives, adverbs, and verbs came to follow placement rules of their own, obscuring the transportation rules of PIE.

4.6. Topicalization.

In topicalization an element in a sentence is marked in such a way that it assumes the most prominent role in the sentence. Differing syntactic devices may be employed to achieve such marking. In Japanese and in Lisu distinctive particles are used. In English distinctive intonation may be used. In PIE the syntactic device used was arrangement. Delbrück has identified the patterns of arrangement which are employed to achieve topicalization (1878:13); these consist of moving a syntactic element towards the front of the sentence, often placing it in initial position (see also Schwyzer 1950:690–691; Watkins 1962).

The elements most prominently affected are nouns or pronouns in the role of subject. As we have noted in Chapter 1, subjects are not essential elements in the PIE sentence. When an element is to be marked, however, a pronoun or noun can be introduced as subject and placed initially, as in the following sentence from a Strophic hymn:

132.	RV 7.71.5.	yuváṃ	cyávānaṃ	jaráso	'mumuktaṃ
		you-two	Cyavāna	from-old-age	you-two-released
		'You two released Cyavāna from old age.'			

This stanza of the hymn, highlighting the two Aśvins, follows one in which the chariot of the Aśvins is emphasized, by a more elaborate pattern discussed below.

The hymn begins with a stanza depicting the time of day, the dawn. Stanza 2, which asks the Aśvins to come to the suppliant, has the verbal action topicalized:

133.	RV 7.71.2.	upā́yātaṃ	dāśúṣe	mártiāya
		you-two-come-here	pious	mortal
		'Come here you two to the pious mortal.'		

Stanza 3 emphasizes the direction of the action, with the particle *ā́* in initial position:

134. RV 7.71.3. ā́ vāṃ rátham . . . vŕ̥ṣaṇo vartayantu
hither your chariot . . . stallions they-must-turn
'Hither the stallions should turn your chariot.'

As these sentences illustrate, any syntactic element—noun, verb, or particle—may be topicalized by initial placement.

While any syntactic element can be topicalized in this way, the major focus of topicalization is on an explicit subject of the sentence. An example may be taken from the Old Hittite purification ritual edited by Otten and Souček (1969:24, § 13–14).

135. adueni akueni nu ^{URU}Hattuša i̯annahhé LUGAL-ša
we-eat we-drink Ptc. Hattuša I-go king-however
^{URU}Arinna paizzi
Arinna goes

'We eat; we drink; and I go off to Hattuša. The king however goes to Arinna.'

The priest who narrates and carries out the ritual does not need a pronoun to refer to his own action. By contrast, the king is highlighted in the following sentence; since the emphasis is on him rather than on the city Arinna, the word for "king" is put in initial position. Similar constructions may be found elsewhere in the ritual, for example p. 18, § 15. Examples from Vedic prose texts are provided by Delbrück (1878:26–32), also for predicate nouns and for nouns in all cases.

A further device to indicate topicalization may be illustrated by the fourth stanza, in which a relative construction highlights the chariot:

136. RV 7.71.4. yó vāṃ rátho nṛpatī́ ásti voḷhā́
which you chariot lords-of-men it-is conveyor

trivandhuró vásumāň usráyāmā
three-seated full-of-riches daybreak-driving

ā́ na enā́ nāsatyā úpa yātam
in us with-that Nāsatyas up you-two-come

abhí yád vāṃ viśvápsnio jígāti
about when you all-nourishing it-may-come

'The chariot which is yours, your vehicle,
three-seated, rich, leaving at daybreak,
with that, Nāsatyas, come to us,
when the all-nourishing [chariot] approaches.'

The topicalization by which subjects came to be included and placed in initial position may be related to the development of the individualizing *-s* added to nouns indicating individuals (Lehmann 1958). This development led to the nominal declension of late PIE and the dialects. As I indicated in my 1958 article, traces of the earlier system are evident in Hittite and in Vedic. With the development of the nominative case to indicate subjects, the topics of sentences were generally indicated by this syntactic category. The further development of a passive inflection permitted the use of the nominative as the case for the topic, whether it referred to the agent or instrument or to the target.

In Example 136 the element to be topicalized, *ráthas,* is introduced in a preposed relative construction. This device is also used in Hittite, as in the following example taken from J. Friedrich (1960:168—see others there):

137.

nu	kuiš	tān	pēdaš	DUMU^{RU}	nu	LUGAL-uš	apāš	kišaru
Ptc.	who	second	rank	son	Ptc.	king	that-one	should-become

'Who is a son of second rank, that one shall become king.'

While such relative clauses are more elaborate devices to indicate topicalization than are preposed elements, they are similar in effect to the patterns discussed above in initial placement. Topicalization in PIE is, then, characterized by placement of the elements topicalized at or near the beginning of the sentence.

4.7. Coordination.

While coordination is prominent in the earliest texts, it is generally implicit. The oldest surviving texts consist largely of paratactic sentences, often with no connecting particles. The Brahmanic passages cited at the end of Chapter 3, notably the passage numbered 56, illustrate such a structure. New sentences may be introduced with particles, or relationships may be indicated with pronominal elements; but these are fewer than in subsequent texts, as examples taken from an Archaic hymn and from Hittite may indicate. Stanzas 3-7 of the Archaic hymn RV 1. 167 are cited and analyzed by Hoffmann (1967:194–197); accordingly only the following stanzas will be included in the last sections of this chapter.

Stanza 8 consists of four sentences, with no connective other than the introductory particle *utá* in the third line:

138. RV 1.167.8.

pā́nti	mitrā́váruṇāv	avadyā́c
they-protect	Mitra-Varuna	from-shame

cáyata	īm	aryamó	ápraṣastān
he-punishes	them	Aryaman-Ptc.	unpraiseworthy

utá cyavante ácyutā dhruvā́ṇi
and they-waver nonwavering firm

vāvṛdhá īm maruto dā́tivāraḥ
he-has-prospered him O-Maruts giver-of-wishes

'Mitra and Varuna protect from shame;
Aryaman punishes the unpraiseworthy.
[Though] the nonwavering and the firm waver,
The worshiper has prospered, O Maruts.'

Neither coordinate subjects, like *ácyutā* and *dhruvā́ṇi,* nor sentences are explicitly connected with particles. In his comment on the stanza, Geldner notes that a hypotactic relationship exists here and occasionally elsewhere between sentences connected by *utá* (1951–1957:I, 244, note to stanza 8, lines *b–c*). The type of relationship must however be supplied by the reader; *utá* itself is a coordinating particle.

Similar patterns of paratactic sentences are found in Hittite, with no overt marker of coordination or of subordination. J. Friedrich states that "purpose and result" clauses are not found in Hittite (1960:163), but that coordinate sentences are simply arranged side by side with the particle *nu,* as in the Hittite Laws (1959:16, § 4):

139. takku ÌR-an našma GEME-an kuiški walhzi na-aš aki *QAZZU*
if slave or female-slave anyone he-strikes Ptc.-he he-dies his-hand

waštai apun arnuzi *Ù* I SAG.DU pai
it-sins that-one he-gives-recompense and one person he-gives

'If anyone strikes a male or a female slave, [so that] the slave dies, his hand is guilty, and he pays recompense for that one and gives one person.'

Here the conditional relationship of the first clause is indicated by the particle *takku.* But the result clause *na-aš aki* does not differ in form from a coordinate clause. Conditional relationships too are found in Hittite with no indication of subordination (J. Friedrich 1960:165).

The subordinate relationships that are indicated, however, have elements that are related to relative particles. Accordingly the subordination found in the early dialects is a type of relative construction, as we will note more fully in § 4.9.

As these examples and these references indicate, no characteristic patterns of order, or of verb forms, distinguish subordinate from coordinate clauses in PIE and the early dialects. Hermann therefore concluded in his celebrated article that there were no subordinate clauses in PIE (1895). The paratactic arrangement which he assumed for PIE, however, is characteristic of OV languages. Hypotaxis in OV languages is often expressed by nonfinite verb forms and by postposed particles, as we will note in the following two sections, where evidence for such patterns in PIE will be cited.

The arrangement of sentences in sequence, as in RV 1.167.8, is a typical pattern of PIE syntax, whether for hypotactic or for paratactic relationships. Expressions for coordination were used largely for elements within clauses and sentences. When used to link sentences, conjunctions were often accompanied by initial particles indicating the beginning of a new clause and also indicating a variety of possible relationships with neighboring clauses. Sentence-connecting particles are, however, infrequent in Vedic and relatively infrequent in the earliest Hittite texts; we may conclude therefore that formal markers of sentence coordination were not mandatory in PIE.

The normal coordinating particle in most of the dialects is a reflex of PIE *k*^{w}*e.* This is postposed to the second of two conjoined elements, or to both, in accordance with conjoined constructions in OV languages (§ 4.5; Delbrück 1897:512–519). Hittite *-a, -i̯a* is used similarly, as in *attaš annaš a* 'father and mother' (J. Friedrich 1960:154–155). The disjunctive particle PIE *wĕ* is also postposed like *k*^{w}*e,* as in Delbrück's example (1897:516):

140. TS 2.4.10.1. náktaṃ vā dívā vā varśati
by-night or by-day or it-rains
'It rains either by night or by day.'

In Hittite, however, besides the postposed disjunctive particles *-ku . . . -ku* 'or', there was the disjunctive particle *našma,* which stood between nouns rather than after the last, as in Example 139. This pattern of conjunction placement came to be increasingly frequent in the dialects; it indicates that the conjunction patterns of VO structure have come to be typical.

With the change in coordinating constructions, new particles were introduced; some of these, for example, Lat. *et,* Goth. *jah,* OE *and,* have a generally accepted etymology; others, like Gk. *kaí,* are obscure in etymology. Syntactically the shift in the construction rather than the source of the particles is of primary interest, though, as noted above, the introduction of new markers for the new VO patterns provides welcome lexical evidence of a shift. The syntactic shift also brought with it patterns of coordination reduction *(Ersparung)* which have been well described for some dialects (Behaghel 1923–1932:III, 497–528). Such constructions are notable especially in SVO languages, in which sequences with equivalent verbs (S, V, O, Conj., S_2, V_1, O_2) delete the second occurrence of the verb (ibid.:525, a MHG excerpt from Tauler):

141.

daz	einer	einez	will	und	ein ander	ein	anderz
'that	one	one-thing	wants	and	another	an	other'

Reduction of equivalent nouns in either S or O position is also standard, as in *Beowulf* 120–123 (Behaghel 1923–1932:III, 512).

142.

. . . Wiht	unhǣlo,
. . . creature	of-evil

. . . gearo	sōna	wæs,
. . . ready	at once	he-was

. . . ond	on	ræste	genam
. . . and	in	sleep	took

þrītig	þegna
thirty	thanes

'The creature of evil was ready at once and seized in their sleep thirty warriors.'

But in the paratactic structures characteristic of Hittite, such reduction is often avoided, as in the early lines of *Muršilis Sprachlähmung* (Götze and Pedersen 1934:4, § 3):

143.

nu-mu-kán	memii̯aš	KAxU-i	anda	tepau̯ešta
now-to-me-within	word	mouth	in	it-became-little

nu-mu-kán	memii̯aš	tepu	kuitki	šarā	ii̯attat
now-to-me-within	word	little	somewhat	up	it-went

'Now my speech in my mouth became infrequent;
now my speech came upward somewhat slowly.'

In an SVO language the second *memii̯as* would probably not have been explicitly stated, as in: 'now my speech came to be halting and was uttered slowly.' The lack of such reduction, often a characteristic of OV languages, gives an impression of paratactic syntax.

Another pattern seeming to be paratactic is the preposing of "subordinate clauses," either with no mark of subordination or with a kind of relative particle, as in the concluding passage of *Muršilis Sprachlähmung* (Götze and Pedersen 1934:10, § 16). The second from last clause has no mark to indicate subordination; the earlier clauses contain a form of relative particle.

144.

IŠTU	^{GIŠ}BANŠUR-ma-za-kán	kuizza	azikinun
from	table-but-Refl.-Ptc.	from-which	I-was-accustomed-to-eat

IŠTU	GAL-i̯a-kán	kuizza	akkuškinun
from	beaker-and-Ptc.	from-which	I-was-accustomed-to-drink

šašti-i̯a-za-kán	ku̯edani	šeškeškinun	*IŠTU*
in-bed-and-Refl.-Ptc.	in-which	I-was-accustomed-to-sit	from

^{URUD}DU$_{10}$xA-i̯a-za-kán	kuizza	arreškinun
basin-and-Refl.-Ptc.	from-which	I-was-accustomed-to-wash

kuit-i̯a	imma	*ÚNUTU*	anda	u̯erii̯an	ešta	nu	*UL*
what-and	else	utensil	Adv.-Ptc.	mentioned	it-was	now	not

kuitki	dattat	*IŠTU*	DINGIR^{LI}	QATAMMA	SIxDI-at
any	it-was-taken	from	god	likewise	it-was-determined

'The god also determined that nothing more should be used of the table from which I was accustomed to eat, of the beaker from which I was accustomed to drink, of the bed in which I was accustomed to sleep, of the basin in which I was accustomed to wash, and of whatever other article was mentioned.'

In an SVO language like English, the principal clause, which stands last in Hittite, would be placed first. The interpretation of the preceding clause as a result clause is taken from Götze and Pedersen. The initial clauses contain relative particles which indicate the relationship to *kuitki* of the second-from-last clause; they also contain coordinating particles: *a, i̯a.* In this passage the clauses, whether coordinate or subordinate from our point of view, are simply arrayed in sequence. Each concludes with a finite verb which provides no evidence of hypotaxis. The sentence connectives which occur—repeated instances of *a*/*ia*—heighten the impression of coordination.

Such examples may also provide insights concerning the absence in Hittite of verb forms which are cognates of the Vedic and Greek optative and subjunctive. These forms came to be used largely to indicate subordination. Since Hittite was highly consistent in its OV patterning, such verb forms were not required. Hittite however did not forego another device, which is used to indicate subordinate relationship in OV as well as VO languages, the so-called nonfinite verb forms. These are used for less explicit kinds of complementation, much the way relative constructions are used for more explicit kinds, as we note in the following sections.

4.8. Complementation.

The understanding of compound sentences and sentences with complements has been a problem to Indo-Europeanists since the beginnings of their concern with syntax. A citation from Windisch's investigation of the origin of the relative pronoun in the Indo-European languages may assist in understanding their point of view: "For syntax there follows from what has been said the important result, that the simple sentence was indeed developed before the separation of languages, but compound sentences [Satzgefüge] were not" (1869:205). This point of view may be characterized as reflecting the belief that language has gradually become more complex; man first talked in simple sentences, but in time he developed compound and complex sentences. The process of this development was still transparent in the history of PIE and its early dialects. Indo-Europeanists have completely rejected this view; but they have not departed from the attempted explanations of syntactic constructions, such as relative clauses, which were made in line with it. Hittite has now provided the data for understanding the relative constructions which we posit for late PIE (Raman 1973). This understanding, both of complementary constructions in PIE and of their development in the early dialects, is built on observations of typological patterning in language.

Study of typological characteristics has clarified not only the syntactic characteristics of simple sentences but also those of compound sentences in languages of differing types. Compound sentences may result from the embedding of nominal modifiers; in VO languages embedded nominal modifiers follow nouns, whereas in OV languages they precede nouns. This observation has led to an understanding of the Hittite and the reconstructed PIE relative constructions. If we follow the standard assumption that in relative constructions a second sentence containing an NP equivalent to an NP in the matrix sentence is embedded in that matrix sentence, we may expect that either sentence may be modified, as illustrated in § 3.6. A sentence may also be embedded with a dummy noun; the verb forms of such embedded sentences are commonly expressed with nominal forms of the verb, variously called infinitives, supines, or participles. In OV languages these, as well as relative constructions, precede the verb of the matrix sentence.

To illustrate these processes, a relatively simple sentence may be cited from an ancient Japanese story, "Taketori no okina no monogatori"

[Story of the old man of (= who was) a bamboo-hewer] (Dickens 1888: 50);

145.

Mote	itarite	kano	ura	ni	oru	Wokei	ni
having, holding	going-to	that	coast	on	being	Wokei	to

kogane	wo	torasu
money, gold	Ptc.	cause-to-take

As commentary to the sentence and its structure, F. Victor Dickens's translation is quoted: "So Fusamori took the letter and went down to the coast, and delivered it to Wokei, to whom he likewise gave gold" (1888: 16). Dickens's interpretation results from an analysis by which the first reduced coordinate sentence is *mote* 'having'; the second is *itarite* 'going to'; these are "coordinate" with *torasu,* a causative accompanied by an agent and a target. With less interpretation than given by Dickens the sentence may be translated: "Having [the letter] and going to [the coast] he causes Wokei to take the money.' Within this sentence a further sentence is embedded, *kano ura ni oru* 'he is on that coast'. A more literal translation than Dickens's might then read: 'So Fusamori takes the letter and goes and gives [it and] money to Wokei, who is on that coast.' The nonfinite verb forms *mote* and *torite* are loosely connected with the principal verb *torasu.* The attributive or relative-marked verb form *oru* is here closely connected with the following noun Wokei; in another widespread use, forms corresponding to *oru* are connected with a following particle.

If we regard the Japanese sentence as an example of a compound sentence in OV languages, we may expect to find in PIE as well nonfinite verb forms like *mote* and *itarite* preceding the main clause and also relative constructions preceding their antecedents. The Japanese nonfinite forms correspond to participles in the IE languages, like *vásānaḥ* in the last lines of the following Strophic hymn:

146. RV 4.5.15.

rúśad	vásānaḥ	sudṛśīkarūpaḥ
brightly	dressing-himself	beautifully-hued

kṣitír	ná	rāyā́	puruvā́ro	adyaut
dwelling	like	of-riches	much-desired	gleamed

'Dressing himself brightly, beautifully hued,
the much-desired [Agni] gleamed like a dwelling of riches.'

The Japanese nonfinite forms also correspond to infinitives in the IE languages, such as *srávitavā́i* which is used for expressing an embedded complement of result or, according to Macdonell (1916:333), "a final or consequential sense" in the following Strophic hymn:

147. RV 7.21.3. tvám indra srávitavā́ apás kaḥ
you O-Indra for-flowing waters you-make
'You, O Indra, make the waters to flow.'

Also in the poetic texts such infinitives may follow the main verb, as in the following passages:

148. RV 5.1.2. ábodhi hótā yajáthāya devā́n
he-woke-up priest for-sacrificing gods
'The priest has awakened to sacrifice to the gods.'

149. RV 5.39.2. vidyā́ma tásya te vayám
we-wish-to-know your you we

ákūpārasya dāváne
infinite for-giving

'We wish to know you as you [are], infinite in gifts.'

The postposed order may result from stylistic or poetic rearrangement; yet it is also a reflection of the shift to VO order, a shift which is reflected in the normal position for infinitives in the other IE dialects. In the Brahmanas still, infinitives normally stand directly before the verb, except in interrogative and negative sentences (Delbrück 1878:33–35):

150. ŚB 2.1.4.16. tád áśvam ā́netavaí brūyāt
then horse for-bringing he-should-speak
'He should order [them] to bring a horse then.'

On the basis of the Brahmanic order we may assume that in PIE nonfinite verbs used as complements to principal verbs preceded them in the sentence.

Hittite provides examples of preposed complementary participles and infinitives to support this assumption (J. Friedrich 1960:111–112, 142–155, 164). Participles were used particularly with *har(k)-* 'have' and *eš-* 'be', as in the example given above (144): *uerii̯an ešta* 'was mentioned'; the pattern is used to indicate state. Among their various uses, infinitives could indicate result, with or without an object (J. Friedrich 1960:142):

151. 1-aš 1-an kunanna lē šanhanzi
one one to-kill not he-tries
'One should not try to kill another.'

Moreover, infinitives could be used to express purpose, as in the following example, which pairs an infinitive with a noun (J. Friedrich 1960: 143):

152. tuk-ma ki̅ uttar ŠÀ-ta šii̯anna išhiull-a ešdu
to-you-however this word in-heart for-laying instruction-and it-should-be
'But for you this word should be for taking to heart and for instruction.'

Moreover, the infinitive could be loosely related to its object, as in examples cited by Friedrich (1960:143–144), such as the following:

153. apāš-ma-mu harkanna šan(a)hta
he-however-me for-deteriorating he-sought
'But he sought to destroy me.'

The complementary infinitive indicates the purpose of the action; as Friedrich points out, it is attached to the verb *šanhta* plus its object *mu* in a construction quite different from that in subsequent dialects.

These uses are paralleled by uses in Vedic, as may be noted in the work of Macdonell (1916:333–338), from which the following examples are taken (p. 336):

154. agníṃ páristaritavā̆ āha
fire for-enclosing he-says
'He says that the fire is to be enclosed.'

155. RV 5.79.10. etā́vad véd uṣas tvám
so-much or-Ptc. dawn you
bhū́yo vā dā́tum arhasi
more or give you-can
'You can give either so much or more, O Dawn.'

On the basis of such examples in Vedic and in Hittite, we may assume that infinitive constructions were used to indicate a variety of complements in PIE.

Hittite and Sanskrit also provide examples of participles functioning appositionally or as adjectives indicating state (J. Friedrich 1960:164):

156. ammuk-u̯ar-an akkantan *IQ.BI*
to-me-Ptc.-indicating-quotation-him dying he-described
'He told me that one had died.'

This pattern had been noted by Delbrück for the Rigveda, with various examples (1900:327):

157. RV 10.42.3. śiśīhí mā śiśayáṃ tvā śṛṇomi
you-strengthen me being strong, strengthening you I-hear
'Strengthen me; I hear that you are strong.'

The adjective *śiśayá* 'strengthening' is an adjective derived from the same root as *śiśīhí*.

Delbrück also noted that such "appositives" are indicated in Greek by means of clauses. Greek accordingly represents a further stage in the development of the IE languages to a VO order. Yet Greek still maintained preposed participles having the same subject as does the principal verb, as in:

158. Odyssey 5.486. tḕn mèn idṑn gḗthēse
it Ptc. seeing he-rejoiced
'Seeing it, he rejoiced.'

This pattern, preserved in some IE languages to this day, permits the use of two verbs with only one indicating mood and person; the nonfinite verb takes these categories from the finite. As we have noted in examples given above, participles were used in the older period for a great variety of relationships. though also without indicating some of the verbal categories. Dependent clauses are more flexible in indicating such relationships, and more precise, especially when complementary participles and infinitives follow the principal verb. Possibly this was largely the reason for their great expansion in the dialects. The description of these and of their development in the early dialects will be discussed in the following section.

4.9. Subordinate Clauses.

In an OV language a subordinate clause proper consists of a finite verb form preposed to another word, often a particle. For example, the verb *oru* 'be' is preposed to *ni* 'in, on, when' in the following sentence from the story of the old bamboo-hewer (Dickens 1888:49):

159. kore wo mo awareto mite oru ni Taketori
this Obj.-Ptc. Ptc. sadly seeing be on, when bamboo-hewer

no Okina hashiri irite iwaku
Ptc. old-man running coming-in say

'When she looked with sadness at this, the old bamboo-hewer comes in swiftly and says . . .'

The form *oru* is the same as that in the sentence cited above (Example 145). In that sentence the relationship corresponds to that between a noun and a relative clause. By contrast, in the sentence cited here the relationship corresponds to that between a temporal subordinate clause and a principal clause. These Japanese examples may illustrate the relationship between relative clauses and subordinate clauses in an OV language.

Indo-Europeanists have long recognized the relationship between the subordinating particles and the stem from which relative pronouns were derived in Indo-Iranian and Greek. Thus Delbrück has pointed out in detail how the neuter accusative form of PIE *yo-* was the basis of the conjunction **yod* in its various meanings: (1) temporal, (2) temporal-causal, (3) temporal-conditional, (4) purpose (1900:319–333). He also recognized the source of conjunctional use in sentences like:

160. RV 3.48.2.

yáj	jā́yathās	tád	áhar	asya	kā́me
which	you-were-born	that	day	of-it	in-desire

'ṅśóḥ	pī́yū́ṣam	apibo	giriṣṭhā́m
of-plant	milk	you-drank	be-on-mountain

'On the day you were born you drank the mountain milk out of desire for the plant.'

161. RV 7.86.4.

kím	ā́ga	āsa	varuṇa	jyéṣṭhaṃ
what	sin	it-is	O-Varuna	terrible

yát	stotā́raṃ	jíghāṅsasi	sákhāyam
which	singer	you-want-to-kill	friend

'What is the terrible sin, O Varuna, because of which you reject the singer, your friend?'

Although Delbrück recognized the source of the conjunction **yod* and other conjunctional forms based on the relative-pronoun stem *yo-* he did not provide an explanation for this development from a relative clause to a subordinate clause.

Comparison with the OV structures illustrated in the Japanese sentences illuminates the relationship. In an OV language the relative-clause relationship is parallel with that in subordinate clauses: Modern Japanese for example simply preposes a finite verb before either a noun or an adverbial particle to indicate some kind of modifying relationship of the clause concluded by the verb. Ancient Japanese provides an illustration of a variant device, for it contained a special, attributive verb ending to mark the relationship, exemplified in the *-u* ending of the verb *ori.* If such a situation applied in PIE when it was OV in structure, upon the shift to a VO structure PIE might have been expected to use one and the same device to indicate linking with a following clause. This device was the so-called relative pronoun.

Delbrück's preliminary explanation of relative and subordinate clauses in PIE has been supported by closer analysis of the use of *ya* in the old sections of the Rigveda (Porzig 1932:210–303) and by parallel developments in Hittite. Walter Porzig's interpretation of the relative clauses in the Rigveda must be viewed in accordance with the clarification that has been provided by the more archaic Hittite texts. But even without drawing on this clarification, Porzig's conclusions are valuable. Arguing in part on the basis of the verbal accent in subordinate clauses, Porzig concludes that relative clauses must have stood before the main clause originally and, further, that the earliest type of subordinate *ya-* clauses must have been the preposed relative constructions (1932:292). On the basis of his own investigation, then, Porzig supports Delbrück's derivation of a variety of *ya-* clauses from a relative nexus.

This conclusion receives striking support from Hittite, for in it we find the same syntactic relationship between relative clauses and other subordinate clauses as is found in Vedic, Greek, and other early dialects. But the marker for both types of clauses differs. In Hittite it is based on *$*k^{w}id$* rather than **yod;* thus, Hittite too uses the relative particle for indicating subordination. The remarkable parallelism between the syntactic constructions, though they have different surface markers, must be ascribed to typological reasons; we assume that Hittite as well as Indo-Aryan and Greek was developing a lexical marker to indicate subordination, in contrast with simple preposing of the subordinate construction like that in Japanese. Since Delbrück has provided many example of *ya-* constructions (1900:319–333), the citations here are largely Hittite *kuit* clauses, together with excerpts from the Archaic hymn 1.167.

As does *yad* in Vedic, Hitt. *kuit* signals a "loose" relationship between clauses which must be appropriately interpreted; an example from the Old Hittite Šaušgamuwa Treaty may illustrate the Hittite nexus (Kühne and Otten 1971:8, line 8):

162.	tuk-ma-za	$^{[m]D}$*IŠTAR*-A.A.-an	^{LÚ}*HA-DA-A-NU*
	you-however-Refl.	Šaušgamuwa	brother-in-law

kuit	DÙ-nun	nu	^{D}UTU^{ŠI}	*AŠ-ŠUM*	EN-*UT-TI*	pahši
"that"	I-made	Ptc.	my-sun, me	concerning	rule	you-protect

'Protect me in my rule, [regarding the fact that = because] I made you, Šauš-gamuwa, my brother-in-law.'

This is part of a statement made by the king of the Hittites; the first line recapitulates a statement he has made earlier in the text. In contrast with the two earlier occurrences, the recapitulation is related to the *nu* clause by means of *kuit,* which the editors translate 'because'. As J. Friedrich has stated (1960:163), *kuit* never stands initially in its clause. Sentences in which it is used are then scarcely more specifically interconnected than are conjoined sentences with no specific relating word, as in examples cited by Friedrich (ibid.):

163.	nu	taškupāi	nu	URU-aš	dapii̯anzi	išdammašzi
	Ptc.	you-shout	Ptc.	city	whole	it-hears

'Now cry out [so that] the whole city hears.'

Like this example, both clauses in a *kuit* construction generally are introduced with *nu* (J. Friedrich 1960:159). We may assume that *kuit* became a subordinating particle when such connections were omitted, as in Friedrich's example (ibid.):

164.	*ABU.KA*-mu	kuit	tuēl	*ŠUM*-an	memiškit	nu-tta
	father-me	because	your	name	he-said-repeatedly	now-you
	appaddan	EGIR-an	šan(a)hhun			
	for-that-reason	therefore	I-cared-for			

'Because your father mentioned your name to me again and again, for that reason I concerned myself about you.'

The relationship expressed by *yád* in the following Strophic hymn is similar, though *yád* can also be analyzed as a relative pronoun still:

165.	RV 1.131.4.	vidúṣ	ṭe	asyá	vīryàsya	pūrávaḥ
		they-know	you	of-this	manliness	Purus
		púro yád		indra	śā́radīr	avā́tiraḥ
		cities because, when		O-Indra	autumnal	you-tore-down

'The Purus know this heroic deed of yours, Indra, since you tore down the autumnal cities.'

These examples illustrate that both *yád* and *kuit* introduce causal clauses, though they do not contain indications of the origin of this use.

We assume that the use of *yád, kuit,* and other relative particles to express a causal relationship arose from subordination of clauses introduced by them to an ablative, as in the following passage:

166. RV 7.89.5.

ácittī	yát	táva	dhármā	yuyopimá
unknowing	that, because	your	law, order	we-have-disturbed

mā́	nas	tásmād	énaso	deva	rīriṣaḥ
not	us	because-of-that	because-of-sin	O-god	you-harm

'Do not harm us, god, because of that sin [that] because unknowingly we have disturbed your law.

As such relationships with ablatives expressing cause were not specific, more precise particles or conjunctions came to be used. In Sanskrit the ablatival *yasmāt* specifies the meaning 'because'.

Further, *yadā́* and *yátra* specify the meaning 'when'. In Hittite, *mān* came to be used for temporal relationships, possibly after combined use with *kuit; kuitman* expressed a temporal relationship even in Late Hittite, corresponding to 'while, until', though *mahhan* has replaced *mān* (J. Friedrich 1960:164–165 gives further details). The conjunction *mān* itself specifies the meanings 'if' and 'although' in standard Hittite. In both Hittite and Vedic then, the "loose" relative-construction relationship between subordinate clauses and principal clauses is gradually replaced by special conjunctions for the various types of hypotactic relationship: causal, temporal, conditional, concessive. Just as the causal relationship developed from an ablative modified by a relative construction, so the temporal and conditional relationship developed from a clause modifying an underlying time node.

The less differentiated and less precisely related subordinate clauses are often still evident, however, as in *yád* clauses of the Archaic hymn, Rigveda 1.167. For conciseness, only *yád* clauses will be cited here, with Hoffmann's interpretation of each; the entire stanzas and their translations are given by Hoffmann (1967:194–197).

167. RV 1.167.5.

jóṣad	yád	īm	asuryā̀	sacádhyai
she-desires	when	them	Asuryan	to-follow

'when the Asuryan will desire to follow them'

RV 1.167.6.

arkó	yád	vo	maruto	havíṣmān
song-of-praise	whenever, if	for-you	Maruts	accompanied-by-libations

'if the song of praise accompanied by libations is designed for you, Maruts'

RV.167.7.

sácā	yád	īṃ	vṛ́ṣamaṇā	ahaṁyú
together	because	them	manly-minded	proud

sthirā́	cij	jánīr	váhate	subhāgā́ḥ
rigid	though	women	she-drives	well-favored

'because the manly minded, proud, yet stubborn [Rodasi] brings along other favored women'

In these three stanzas *yad* introduces subordinate clauses with three different relationships: temporal, conditional, causal. Such multiple uses of *yad* belong particularly to the archaic style; subsequently they are less frequent, being replaced by more specific conjunctions.

In addition to the greater specificity of subordinate relationship indicated by particles, the early, relatively free hypotactic constructions come to be modified by the dominant subjective quality of the principal verb. The effect may be illustrated by passages like the following from a Strophic hymn, in which the verb of the principal clause is an optative:

168. RV 1.38.4.

yád	yūyám	pṛṣnimātaro
if, when	you	having-Prsni-as-mother [Maruts]

mártāsaḥ	syā́tana
mortals	you-would-be

stotā́	vo	amṛ́taḥ	syāt
singer	your	immortal	he-would-be

'Your singer would be immortal if [= in a situation when] you Maruts were mortals.' (That is, if our roles were reversed, and you were mortals, then you would wish me to be immortal.)

This passage illustrates how the use of the optative in the principal clause brings about a conditional relationship in the subordinate clause (see also Delbrück 1900:329–330). Through its expression of uncertainty the optative conveys a conditional rather than a temporal meaning in the *yad* clause.

Lacking verb forms expressing uncertainty, Hittite indicates conditional relationships simply by means of particles (J. Friedrich 1960:165–167). Although several particles are used in Hittite to indicate various types of conditional clauses–*man . . . mān* for contrary-to-fact, *takku* and *mān* for simple conditionals–Hittite did not develop the variety of patterns found in other dialects. These patterns, as well described in the handbooks, are brought about not only by differing particles but also by the uses of the various tense and mood forms. Constructions in the dialects which have developed farthest from those of PIE are those in which the tense, mood, or person is modified in accordance with rules based on the verb form of the principal clause. Such shifts are among the most far-reaching results of the subjective quality of the Indo-European verb (Delbrück 1900:437–445).

Differences between the constructions in the various dialects reflect the changes as well as the earlier situation. In Homer, statements may be reported with a shift of mood and person, as in the following line:

169. Odyssey 3.19. líssesthai dé min autós, hópōs nēmertéa eípēi
request Ptc. him self that true-things he-may-say
'You yourself ask him so that he tells the truth.'

The form *eípēi* is a third-person aorist subjunctive. If the statement were in direct discourse, the verb would be *eîpe,* second-person imperative, and the clause would read: *eîpe nēmertéa* 'tell the truth'. Such shifts in person and mood would not be expected in an OV language; in Japanese, with *to* following quotations, the statement is repeated without change. This is also the situation in Vedic, in which statements are repeated and indicated with a postposed *iti,* as in the passage (Example 56) of Chapter 3. The shifts in the other dialects, as they changed more and more to VO structure, led to intricate expression of subordinate relationships, through shifts in person, in mood, and in tense, as well as through specific particles indicating the kind of subordination. The syntactic constructions of these dialects then came to differ considerably from that even in Vedic.

The earliest poems of the Vedas are transparent in syntax, as may be illustrated by Stanzas 9 and 10 of Hymn 1.167:

170. RV 1.167.9. nahí nú vo maruto ánty asmé
never Ptc. your Maruts near from-us

ārā́ttāc cic chávaso ántam āpúḥ
from-far or of-strength end they-reached

té dhṛṣṇúnā śávasā śuśuvā́ṅsó
they bold power strengthened

'rṇo ná dvéṣo dhṛṣatá pári ṣṭhuḥ
flood like enmity bold against they-stand

'Never have they reached the limit of your strength, Maruts, whether near or far from us. Strengthened by bold power they boldly oppose enmity like a flood.'

RV 1.167.10. vayám adyéndrasya préṣṭhā vayám
we today-Indra's most-favored we

śvó vocemahi samaryé
tomorrow we-wish-to-be-called in-battle

vayám purā́ máhi ca no ánu dyū́n
we formerly great and us through days

tán	na	ṛbhukṣā́	narā́m	ánu	ṣyāt
that	us	chief	of-men	to	may-he-be

'We today, we tomorrow, want to be called Indra's favorites in battle. We were formerly. And great things will be for us through the days; may the chief of men give that to us.'

Although the hymn offers problems of interpretation because of religious and poetic difficulties, the syntax of these two stanzas is straightforward; the verbs in general are independent of one another, in this way indicating a succession of individual sentences. Such syntactic patterns, though more complicated than those of prose passages like Examples 56 and 64 of Chapter 3, lack the complexity of Classical Greek and Latin, or even Homeric Greek. These early Vedic texts, like those of Old Hittite, include many of the syntactic categories found in the dialects, but the patterns of order and relationship between clauses had already changed considerably from the OV patterns of PIE. After we review the categories and their methods of expression (Chapter 5), and after we then examine characteristic lexical patterns of PIE (Chapter 6), we will summarize the principal syntactic developments between PIE and the dialects (Chapter 7).

5. Syntactic Categories of PIE

5.1. Means of Expression for Syntactic Categories.

Syntactic categories may be expressed by any of the syntactic devices: arrangement, selection, intonation, or modification. They may also be expressed lexically; in early PIE, for example, the root *ˀed-* 'eat' expresses durative aspect, while the root *peγ-* > *pō-* 'take a drink, swallow' expresses nondurative aspect. The previous three chapters have dealt with the PIE sentence, its basic elements and their modifiers, noting especially syntactic features and their means of expression through patterns of selection, with some reference to arrangement and intonation. The term *feature* is used here to refer to universal syntactic phenomena, such as interrogation and negation. Classes representing such features in a given language are referred to as *categories*. This chapter examines the principal syntactic categories of PIE. It will accordingly deal further with some of the topics discussed in the three preceding chapters. Moreover, since the means of expression for syntactic categories may change in the history of a language, an account of the syntactic categories of PIE involves consideration of such means of expression in various stages of PIE and its dialects. The changes in syntax will however be sketched more explicitly in Chapter 7.

The expression of syntactic categories by means of modificational devices has been thoroughly studied in Indo-European, particularly the ablaut variations and how they came to be utilized to express verbal aspects (Saussure 1879; Hirt 1921–1937:II; Lehmann 1952; Kurylowicz 1968).

Among the most distinct uses of ablaut is that of zero grade to express nondurative aspect, as in *wid-* 'recognize' as opposed to *weyd-* 'see'. Another distinct use is that of the *o* grade to express stative, resultative aspect, as in *woid-* 'know < have seen'. Yet not all instances of these modifications are used to express these same syntactic categories, no more than a given ending, such as the verbal ending *-te,* is always used to express one and the same syntactic category. For example, the *o* grade in roots of causatives made with *-eyo-* suffixes does not express resultative aspect. Nor does the zero grade in the plural of perfects express nondurative aspect, or even stative aspect. In much the same way other means of expression for a given syntactic category are not necessarily used solely to indicate that category. Accordingly in the study of syntax one must start from an examination of the categories rather than from the surface expressions.

Yet the examination of syntactic categories cannot be limited to those which are expressed by inflection, however central this device may be. For, as Wackernagel indicated with reference to Brugmann, some categories, such as tense, could be expressed lexically in early Greek and Vedic, and presumably in PIE as well (Wackernagel 1926:47, 158–159; see also Delbrück 1897:265–268). To understand PIE syntax and its development we must be prepared for dealing with the means of expression for syntactic categories which may be vestiges of an earlier system and also with those which, like ablaut, have come to be central.

Comparison with selected OV languages may illustrate further possibilities of expression of syntactic features. In Lisu "the various logical predicates are all expressed by verbs in the surface structure," as in the following example (Hope 1972:147–148):

1.	. . . dzwa	kə̪le	tyə̪	nyi̪	-a̪
	. . . help	happen	cause	try	-Dec.

'try to cause it to happen that *x* helps'

Negation is also expressed lexically in Lisu; the negative is placed "in front of the leftmost verb" (Hope 1972:155–156), as in:

2.	ása	mà	tə̌	yæ̪̀	ye	tyǎ
	Asa	not	run	descend	go	Cont.

'Asa is not in the process of running away downhill.'

The lexical expression for 'not' is *mà,* except in imperative sentences, which have *thà.* Aspect markers, e.g., *tyǎ* in Example 2, are also lexical; unlike the negative, they are not moved in front of the verb. The marker for the declarative, -$\underset{\frown}{a}$ in Example 1, is however a bound element, as are the markers for interrogative and imperative; Hope labels these markers performatives (1972:158). In contrast with Lisu, the OV languages Japanese and Turkish express the negative by means of an inflectional suffix, a device used also for other verbal categories in these languages (Lehmann 1973*a*). Accordingly we cannot expect to find the same means of expression for syntactic categories from language to language, nor even in typologically similar languages. PIE resembles Lisu in having lexical elements to express negation and in having these placed before verbs. On the other hand it resembles Turkish in having the feature of reflexivity expressed by means of an inflectional suffix. In order to survey the syntactic categories of PIE systematically, the verbal features will be discussed below in the sequence of primary categories, followed by voice, mood, aspect-tense, and thereupon the deictic categories. Syntactic features associated with substantives will then be treated. When features and their means of expression have been discussed extensively above, corresponding syntactic categories will be treated only briefly here.

5.2. Syntactic Categories Expressed in Conjunction with Verbs.

The primary syntactic features associated with verbs are declarative, interrogative, and negative. Sentences with verbs expressing these features may be statements or questions, both positive and negative; when marked any of these may be exclamations.

Relationships between verbs and nominal elements may also be expressed by means of verbal categories. Characteristic relationships with the subject are expressed through reflexive or reciprocal features. Relationships with objects, such as transitivity, were lexically expressed in PIE, and causative relationships were indicated through various affixes. Categories that express attitudes by means of verbs are referred to as moods. For PIE the characteristic modal categories were the imperative, the subjunctive, and the optative. A prominent derivational suffix also indicated the desiderative. And in late PIE the affix used earlier to mark +Dec. came to mark the indicative as opposed to other moods.

Since verbs are the elements which are generally used to express action (or -action, i.e., state) and process, additional features are commonly associated with them, having to do with degree of completion of the action or state. Categories expressing these features are known as aspects or, when measured by time, as tenses. PIE and the early dialects were marked for aspect.

In the generation of sentences, features of tense are introduced through nominal elements; the categories of inflection for tense were, however, expressed with verbs in PIE. By contrast, other verbal features came to be expressed nominally, notably reflexivity. Some Indo-Europeanists have also assumed the ergative relationship between nouns and verbs in early Indo-European (Vaillant 1936; cf. Lehmann 1958:190), but evidence for that assumption is inadequate. Apparently then the relationship between the kind of action expressed by the verb, or its voice, and the subject was not marked by nominal inflections.

From late PIE the categories of person and number were expressed with verbs, and accordingly Indo-Europeanists often assume these categories to be characteristic or even necessary for verbal forms. Yet in many languages they may not be expressed at all or may be expressed lexically, even with nouns. Thus in Japanese the category of person is indicated by means of honorifics, that is, by lexical devices; lexical devices also indicate number. From internal evidence we assume that in early PIE person and number were also expressed lexically, or not at all.

These categories, as well as the nominal categories of case and gender, will be examined in detail below, as well as their roles in PIE syntax.

Syntacticians have dealt with these categories and their means of expression according to various points of view, some emphasizing to a greater extent surface forms, for example Brugmann (1897–1916, 1925) and Eugene A. Nida (1949); others emphasizing to a greater extent underlying forms, for example Jespersen (1924) and Wackernagel (1926–1928). Whatever their emphasis, they have noted that direct correlations between surface forms and underlying features are only partial, as is strict delimitation of the various categories. The treatment of English passive constructions in transformational grammar provides a recent illustration. The earliest treatments were based largely on surface phenomena (Chomsky 1957). Subsequent treatments have concentrated more heavily on underlying phenomena (Chomsky 1965 and others). This shift in approach of the interpretation of a relatively simple syntactic construction which was made in a short time even under a severely rigorous methodology may serve to illustrate that any systematic presentation is based to some extent on arbitrary decisions, since the relationship between surface expression as represented through syntactic categories and underlying phenomena viewed through features is not direct, and since that relationship varies from language to language as well as from one stage of a language to another.

5.2.1. The Primary Syntactic Categories Associated with Verbs. In PIE the declarative feature was expressed by the affix *-i,* in contrast with a zero affix. The contrast is still evident in Vedic texts which have maintained injunctive forms. As Hoffmann has pointed out (1967:278–279, 1970), the injunctive serves to mention an action *(Erwähnung),* while the indicative, which differed only by the addition of *-i,* indicates a report *(Bericht).* At any early stage of PIE, *-i* was accordingly comparable to declarative affixes in Squamish and in Lisu (§ 4.1.4).

By the time of the early dialects the verb forms marked with *-i,* that is, the indicative, indicated reality or neutrality with regard to mood (Wackernagel 1926:224). The function of *-i* had accordingly been modified, as is also evident from the abandonment of the use of *-i,* or primary endings, in the subjunctive. As subjunctive forms came to be characteristic of subordination, they had secondary rather than primary endings (Brugmann 1904*a*:552–554). And since the use of the indicative to indicate reality was confined to the present system, even the indicative inflection cannot be defined as representing the declarative feature. Rather, the declarative was expressed by other devices.

In late PIE and the early dialects this device was intonation. For expressing -Dec., particles were used, such as *án* and *ke* in Greek (Wackernagel 1926:224, Brugmann 1904*a*:615, 620; 1925:86).

Marking of -Dec. is found in conjunction with the primary category of interrogation. For example, cognates of *an* were used to indicate interrogation in Italic and Germanic. Generally, in Gothic, *an* is used in conjunction with interrogative markers like *hwas* 'who', but, as in the following passage, *an* may be found without such markers (Streitberg 1920:219).

3. John 18:37. an nuh þiudans is þu
? indeed king are you
'Are you a king then?'

By the time of the dialects, then, specific lexical devices were used for expressing -Dec., and these were also used to indicate interrogation.

Clarification questions were marked lexically in PIE by forms of *$*k^wo$-, k^wi-, k^wu-* (Brugmann 1904*a*:402; 1925:193, 224) and by other interrogatives. It is unclear whether at an early period these were accompanied by a specific interrogative particle placed at the ends of sentences, such as *ka* in Japanese, and whether confirmation questions as well were so marked. The use of final interrogative particles is attested in late dialects, especially Latin and Slavic, though it is sporadic. We may most safely assume that confirmation questions were first marked in PIE by means of a special interrogation pattern and only later by presuppositional particles. This assumption is supported by the use of the *pluti* pattern in some Vedic questions (Brugmann 1925:221) and by various particles in the several dialects. Questions presupposing a "yes" answer generally have a negative particle, *na* in Indic, *ou* in Greek, *nonne* in Latin, *ni* in Gothic, and so on; questions presupposing a "no" answer have a variety of particles, *mḗ* in Greek, *num* in Latin, *ibai* in Gothic (§ 4.3.2; Brugmann 1925:222–224). Particles, then, as Brugmann pointed out (1925: 224), came to be highly prominent in expressing interrogation.

To express negation, lexical devices were used. Before the development of inflectional forms to indicate necessitative and obligative features, and while injunctive forms were still in use, a distinct negative, PIE *mē*, was used to express the negative of these features; **ne* was used elsewhere (Brugmann 1904*a*:582, 612). The PIE contrast between *mē* and *ne* was maintained in the most archaic dialects, in some with changed surface markers (§ 4.3.3). These dialects were Hittite, Indic, Greek, and another which retained the OV pattern, Armenian.

But even in Vedic and Greek the PIE contrast was modified. In Vedic, *na* was used with the subjunctive even when it had necessitative force, thus assuming one of the uses of PIE *mē*. In Greek, on the other hand, *mē* was maintained in sentences having subjunctive verb forms with necessitative meaning, though not with subjunctives expressing likelihood (Brugmann 1904*a*:581–582). The distinction between negative modal statements and simple negative sentences was accordingly no longer expressed as it had been in PIE, even though reflexes of the negative particles were maintained. In some dialects, as in Latin with *nī* contrasting with *ne*, differing negative particles had to do with emphasis.

Emphatic, or marked, variants of declarative, interrogative, and negative features were characterized lexically by means of particles or by marked word order (see Brugmann 1904*a*:614–622 for a list of such particles, and also Delbrück 1897:497–511). Initial position, especially of verbs, conveyed emphasis for the element in question, as in many examples.

4. RV 1.10.1. gā́yanti tvā gāyatríṇó 'rcanty arkám arkíṇaḥ
they-sing you singers they-chant song praisers
'Celebrating you are the singers; singing a song of praise, the praisers.'

Since interrogative particles and pronouns are often emphatic, they generally stand in initial position in the clause, as in Examples 52 and 55 of Chapter 4; similarly, negation can be emphasized by means of initial negative particles, as in Example 170 of Chapter 4.

Although declaratives, interrogatives, and negatives may in this way be emphatic, emphatic sentences are particularly associated with exclamations and commands, as in Brugmann's example (1904*a*:680).

5.	RV 1.14.12.	yukṣvā́	hy	áruṣī	ráthe	haríto	deva	rohítaḥ
		you-yoke	now	ruddy	to-chariot	yellow	O-god	red-horse

tā́bhir	devā́ñ	ihā́	vaha
with-them	gods	here	you-bring

'Yoke the ruddy, tawny, red horses to the chariot, god!
With them bring hither the gods!'

The frequent use of emphatic patterns for commands led Brugmann to classify sentences into three principal types; exclamatory, declarative, and interrogative (1904*a*:647–649); this classification, according to Brugmann, was based on fundamental psychological functions. The identification of exclamatory sentences as a separate class has the advantage of accounting for abbreviated utterances, as well as vocatives and interjections (1904*a*:687–697). Yet, since all kinds of sentences, declarative and interrogative as well as imperative, volitional, and so on, can be emphatic, the analysis of sentences into marked and unmarked types provides a more satisfactory classification than does that of Brugmann, removing at the same time the need for the exclamatory type.

Summing up the syntactic devices for expressing the primary syntactic categories in late PIE, we note that these devices were for the most part intonation and lexical. The extensive system of verbal inflection was used to express other verbal categories.

5.2.2. Voice and Its Means of Expression. Relationships between verbs and nouns were expressed primarily through case forms of nouns. Accordingly early PIE did not have inherently transitive or intransitive verbs. The lack of such a distinction is reflected in dialects as late as Latin, in which the accusative can be used to indicate the goal of the action with "intransitive" verbs (Hale and Buck 1903:203, 206–207):

6.	Vergil, Aeneid 1.2.	Ītaliam	vēnit
		'[to] Italy	he-came

7.	Cicero, Catiline 4.1.2.	multa	tacuī
		'[with regard to] many things	I-have-been-silent'

In the early dialects specific case forms came to be associated with specific verbs, such as the accusative for direct objects. From this time verbs are classified as transitive or intransitive; the classification, though in part related to derivational affixes, is for the most part lexical.

The distinction between + and –transitive verbs, however, came to be associated to an increasing extent with inflectional classes. Since the perfect inflection indicated state, accusative nominal forms were less commonly associated with it than with verb forms of the *m* class. Moreover, accusatives were generally not used with middles. Both of these inflections are comparable in this way to intransitives; this characteristic has led to the assumption of a relationship between the perfect and the middle. As the statements presented above indicate, however, the relationship is only secondary: the middle, with its basic meaning of reflexivization and reciprocality, is comparable with the resultative perfect primarily in lacking an accusative object, Since however transitivity was not a category of the PIE verbal system, the middle and perfect should not be related to one another but treated as categories independent of one another.

Some prominent derivational affixes, notably *-yo-* and *-ē-* < *-eʔ-*, expressed state and accordingly were comparable to intransitives (Brugmann 1904*a*:492, 527; Delbrück 1897:26–40, esp. 34–35). Yet it is instructive to note that, in keeping with the autonomy of individual words and with the patterning of the case system, verbs with these suffixes may be accompanied by nouns in the accusative. Delbrück gives excellent examples, such as the following for the Sanskrit root *as-* + *-ya-* 'hurl, throw':

8. RV 2.24.8. tásya sādhvī́r íṣavo yā́bhir ásyati
his accurate arrows with-which he-shoots
'Accurate are his arrows, with which he shoots.'

9. RV 10.168.1. utó eti pṛthivyā́ reṇúm ásyan
and it-goes on-earth dust throwing
'And [the wind] goes along the earth, throwing up dust.'

The essential of such *-yo-* verbs is the expression of a state or process, whether they are intransitive and accompanied by noun in an adverbial sense, as in Example 8, or transitive and accompanied by a noun that can be regarded as the object, as in Example 9. With these possibilities, both affixes were employed in passive formations, after the passive was introduced as a verbal category: the *-yo-* especially in Indic, the *-ē-* in

Greek. The passive as a separate category developed, however, primarily from the middle.

As we have noted above, § 4.3.4, the middle was a distinct voice category in PIE. It has at least the following meanings. Some roots always had the middle affix, and in these the action or process was viewed as taking place with reference to the subject; see Delbrück (1897:417–425) for examples of such roots. The middle affix was also used in contrast with the active to convey reflexive or reciprocal meaning, as in Examples 76 and 77 of Chapter 4. When late PIE began to assume VO characteristics, pronominal elements were introduced for reflexive and reciprocal meaning. The central meaning of the middle became that of passive voice.

A passive proper requires the presence of an agent, whether animate or inanimate (Gonda 1951*a*:73–78). In our early texts we find examples of middle verbs used with agents and thus having passive force (Delbrück 1897:432–435), such as the following with the verb *epeígomai* 'set oneself in motion, hasten, be beset':

10. Iliad 6.363. allà sú g' órnuthi toûton, epeigésthō dè kài autós
but you Ptc. rouse him he-should-hurry Ptc. and self
'But you stir him up, and he himself should make haste.'

11. Iliad 5.622. epeígeto gàr beléessi
he-hastened, he-was-beset for with-missiles
'For he was beset with missiles.'

In Example 11 the inclusion of an instrument gives a passive meaning to a verb which when not accompanied by a noun indicating an agent or instrument is simply a middle. From such uses the passive arose as a separate category.

A passive is not likely to arise as a separate category, however, except when a language includes causative constructions; for these require the presence of an agent or instrument as well as a direct object. Parallelism between the passive and increasing frequency of causatives is evident in our Sanskrit texts (Whitney, JAOS 13:xxxiv). The number of roots found only in the oldest texts with the passive is less than half that of roots found with the passive in both earlier and later texts (37 vs. 105); and this number is lower than that of roots with the passive found only in the later, epic and classical language (117). The proportions between attested causative forms are comparable: 111 vs. 247 vs. 207. The increase in the number of passives made from causatives is even more striking: 9 vs. 28 vs. 110. These figures support the assumption that the passive developed only after PIE, in the various dialects.

This assumption is also supported by the diversity of passive formations, such as: the middle forms in Gothic and Greek, supplemented in Greek with *-ē-* and *-thē-* forms; the *-yo-* forms with middle endings in Sanskrit; the *r* forms in Italic and Celtic (Leumann 1963:306–308). Such forms are concerns of studies dealing with the individual dialects. Here we have been examining the evidence for voice categories in PIE. On the basis of verbal inflection we may assume only a middle and an active. Derivational affixes could be used to indicate other meanings comparable to voices, such as the causative and the factitive (§ 4.4.3). These, like the middle, underwent various modifications in the individual dialects, leading to different alignments of categories for voice.

5.2.3. Moods and Their Means of Expression. The inflectional suffixes which were most prominent in PIE indicated moods: *-e/o-* with necessitative and obligative force, *-yeʔ-* with voluntative (§ 4.3.5–4.3.6). The dubitative and voluntative meanings of these suffixes became highly frequent, and from these uses the two moods were named subjunctive and optative. The subjunctive and optative were employed particularly in subordinate clauses, in which their meanings were determined in part by the relationship of the subordinate clause to the principal clause, a relationship which was also indicated by introductory particles. In view of the effects of these interrelationships and of particles such as conjunctions, the uses of modal forms in the dialects provide some of the greatest complexities in Indo-European grammar (see such specialized monographs as Goodwin 1893, Gonda 1956, and the bibliographical survey of Calboli 1966–1968). We have assumed however that the subjunctive in PIE had basically an obligative meaning, the optative a volitional, and that these meanings were modified as the individual dialects developed.

The uses of the optative and subjunctive were associated with that of a third mood, the imperative, marked by distinctive endings and used to express commands. The difficulties involved in attempting to determine the uses of these three moods in PIE are compounded by the presence of derivational affixes and by syncretism of the moods among one another and with derivational forms.

The most notable derivational affix with modal meaning was *-s-*, which expressed desiderative force (Brugmann 1904*a*:518–519, 529). In Indic, forms with *-s-* assumed the status of a modal category, although desiderative forms never were very frequent. In other dialects which maintained

-s- forms, these fell together with the tense system, expressing the future, or with the subjunctive (Delbrück 1897:242–255, 306–308, 321–330).

In Sanskrit the subjunctive merged with the imperative, so that this mood had first-person forms (see Whitney 1896:215–220 on this merger and the uses of the modes in general). Hittite underwent a similar merger, though here the first singular *-l-* forms were based on a derivational affix with "imperative" force (Solta 1970:44–84). These mergers extended the meanings of the modal forms which survived in the various dialects, whether the so-called subjunctive based on an IE optative in Germanic or the so-called imperative in Hittite; and because of such broadening of meaning, it is difficult to be certain of the meanings of the moods in PIE.

Besides inflectional and derivational affixes, modal meanings were also expressed lexically. In some dialects such lexical expression serves primarily to support the meaning of a modal form, as does *hí* in the following (see Grassmann 1872:1664–1665 and also Denniston 1966*b*:xxxvii).

12. RV 5.4.6.	vadhéna	dásyum	prá	hí	cātáyasva
	with-weapon	dasyu	away	indeed	you-repel
	'Drive away the Dasyu with your weapon.'				

In Hittite such particles have independent meaning, as does *man* for the expression of potentiality (J. Friedrich 1960:140):

13.	man-	u̯ar-aš-mu	LÚ*MUTI.I̯A*	kišari
	'may'	quote-he-me	spouse	he-is
	'He could become my spouse.'			

From such modal uses of particles in independent sentences we may assume lexical indications of mood in PIE.

Such an assumption is supported by the use of reflexes of **mē,* especially in Vedic. For with injunctive forms *mā* is the sole indication of modal meanings, chiefly necessitative but also voluntative (Hoffmann 1967:46–92, 101–106):

14. RV 8.48.14.	mā́	no	nidrā́	īśata,	mótá	jálpiḥ
	may not	us	sleep	it-overpowers	may-not-and	chatter
	'May sleep not overpower us, nor chatter.'					

The first clause illustrates a necessitative use of *mā́* with the modally unmarked injunctive. The second, verbless clause suggests that *mā* alone could have negative modal force; here however one may assume conjunction reduction of the second use of *īśata,* though Hoffmann gives other examples of *mā* without a verb (1967:65). Although no modal particle with positive meaning is as prominent in the early texts as are the reflexes of PIE *mḗ*, such examples as Gk. *án* and *ke* support the assumption of lexical as well as inflectional indication of modal meaning in PIE (Wakkernagel 1926:224). The primary indicators of mood in PIE however were the inflectional categories known as the subjunctive, optative, and imperative.

5.2.4. Aspects and Their Means of Expression. As noted in § 4.4, the primary contrast in aspect was one of imperfective versus perfective. In early PIE the distinction was expressed through the contrasting endings; *m s t* versus *x the ϕ*. Another aspectual contrast, that between momentary and durative, was expressed primarily through forms of the root: durative by an accented and accordingly *e* vowel in the root; momentary by lack of principal accent on the root and accordingly *ϕ* vowel, or *o* vowel when the root received secondary accent on shift of the principal accent. Through subsequent syncretism and shift from aspect to tense, this early aspect was disrupted.

Contrasts between the aspects in the early system are clearest in Vedic injunctives, as opposed to aorists and perfects of a given root or of an extended root like **wey-d-* < **wey-* + *-d-*. The simple injunctive form *vet* < **weyd-t* expresses imperfective, durative aspect; its single attestation, RV 10.53.9, may be translated 'he understands'. The aorist *vidát* < **wid-ét* expresses perfective, +momentary aspect; as in RV 1.62.3, it may be translated 'he found'. The perfect *véda* < **wòid-e* expresses perfective, –momentary aspect; as in RV 10.169.2, it may be translated 'he knows < he has seen and accordingly he understands'. These contrasts may be illustrated more precisely by citing the sentences in which these forms occur:

15. RV 10.53.9.
 tváṣṭā māyā́ ved
 Tvaṣṭr changes understands
 'Tvaṣṭr understands the changes.'

16. RV 1.62.3.
 índrasyā́ñgirasāṃ ceṣṭhaú
 of-Indra-of-Angiras and-at-request
 vidát sarámā tánayāya dhāsím
 he-found Sarama for-descendants nourishment
 'At the request of Indra and the Angiras
 Sarama found nourishment for their descendants.'

The perfective, momentary meaning is equally implicit if one follows the interpretation of Geldner (1951–1957:I, 80): 'Als Indra und die Angiras' auf der Suche waren, fand . . .' The stative, resultative meaning of the perfect form *véda* is pointed up by the instrumental *íṣṭyā* in RV 10.169.2, for this indicates that 'finding' was made at a definite time in the past, leading to knowledge:

17.	RV 10.169.2.	yā́sām	agnír	íṣṭyā	nā́māni	véda
		whose	Agni	through-sacrifice	names	he-knows

'Whose names Agni has found out (and thus knows) through the sacrifice.'

By contrast the injunctive form simply indicates a situation; in Hoffmann's term it has a "memorative" meaning, in T. Elizarenkova's a "mentioning," an interpretation like Hoffmann's *Erwähnung* (Hoffmann 1967: 279, Elizarenkova 1972:250–253, with reference to her earlier work of 1960). And the aorist form in RV 1.62.3 refers to a single action that has been completed.

While these distinctions were expressed unambiguously in the distinct, contrasting forms of the singular, the dual and plural forms were not unambiguous; they had neither contrasting endings throughout for each of these aspectual categories nor characteristic root forms. The zero grade of the root was found in the dual and plural of the perfect as well as in the aorist, and in athematic presents as well, a vocalism applying also to injunctives. Accordingly the contrasts between ±perfective and ±momentary were not marked throughout a paradigm (present versus aorist/perfect; aorist versus perfect). The lack of contrast in many forms of the dual and plural numbers resulted in syncretism also in the singular, as is evident from the reflexes of these aspectual forms in the dialects. In some dialects the distinction between the +perfective and the –perfective became predominant, as in Slavic, which has a verbal system with principal distinction between these two verbal aspects. In other dialects, as in Sanskrit and Greek, the contrast between –momentary (durative) and +momentary became predominant, leading to a contrast between ongoing action, or present tense, on the one hand, and punctual and stative action, or aorist and perfect tense, on the other hand. Whichever features predominated, all dialects showed syncretism; and in most dialects the aspectual system gave way to a tense system.

Other aspects, such as iterative, intensive, frequentative, and inchoative, never occupied as prominent positions in the PIE verb systems as had ±perfective and ±momentary. These other aspects were expressed by verbal affixes, some of which became productive in specific dialects but are found only sporadically in others. An iterative with *-ske-* affix is especially prominent in Hittite (J. Friedrich 1960:140–141), where it has durative meaning and indicates action carried out in several steps, as in:

18. anniškimi kuin
 'which I carry out (in several ritual acts)'

This example and others given by Friedrich illustrate that even in Hittite the *-ske-* affix had various functions. We may make the same assumption for PIE, although the iterative meaning may have predominated in *sk-* forms.

By Dressler's view, the intensive, distributive, and durative developed from the iterative (1968:233). In accordance with this view the various meanings exhibited by *sk-* formations in the several dialects had their origin in the iterative, such as the inchoatives of Latin, which presumably arose from distributive uses like that in the Hittite example above (18) (see also Brugmann 1913:350–361; Delbrück 1897:59–64). And the causative formation in Tocharian marked by this affix was attributed by Holger Pedersen to an iterative developing through a factitive (1941:168).

Frequentative, iterative, and also intensive aspect was expressed by reduplication, a process which came to be productive especially in Sanskrit (Delbrück 1897:16–26), as in *jigā́ti*, Gk. *bíbāmi* 'walk, stride', as opposed to the simple root in the aorists *ágāt, ébē* 'put one's foot down'. Aspectual categories may then be regarded as compounds of features.

Such a view of aspects as composites rather than single semantic features has been explored by H. J. Verkuyl (1972), as well as the interrelationships of aspects with elements which, by our model of language, are introduced through the nominal constituents of the proposition (see also Anderson 1971). For Verkuyl, durative aspect is composed of "elementary semantic verbal" features, such as "MOVEMENT, AGENTIVE, PERFORM, TAKE, ADD" (1972:96); moreover, it also involves a "nominal node . . . containing quantificational information." Durative aspect then allows the introduction of "durative adverbials." And a verb with durative aspect is associated with the feature "unspecified quantity," while a nondurative is associated with the feature "specified quantity." We may illustrate something of the "compositional nature of the aspects" by comparing examples of the durative verb 'eat' and the nondurative 'bite'.

19. The dogs were happily eating their biscuits.

20. The dogs quickly bit three of the chilren.

As in the numerous examples given by Verkuyl, the perfective verb of Example 20 is associated with a specified quantity, unlike the durative "were eating" of Example 19. Moreover, if perfective meaning is included in a sentence including 'eat', as through an adverbial element like 'quickly', the simple past is used:

21. The dogs quickly ate their biscuits.

By contrast, the past progressive with 'quickly' implies repeated, iterative action, as in:

22. The dogs were quickly eating their biscuits.

These examples illustrate that aspect, though conveyed lexically in English, involves contrasts between manners of action which can be readily introduced; we may make a similar assumption for PIE, though expression of such contrasts in PIE was primarily suffixal. These English examples also illustrate the close relationship between aspect and tense; as Verkuyl cautiously puts it, "the underlying V-node involved in the composition of the Nondurative Aspect has something to do with what I have called 'the temporalization of abstract entities'" (1972:176). Aspects, then, as Dressler and Verkuyl have demonstrated, cannot be viewed as simple features associated only with the verb; they extend to other elements of the proposition as well and include temporal features as well as features pertaining to manner of action. Because of these relationships to all elements of the proposition, and because of their various means of expression, they are best treated as Q constituents.

In the course of syntactic change a given feature may come to predominate, somewhat as a given phonological feature may change in sound. In late PIE, features of tense became predominant: present tense rather than durative aspect, preterite rather than nondurative. The aspectual meanings thereupon were expressed lexically or by derivational processes. Forms in which the shift from a predominant aspectual to a tense meaning was not carried out provide excellent evidence for the development. Among such forms are the Germanic preterite-presents. In preterite-presents, like Gothic *kann* 'I am able to do < I have acquired knowledge', the shift was carried out lexically. Various reflexes of the perfect of **weyd-* provide illustrations in a number of dialects. Vedic *véda,* Gk. *oîda,* Goth. *wait* 'I know' reflect the PIE resultative, –momentary meaning lexically; Latin *vīdi* 'I have seen' on the other hand illustrates the normal shift to a "preterite" tense, a shift also exemplified in Armenian *egit,* which corresponds to Skt. *ávidat* 'he found'. Thus, both of the PIE perfective aspect forms, the aorist and the perfect, were shifted to preterite-tense forms as opposed to present-tense forms, which normally had their origin in imperfectives.

In some dialects, notably Sanskrit, Greek, Italic, and Baltic, the tense system was amplified by a future, which developed from forms indicating doubt, such as *s*- suffixed forms and subjunctives. PIE itself had no future tense, in contrast with the views of some scholars (see Brugmann's interesting observations [1917] on the lack of a word for 'tomorrow' in PIE, though words for 'today' and 'yesterday' can be reconstructed; see also Gonda 1971:92–93). Reference to time of the action was indicated by means of adverbial or nominal elements; the verbal forms associated with these elements were aspectual. Verbal affixes and endings accordingly indicated aspects in PIE; but the meanings of individual forms were determined in part by lexical features, as we will note in Chapter 6, and also by the case forms of substantives in the proposition.

5.3. Syntactic Categories Expressed in Conjunction with Substantives.

In late PIE, inflection of nouns, pronouns, and adjectives, that is, substantival inflection, was made for case, gender, and number. The primary uses of gender and number were for indication of congruence, gender in nominal constructions, number in nominal and verbal constructions. Number also carried lexical meaning, both with verbs and with substantives. Case was particularly important in specifying the lexical meaning of nominal elements and of verbal elements associated with them, though with some verbs specific case forms were regulated by patterns of government (Meillet 1937:338–341). Yet the central uses of cases marked nominal forms for specific functions in sentences, as the selected examples in the following section illustrate.

5.3.1. Uses of the Case Categories. With its large number of inflections, the PIE substantive had overt markings for many of the features introduced in the nominal constituent of the proposition.

Of the eight cases, only one, the genitive, served primarily to indicate relationships between substantives. Another, the vocative, marked nouns as being independent of other elements. In this way the vocative preserved longest the earlier situation in which nominal forms with characteristic endings had a self-contained meaning, independent of other elements in the sentence (Meillet 1937:151). It is the case of address, with both independent and included nouns. When independent the vocative was always accented; when included in a clause, it was not. Accentuation however did not affect its meaning.

The six remaining cases expressed meanings largely with regard to the verb. The accusative indicated the target of the verbal action; the dative indicated the receptor. When the agent of the action was animate, it was indicated by the nominative; when inanimate, by the instrumental. As passive forms were introduced, the instrumental was also used for animate agents. Closely related to its use for the instrument of the action is that for accompaniment; accordingly the instrumental is also referred to as the sociative. To indicate a point in time or place, the locative was used; to indicate contrast with an element or departure from a point in time or place, the ablative. These six cases correspond closely with underlying syntactic categories referred to as *target, receptor, agent, instrument, place, time, source.* Yet they also had additional uses, as described in the handbooks (Delbrück 1893:173–400; Meillet 1937:341–349; and many others, such as Krahe 1972:56–108). Moreover, their uses with specific verbs which draw on their central meanings are illustrated in Chapter 2.

If these additional uses are treated independently of their contexts, or if a case is analyzed from an item approach rather than a process approach, each case will be described as having a multitude of meanings. When, for example, the genitive was analyzed in this way, it was assumed to have more than a score of uses. A study by Benveniste, however, indicates both how a case is to be described in a syntactic discussion and how the genitive can be characterized in a unified way (1966:140–148).

Starting from an article on the Latin genitive by A. W. de Groot, who proposed "eight regular grammatical uses" after a review of the "thirty or so distinct uses" recorded in earlier classifications, Benveniste defines the genitive as follows: "The genitive is the case that in a construction consisting of two nouns takes on the function which either the nominative or the accusative has in a sentence with a finite verb; all other uses... derive from this use" (1966:148; 1971:127). If the verb is intransitive, the noun accompanying it must be in the nominative; and if the verbal construction is changed to a nominal construction, the nominative becomes the so-called subjective genitive, as in *patientia animi* 'patience of spirit' from *animus patitur* 'the spirit is patient'. If the finite verb is transitive, the result of a modification of the accusative is the so-called objective genitive, as in *patientia doloris* 'endurance of suffering' from *pati dolorem* 'to endure suffering' (see also Kurylowicz 1964:186–189). In his discussion Benveniste also indicates how the other uses of the genitive in Latin are related to its basic function and how they are to be treated under specific syntactic constructions; thus the "genitive of locality" is to be treated in connection with toponyms, for it occurs only with these. And the "genitive of quality" is a "syntactic derivation . . . of the normal use of the genitive," as in *aedes regis* 'palace of the king', with a following infinitive (Benveniste 1971:125):

23. pauperis est numerāre pecus
of-the-poor-man it-is to-count cattle
'It is a characteristic of the poor man to count cattle.'

Benveniste's conclusions are accordingly based on a generative syntactic approach, as are also those of Jerzy Kurylowicz. These conclusions have important theoretical implications for the view of grammar maintained here.

The characterization of the genitive as derived from either the nominative or the accusative indicates that the genitive occupies a particular hierarchy in the system of cases and in this way demonstrates that there is indeed such a hierarchy. In this hierarchy the underlying case categories differ from verbal categories and especially from those introduced under Q. For the genitive case is subordinate to other cases, and these in turn are subordinate to the verbal element with its categories. Only the vocative, which is independent, is an exception. The position of the genitive, then, supports the analysis of the proposition into a verb and abstract case categories, as well as the analysis of the sentence into a Q and a Prop. constituent. Moreover, this approach clarifies the positing of a central meaning for a case.

Benveniste's conclusions on the "meaning" of the genitive are much like those of earlier Indo-Europeanists who have proposed "basic meanings" *(Grundbegriffe)* for the cases (Delbrück 1893:185–187, 333–335, with references to Grimm and Gaedicke; Sommer 1959:10, cited by Krahe 1972:56–57). Thus, for Ferdinand Sommer, "the genitive denotes the sphere of a verbal process or that of a further noun." With greater use of a generative approach, Benveniste's definition is more precise, though still comparable with that of Sommer. Moreover, in contrast with some earlier Indo-Europeanists, Benveniste is not giving the "basic meaning" of the genitive in a supposedly primeval stage of Indo-European; rather, the meaning proposed by him is that added by the selection of a genitive case form in a particular construction. More elaborate statements of the choice of a particular case in specific constructions, and in connection with specific lexical elements, such as those given at length by Delbrück (1893:308–333), belong in the lexicon rather than the syntactic component of an account of PIE or of any language. The same procedure must be used in the study of other case forms.

Care must also be taken to distinguish possible differences between the basic use of the genitive in PIE and that in a dialect like Latin. In his study of the genitive as examined by other scholars, including Wackernagel, Kurylowicz, and Benveniste, and as occurring in other languages, Calvert Watkins concluded that Roman Jakobson's analysis of the meaning of the case is to be assumed for PIE (Watkins 1967:2191–2198). The primary function of the genitive in PIE then relates to "the extent of participation of the entity in the message"; the transformationally derived subjective and objective genitives are secondary to a "genitive of belonging." The question is partly one of chronology, partly one of focus. The meaning "extent of participation" is a semantic characterization, in contrast with Benveniste's syntactic definition. We may relate the definitions of Watkins and Benveniste by noting that the genitive, as a nominal form derived from nominatives or accusatives with given verbs, indeed indicates the extent of participation of a given substantive in a verbal action. If one seeks a still earlier use of the nominal forms which are the etyma of the genitive in PIE, one may find it in connection with a definition of the nominal suffix *-s* in pre-IE; *-s* was used to specify an individual (Lehmann 1958:190). In late PIE the genitive had the syntactic function indicated by Benveniste. This then was its "basic meaning" for PIE, comparable to the basic meanings given for the vocative and the six other cases at the beginning of this section.

From these basic meanings secondary uses arose in specific contexts, and other means of expression than case suffixes, as we may note briefly. We have proposed in Chapter 2 that a verb is characteristically accompanied by one case form in PIE, in addition to the person expressed in the verbal ending. Meillet characterized the accusative as "determining the meaning of the verb" (1937:343). But as the following examples with Skt. *vidh-* demonstrate, other cases also function in this way. Accompanied by the accusative, *vidh-* may be translated 'honor'.

24.	RV 8.96.8.	śúṣmaṃ	ta	enā́	havíṣā	vidhema
		power	of-you	with-this	with-offering	we-would-honor

'We would honor your power with this offering.'

Various other examples could be cited with a similar use of the accusative, including the examples given by Meillet, such as those with the Greek verb *bállō* 'throw':

25.	Odyssey 2.80.	potì	dè	skêptron	bále	gaíēi
		toward	Ptc.	staff	he-threw	to-ground

'And he threw the staff down to the ground.'

Complementing or determining the meaning of the verbs *bállō* and *vidh-*, the accusatives indeed fulfill the function stated by Meillet. But they also specify the element which is the target of the verbal action. This use as target is then the basic meaning of the accusative. It applies also in connection with other verbs, such as verbs of motion like Lat. *īre* in *Rōmam īre* 'go to Rome'. Especially when discussed independently of verbs, such uses are taken as secondary and treated independently, often with separate labels, but, as Meillet indicates, these uses derive from the basic meanings, in association with certain verbs. We may illustrate such developments with other cases as well, as in the dative accompanying *vidh-*.

Like Example 24, RV 8.48.13 would be complete with the verb form and the dative *(te > ta)*; *tásmai* is appositional to *ta.* The vocative *Indo* is independent.

26.	RV 8.48.13.	tásmai	ta	indo	havíṣā	vidhema
		that, such-a	you	Indu	with-oblation	we-would-worship

'We would worship you, such a one, O Indu, with oblation.'

As Meillet has stated (1937:347), the dative does not indicate the target of the action, as would the accusative, but rather the person (or object) in view of which the action was carried out. In Example 26 then *vidh-* is specified for the receptor of the act of worship. The dative may thus determine the meaning of the verb as does the accusative. Moreover, the dative is characteristically found with certain verbs, like those of 'hearing'. This use simply supports the proposal that the basic meaning of the dative is as receptor.

Both Example 24 and Example 26 have *vidh-* with its primary noun accompanied by an instrumental. In these sentences the instrumental has its primary meaning, indicating the instrument of the action (Schwyzer 1943:16). As another example in this poem indicates, this meaning could readily be used in the sense of accompanied by. The minimal sentence of this example states that the speaker would partake of the pressed-out soma, *bhakṣ-* governing the genitive *te,* which is accompanied by the appositional *sutásya:*

27. RV 8.48.7. iṣiréṇa te mánasā sutásya
devoted you with-mind pressed

bhakṣīmáhi
we-would-partake-of

'With devoted mind we would partake of you pressed-out.'

In this passage the instrumental indicates "accompanying circumstances" (Delbrück 1893:238–240), though its relationship to the basic meaning is transparent. In the following stanza the instrumental *suastí,* though indicating the instrument of the action, is virtually equivalent to a dative, indicating purpose:

28. RV 8.48.8. sóma rājan mṛḷáyā naḥ suastí
Soma king you-be-gracious to-us through-means-of-well-being
'King Soma, be gracious to us for our welfare.'

These examples taken from an Archaic hymn may illustrate how the instrumental came to be used to express meanings other than its central meaning.

The ablative likewise is used in accordance with its basic meaning of the starting point of the action. As Gonda points out (1971:119), it is excellently characterized by Panini (1.4.24–31) as the "case of the item which remains in its own place when another item is removed from it." This meaning is figurative as well as literal; the figurative use is found widely in comparison, with or without a comparative suffix on the adjective:

29. RV 1.57.4. nahí tvád anyó girvaṇo gíraḥ
not-indeed from-you other desiring-praise songs-of-praise

sághat
can-endure

'For no one but you can endure the songs of praise, you who desire praise.'

In another figurative use it also expresses the reason for an action (Macdonell 1916:318):

30. RV 7.89.5. mā́ nas tásmād énaso deva rīriśaḥ
not us from-that from-sin O-god you-punish
'Do not punish us because of that sin, O god.'

These secondary uses of the ablative conform with its limitations of a distinct form only in the singular, notably the comparative, which represents a contrast between two items. Its limitation to the singular may have been largely responsible for its loss, in both its primary and its secondary meanings.

For the other cases, any of these secondary meanings could become more prominent, as study of the dialects indicates. Thus in Lithuanian and the Slavic languages the instrumental is used predicatively as a resultative, as in the example below (see Delbrück 1893:262–268 and Senn 1966:429, who gives examples such as the following):

31. sniẽgas pavir̃sta vándeniu
snow it-becomes water
'The snow turns to water.'

Such developments of individual case forms would require extensive discussion if the various details were to be presented, as they have been by Delbrück (1893:200–400). Here only the principle behind the developments is presented: when a second or third case form was used in sentences, its meaning was extended beyond the basic meaning, and eventually the secondary meanings might become prominent.

The meaning involved could also be specified by particles, which accompanied case forms in particular passages. An example from the cited Archaic hymn may illustrate such uses of postpositions; in the following example, the locative *máda* < *máde* would adequately express the meaning 'in . . .', but the postposition *ā́* 'in' is included, apparently to specify this meaning more clearly:

32. RV 8.48.6. áthā hí te máda ā́ soma mánye
then for your intoxication in Soma I-think-of-myself
revā́m̐ iva
bring-rich as

'For then in intoxication with you, Soma, I consider myself rich.'

The development of particles like *ā́* as postpositions, subsequently prepositions, has been described as thoroughly as have the uses of the case forms (see for example Delbrück 1893:643–774; Meillet 1937:345–349).

In his extensive treatment Delbrück has pointed out how particles were combined with verbs as well as nouns. Thus *ánu* in the following line is interpreted as a verbal particle accompanying the root *tan-* 'extend' and the particle *ā,* with the accusative maintaining its independent meaning:

33. RV 8.48.13. ánu dyā́vāpṛthivī́ ā́ tatantha
over heaven-earth to you-have-extended
'You have extended yourself over heaven and earth.'

In the following example *ánu* may be interpreted as a postposition as readily as a verbal particle:

34. RV 10.97.19. viṣṭhitāḥ pṛthivī́m ánu
spread earth over
'spread throughout the earth'

When such particles came to be placed before nouns, they developed into prepositions, such as those in the later dialects; the cognates of *ánu* are attested in numerous dialects: Avestan *ana,* Gk. *aná,* Lat. *an,* Goth. *ana,* Slav. *na,* Lith. *nù.*

35. Odyssey 9.209. hén dépas emplḗsas húdatos anà eíkosi métra
one cup having-filled water over twenty measures
kheû
he-poured
'after filling one cup [with wine] he poured it on twenty measures of water'

In this way particles first supplemented case forms as postpositions, then as prepositions, and eventually in many IE dialects as the sole markers of relationships between verbs and nouns. Such postpositional and prepositional phrases have been equated with inflectional forms representing underlying case categories. The shift from inflected nouns to noun phrases including postpositions or prepositions is thus a matter of surface syntax.

There are various reasons for the shift from an inflectional system marking cases to the use of prepositions; these reasons were phonological and morphological and, not least, syntactic. The phonological reasons are primarily a result of a shift to stress accent, because of which characteristic final endings were weakened and merged or lost. The phonological syncretism was intensified by systemic morphological realignment of the eight-case singular system with the smaller system of the plural and dual. Most influential in the placement of particles in preposed position and accordingly prepositional constructions was the shift to a VO structure; for prepositional phrases are the characteristic nominal constructions to indicate case relationships in VO languages.

Although these changes led to the indication of substantival relationships to verbs largely through prepositional phrases, the indication was marked in part by arrangement, notably of the subject and object. Already in the early dialects the subject or object relationship of duals and of neuter nouns to verbs in the third person was determinable chiefly from their position and clarified by the presence of other elements in the clause which were unambiguous. When first- and second-person forms of the verb merged with third-person forms, the position of a substantive often was the only means of distinguishing its role. Word order then became fixed. Thus in spite of the unambiguous syntactic use of *he* as opposed to *him*, one must put the English subject initially in translating the following German sentence:

36. Die Tóchter hat er gesehen.
He saw the dáughter. NOT The dáughter he saw.

The changing role of case categories thus is related to general syntactic changes, and these also involve the other nominal categories.

5.3.2. Gender. Although gender distinctions are expressed in the substantives of all Indo-European dialects, it is clear that the gender category was developed late in PIE. The decisive evidence for this conclusion was given by Johannes Schmidt in his study of the plural formations of IE neuters (1889; see also Lehmann 1958; Kurylowicz 1964:207–226). According to Schmidt's study, neuter plurals originated from singular collectives. Since feminine singular collectives had the same forms and the same meanings as did neuter plurals, we must assume that an earlier system of endings did not indicate gender categories but rather specific semantic meanings. These meanings I have characterized as follows: *-s* = individual, *-m* = resultative (or result), *-h* = collective (Lehmann 1958: 192). As the nominal system of late PIE developed, these endings were aligned in the gender, number, and case paradigms found in the various IE dialects.

In examining gender, we must note that in PIE and the dialects its function was the indication of congruence. Gender may also have different uses, as T. F. Mitchell has recently demonstrated in an important paper on concord, especially in Sindhi and Cairene Arabic (1973). Concord in Arabic is determined by number as well as gender; and gender conveys the additional force of "marking the role and status relations of interlocutors," as Mitchell illustrates. In IE, however, gender is a means to express congruence, primarily a syntactic category to indicate the bounds of the nominal phrase when nouns, adjectives, and adjectival pronouns are involved; gender also permits precision of pronominal reference (see also Brugmann 1891).

Many studies have been carried out in attempts to account for the origin of gender as a category in PIE, generally relating it to sex distinctions. The initial distinction is assumed to be animate versus inanimate, with a subsequently introduced distinction between animate male and female. The basic assumption of these studies must be rejected, for they disregard Schmidt's conclusions, relying instead on a fanciful notion of primitive speakers introducing linguistic distinctions on the basis of their understanding of the world around them. If the animate-inanimate distinction were so fundamental in early PIE, we would expect far more extensive marking than the lack of the *s* ending in the nominative singular to indicate inanimate nouns (see Lehmann 1958 for details). Since however the basic distinction in the early nominal endings is for syntactic purposes, we must look to a different explanation. We find this in changes resulting from the shift toward a VO structure.

It is readily understandable that expression for congruence is less important in OV languages than in VO languages. For, in OV languages, nominal modification, whether of demonstratives, adjectives, or relative constructions, is indicated simply by preposing. Thus neither Turkish nor Japanese has markers to indicate congruence, nor did Classical Armenian (Jensen 1959:47); I assume that early PIE also lacked expression for congruence. The gender distinctions as we know them, especially from the early dialects (Delbrück 1893:89–133), were developed when nominal modifiers and anaphoric elements came to stand in other positions than the prenominal. For when adjectives are placed after nouns, or when anaphoric pronouns stand at some distance from them, expressions to mark the relationship are highly useful. The syntactically simple first line of the Odyssey may serve as illustration:

37. Odyssey 1.1. ándra moi énnepe, moûsa, polútropon, hòs mála pollà
man to-me you-tell O-Muse much-turned who very many
'Tell me of the man, O Muse, of many devices, who [traveled] through very many places.'

The masculine endings of *polútropon* and *hòs* relate these modifiers to *ándra,* excluding possible relationship with another substantive, such as *moûsa.* Although we cannot account for innovations through poetic use, inasmuch as poets normally utilize the devices their languages provide rather than introduce new ones, nonetheless, it is difficult to conceive of Vedic poetry as we find it without the device of congruence. For virtually every stanza would be unintelligible if there were no congruence markers to relate nominal expressions. We account for the development of the IE gender system, then, as one process in the shift from an OV structure toward a VO structure.

The development of the surface markers of the gender system has been well described (Brugmann 1911:82–109, Kurylowicz 1964:207–226). It is also well known how the expression for gender meshes with that for case and number. Such morphological details are not of concern in determining the reasons for the introduction of gender distinctions in PIE. The situation in Hittite may however still be noted.

Hittite has no expression for the feminine gender. Following established terminology, some Hittite scholars labeled the two congruence classes of Hittite substantives *masculine* and *neuter* (Sturtevant 1951: 82–83). Today, however, the terms *common* and *neuter* are generally used. As Sturtevant pointed out, however, a neuter ending is found only for *a* stems, which have *-n* in the nominative. And nouns may be used adjectivally without indication of congruence; *kurur* means 'inimical' as well as 'enemy' and 'enmity'. Hittite apparently, then, maintained an older stage in which the feminine category had not yet been introduced, though Hittite did introduce innovations by marking a neuter category in one nominal inflection and in pronouns (Sturtevant 1951:111). Hittite was then even more archaic than Vedic, in which neuter nouns could "function syntactically as singulars as well as plurals" (Gonda 1971:62; see also Delbrück 1888:80).

38. RV 1.64.5. ū́dhar divyā́ni
udder heavenly (pl.)
'celestial udders'

Moreover, Hittite has a neuter plural *-a*, which corresponds to the ending identified by Schmidt as a collective; yet neither this ending nor the neuter category, is as well developed as in the other early dialects (J. Friedrich 1960:115–118). The "nominative-accusative neuter (of pronouns) both singular and plural, often refers to plural antecedents of either gender" (Sturtevant 1951:111). Hittite therefore has a nominal system in which the so-called neuter plural resembles a collective rather than the gender marker known from the other early dialects. Accordingly we may conclude that "the lack of a special feminine in Hittite is to be considered as an archaism" rather than "as an innovation" (Kurylowicz 1964:217). Hittite as a relatively consistent OV language had not yet developed fully the congruence markers which are found in the nominal phrase of other IE dialects. But in pronouns, where anaphoric referents were often widely separated from antecedents, as in relative constructions, an incipient congruence system was introduced.

In other dialects this system came to be extended. Whether it was ever extended in Ancient Armenian is unclear. But by the time of the texts which have survived in the other early dialects, a threefold congruence system had been developed for the nominal phrase, though it was not marked in all nominal forms. Through archaisms in the various dialects we can determine that this gender system arose in late PIE. As a syntactic congruence category, it is marked most clearly in those case forms which have essentially grammatical functions: the nominative and the accusative. In the late declensions, notably the *o* stems and the *ā* stems, however, the gender markings have been extended also to the oblique cases, notably the genitive.

5.3.3. Number. Like gender, number is a congruence category; in PIE and the dialects it differs from gender in applying to verbs as well as substantives. Number, then, is a device for relating subjects with their verbs as well as the constituents of nominal expressions and anaphoric markers. Late PIE had three numbers: singular, dual, and plural. For the most part the uses of each of these categories corresponded with their natural meanings. Dual forms were used in connection with two items, especially when these formed a pair, such as the eyes or a divine couple (Meillet 1937:188, 338–339). Plural forms were used for more than two items; singular forms for one. As Meillet points out, however, a "singular" item composed of two or more elements could be in the plural, such as Homeric Gk. *zeiaí* 'spelt(s)'; Vedic *dúraḥ,* Lat. *forēs,* etc. 'door(s)'. Variations from natural uses also reflect older patterns of the language or foreshadow new ones (Delbrück 1893:133–172).

The system of verb endings clearly points to an earlier period in which there was no verbal inflection for number (see Kurylowicz 1964:57, 150). For the dual and plural endings are obviously defective. We cannot reconstruct endings in these two numbers which are as well supported as are those of the singular, except for the third plural.

39.

	m inflection	*h* inflection
1 sg.	m	x
2 sg.	s	th
3 sg.	t	ϕ
3 pl.	nt	r

Only the third plural, as indicated, can be posited for an early period of PIE. The development of precisely third-person forms to express number supports the assumption that the number category was used for congruence.

The number system is defective in substantival as well as in verbal inflection. The personal pronouns never did introduce expressions for plurality, as suppletive paradigms indicate, e.g., Hitt. *uk* 'I', *uēš* 'we', etc., in contrast with demonstratives, e.g., *kāš, kē* 'this, these', and nouns, e.g., *antuhšaš, antuhšeš* 'man, men'. In the system of nominal inflection the most notable reflex of an older prenumber system is the ending *-a,* used in the nominative singular feminine and the nominative-accusative plural neuter. This use, discussed at length by J. Schmidt (1889), reflects a collective ending *-h,* which was lost in late PIE with the change of the preceding *-e-* to *-a-* (Lehmann 1958:191). The earlier use has left reflexes in various dialects, such as: the Hittite and Greek neuter plural subjects accompanied by verbs in the singular; Latin neuter plurals like *loca* accompanying masculines, i.e., *locus* 'place'; the use of neuter plurals in Germanic for collectives consisting of masculine and feminine nouns (Lehmann 1957). Number accordingly was not consistently applied in late PIE and the early dialects in accordance with natural reference. Subsequently application became more regular, and number congruence was carried out for both substantives and verbs.

When the category of number came to be more fully established in the inflectional system, a threefold set of forms was introduced for comparison of adjectives: the comparative when two persons or items were involved, as in the dual; the superlative for more than two, as in the plural; and the positive for one. The absence of markers for comparison in Hittite and the variation in markers from dialect to dialect and within dialects like Greek indicate that comparison was late (Brugmann 1904*a*: 320–324); other evidence is found in suppletive forms throughout the dialects, some surviving as late as NE *good, better, best.*

The late development of the number system in the noun is also clear from the lack of parallelism between the forms of the dual, for which only three forms developed, and the forms of the singular and plural. Moreover, the oblique endings of the plural and the dual instrumental, dative, and ablative were added in accordance with the rules for external rather than internal sandhi (Macdonell 1916:39). Accordingly the dual was never developed as fully as were the other two numbers. The formal aberrancy and its restriction in use to pairs apparently led to its early loss. The number system, both in the noun and in the verb, came to be reduced to two categories, with eventual loss of uses and inflections corresponding to dual number, such as a distinct adjectival comparative as opposed to a positive and a superlative.

5.4. Surface Classes in Which These Categories Are Marked.

In late PIE the two major classes of words, verbs and nouns, were sharply distinguished, as Meillet emphasized (1937:187–192). Person was the dominant category in verbs, case in nouns. Accordingly, even though the two classes shared the category of number, and though they could be built on the same roots, verbs were characterized by their categories and the means of expression for these. Nouns and the other two substantival classes, pronouns and adjectives, were marked for the nominal categories. The numerals were in part nominal, in part adjectival.

5.4.1. The PIE Root. Indo-Europeanists have been greatly concerned with the description and role of the PIE root. Two brilliant studies, both published in 1935 (Kurylowicz 1935; Benveniste 1935), dealt with the description of the root, taking into consideration the huge amount of earlier work as represented in the standard handbooks (Hirt 1921–1937; Meillet 1937; and many others). The monographs of Kurylowicz and Benveniste may be viewed as definitive, because they were able to solve perplexing problems by the assumption of laryngeals in the PIE phonological system. Accordingly, roots which had seemed aberrant, such as *dhē-* 'place' and *es-* 'be', were shown to conform to the pattern found in *bher-* 'bear' and were reconstructed *dheʔ-* and *ʔes-*. The canonical root form for PIE was accordingly C*e*C-.

Roots could be extended by means of suffixes, either suffixes accompanied by a vowel or consonantal suffixes. Such suffixation resulted in a restricted number of extended roots for verbs. The possibilities were summarized in *Proto-Indo-European Phonology* (Lehmann 1952:17-18); only a chart of the possible canonical root forms of primary verbs will be presented here:

40.	Unextended root:	C*e*C-		
	Extended root:	I		II
		C*e*C-C-		CC-*e*C-
			II*a*.	CC-*e*C-C-
			II*b*.	CC-*n*-*e*C-

If further suffixes were added, the form was nominal rather than verbal.

In opposition to these conclusions it has been proposed that this scheme is far too mathematical, that languages do not conform so strictly to canonical shapes. Any Indo-Europeanist would admit exceptions, some probably results of borrowing. Yet the preponderance of the IE vocabulary can be analyzed in accordance with the assumptions on which the forms in Example 40 are based. We may therefore conclude that this description is correct and that the IE lexicon should be analyzed as based on roots which were affixed as indicated in Example 40.

The skepticism concerning this conclusion has resulted partly from statements on the role of the proposed root. The statements which seem dubious were based on the assumption that the reconstructed parent language was primitive, that if taken back far enough it could enlighten us on an early period in which man spoke in monosyllables. Archeological work in the past decades, or even the past century, has totally destroyed any assumption that language was introduced only a brief time before the period of PIE. Accordingly, PIE must not be viewed as a form of language close to the primeval period of man, nor even as a primitive language; actually we have no evidence of any primitive language, even though this term is still encountered in publications. We are then apparently left with the alternative of either considering the PIE root as a convenient fiction for IE grammatical study or trying to account for it in relation to similar elements in other languages.

The PIE root agrees nicely with comparable forms of OV languages. If, for example, we compare Japanese, we may note that two types of roots can be derived from verbs: roots ending in consonants, like *yom-* from *yomu* 'read', and roots ending in vowels, like *ki-* from *kiru* 'put on, clothe'. These roots may take various inflectional and derivational affixes, which are added in accordance with the phonological principles of Japanese; every syllable must end in a vowel, or in vocalic *n̄*. Thus the past tense, suffixed with *-ta,* is *yonda* for *yomu* and *kita* for *kiru.* Other suffixed forms may be examined in any description of Japanese. Another OV language, Turkish, also has simple roots to which affixes are added, for example, *ver-* 'give', *gör-* 'see', and so on. Like Japanese roots, the Turkish roots are found in their simplest forms in verbs and in nominal compounds. Thus, in Japanese the compounds with *mono* 'thing' of the two verbs cited are *kimono* 'wear-thing > clothing' and *yomimono* 'reading matter'. These examples may clarify the role of the PIE root. It was not first and foremost a free form, though free forms consisting only of the root were possible. In Japanese *ki* 'wearing' can be a free form. The

PIE root was used without suffixes in some imperative forms, as Latin *fer* 'carry' indicates. Although such free forms occur, the root is primarily the basic component of lexical elements which carries the fundamental lexical meaning. The PIE root then is as realistic in PIE grammar as are roots in Japanese, Turkish, and other OV languages.

From any root, extended forms of various kinds could be constructed. The analysis of these is one of the achievements of nineteenth-century linguistics and is amply treated in the handbooks (Brugmann 1906; 1913; Meillet 1937:146–173, 197–223, 252–325; Watkins 1969). When using handbooks and other treatments of PIE, great care must be applied in sorting out forms for various stages of the language. Recent scholarship has been concerned with the identification of such forms for various stages of the language. In general we cannot discuss these problems here, nor even deal with the various derived forms of nouns and verbs. Since any such discussions would greatly extend this presentation, we limit ourselves to brief definitions of verbs and nouns.

5.4.2. The PIE Verb. The verb in PIE was characterized by inflection for person, number, aspect, mood, and voice. The roots and stems on which verbal forms were constructed were strictly limited, as noted in Example 40; these bases were in general simpler than those of nouns. Yet denominative forms of verbs were also possible, particularly in later stages of the language. These were common in the so-called weak inflections. In time they led to a different type of verbal inflection from that of PIE, an inflection characterized by secondary suffixes and composite forms. The early PIE verb is illustrated most clearly in injunctive forms, of which examples have been cited earlier. Forms with the four endings of the *m* inflection given in Example 39 are attested in the Veda, as for *dhā-* (for *dhām* see Hoffmann 1967:150).

41.	1 sg.	dhām	véda
	2 sg.	dhāḥ < dhās	véttha
	3 sg.	dhāt	véda
	3 pl.	dhuḥ < dhur	vidús

Because of subsequent changes, the endings of the *h* inflection have become modified in all the dialects; but they may be reconstructed from Vedic forms like those cited in Example 41 for the extended root *vid-*, as well as from forms in other dialects. More complex finite verb forms have been treated above. Like the forms cited in Example 41, each finite form was inflected for first, second, or third person; for singular, dual, or plural number; for ±momentary aspect; and for one of the moods or voices.

5.4.3. The PIE Noun. The noun in PIE was characterized in inflection for case, gender, and number, Endings indicating these were generally added to extended forms of roots, but some root nouns are attested in the early dialects, such as forms in the Rigveda of the masculine noun *pád-* 'foot' (Example 42). (The forms in parentheses may be posited because of attestations of other nouns; root forms with vocatives have the same forms for these as for nominatives.) The three possible dual forms of *pád-* are attested; in the singular and the plural the nominative and dative forms are not attested, as might be expected for a nonanimate noun.

42.

	Singular	Dual	Plural
Nom.	(pā́t)	pā́dā	(pā́das)
(Voc.	pā́t)		
Acc.	pā́dam		padás
Inst.	padā́		padbhís
Dat.	(padé)		(padbhyás)
Ab.		padbhyā́m	——
Gen.	padás	padós	padā́m
Loc.	padí		patsú

(See Meillet 1937:254–255 for other root nouns.) These inflected forms express the nominal categories which have been discussed above.

5.4.4. Pronouns. Personal pronouns were inflected for case and number. Demonstrative and anaphoric pronouns, which supplied the forms for the third personal pronoun, were also inflected for gender (Delbrück 1893: 460–521; Meillet 1937:332–338). We have noted above that the gender category was late. Pronouns provide evidence for the conclusion that the category of number was also introduced late, as differing roots of personal pronouns in the singular, dual, and plural indicate: **eg-* 'I', **ne-* 'we two', **we-* 'we'; **tew-* 'thou', **we-* 'you two', **yew-* 'you'. Moreover, a different root is used in the cases of the first-person pronoun other than the nominative: **me-* 'me', **nes-* 'us'. This shift in root may be compared with stem changes between the nominative and the oblique cases in heteroclitic nouns, such as the neuter Hitt. *watar,* genitive *wetenaš* 'water', or nouns with *-en-* suffix in the oblique cases, such as Lat. *homō,* accusative *hominem* 'man' (Meillet 1937:262–263; see also Sturtevant 1951:102–108). The shifts are archaisms maintained from the period before development of the case system, and they provide evidence that inflection for case categories was also relatively late.

The reflexive pronoun was late. It developed after the loss of the middle from a root **sew-* 'own'. Meillet has assembled illustrations of the use of this root in compounds and as an adjective (1937:336–338). Patterned after forms of **tew-* 'thou', **sew-* developed a set of singular case forms other than the nominative; these were used to refer to plural as well as singular subjects.

The pronouns also differ from nouns in having enclitic forms. The enclitic pronouns were placed in second position in the sentence and are especially prominent in the Anatolian languages, where sentence-connecting particles are followed by these and other enclitics (Carruba 1969).

Rather than a third-person pronoun parallel with the first and second, PIE had a number of demonstrative stems and, in addition, interrogatives, which were used as the basis of indefinites (Brugmann 1904*b*; Meillet 1937:325–329; Brugmann 1904*a*:399–406). These developed a full set of case forms in the singular, dual, and plural, with the obvious exception of the vocative. The relative lateness of their inflection is clear from the parallelism with nominal *o*- and *ā*- stems, the most recent PIE inflection. Demonstratives and interrogative indefinites differ from the personal pronouns in having adjectival as well as nominal use. Moreover, they developed characteristic endings in part; see Brugmann's chart for details (1904*a*:406); also see Sturtevant (1951:108–115).

The simple demonstrative, or anaphoric pronoun, was **so-, sā-, to-*. Besides this a variety of roots was the basis for a demonstrative indicating objects close to the speaker, notably roots with *k-*, and a demonstrative indicating more remote objects, notably roots with *n*. PIE then had threefold deixis in demonstratives. Brugmann discusses this threefold deixis with reference to the personal pronouns, noting an "I-deixis", a "you-deixis" and the more remote reference deixis (1904*b*). By his approach the personal pronouns are closely connected with demonstratives. The interrogatives and indefinites were based on roots with k^w-.

The use of relative pronouns, like that of reflexives, depends on the structure of the language. Since early PIE was OV in structure, relative constructions were marked simply by preposing. When a marker was necessary to indicate relative clauses (Raman 1973), the k^w- forms were adapted in some dialects: Anatolian, Italic, Slavic, and Baltic; other dialects used demonstrative forms: *y*- forms in Indic and Greek, *s*- forms in Germanic and Celtic (Gonda 1971:75, 138). Since our Celtic materials are from the Insular VSO languages, relative constructions are generally marked by position, or by special verb forms, rather than by pronouns, in keeping with the patterning of other VSO languages.

5.4.5. Adjectives. In late PIE and the early dialects, adjectives were distinguished from nouns and pronouns by inflection for each of the three genders. Many adjective classes, however, did not have distinct inflections for the three genders, as is evident even from Latin grammar; some adjectives of the third declension had distinct endings only for neuter nominative, accusative, and vocative: m.f. *gravis*, n. *grave* 'heavy'; others, including present participles, had the same ending for the three genders in the nominative and vocative singular, such as *memor* 'mindful', *amāns* 'loving'. Adjective inflection accordingly developed only late in IE (Delbrück 1893:400–460).

For an early period of PIE we may assume that adjectives were uninflected, as relic constructions in Hittite indicate; *kurur*, as we have noted above, § 5.3.2, could be used adjectivally by simply preposing it to nouns.

Besides their inflection for the three genders, adjectives also were distinguished by their inflection for comparison. This too was late. In early PIE, adjectives were not a distinct inflectional class by reason of either gender inflection or comparison.

5.4.6. Numerals. The role of adjectives in early PIE may be inferred from that of the cardinal numerals. These were used adjectivally as well as nominally (Brugmann 1904*a*:362–372; Delbrück 1893:522–536). As inflection became more prominent, the numerals most clearly associated with the number category came to be inflected. The numeral for 'one' based on **oy-*, was inflected like an adjective in the singular; so was the root **sem-* 'one', which was used in Greek. The numeral for 'two', based on **dwō-*, was inflected as a dual, subsequently as a plural. The numerals for 'three' and 'four' were also inflected as plurals. The remaining cardinal numerals were uninflected, though in some dialects they came to be inflected (Brugmann 1904*a*:362–370). Ordinals were always treated like adjectives (Brugmann 1904*a*:370–372; Szemerényi 1960: esp. 92); as Oswald Szemerényi has demonstrated definitively, they are late adjectival forms based on the cardinals. The numerals then provide us with important insights into the development of inflected adjectival and pronominal forms from noninflected, preposed modifiers.

5.4.7. Participles and Other Nominal Forms Derived from Verbs. Nominal modifiers were also derived from verbal forms. Based on stems with various meanings, they incorporated the category of voice and the aspectual distinctions (Delbrück 1897:218–220, 250–251, 476–499). We may illustrate the inclusion of such categories in participles with the often-cited line from the Iliad, in which participles of **es-* incorporate active and middle voice, as well as continuous present and future meanings.

43. Iliad 1.70. hòs ḗidē tá t' eónta tá t' essómena
who he-knew those and being those and will-be-happening

pró t' eónta
before and being

'who knew what is, what will be, and what was in the past'

Such nominal forms seem to correspond in use to adjectives and nouns. Yet they retain the functions of finite verbal forms in many of their early uses, as we may indicate by comparing them with participles in a VSO language like Ancient Egyptian.

A well-known use of participles, in which they correspond to clauses of circumstance or time, may be illustrated with a frequent formula in Homer:

44. Odyssey 1.63. tḗn d' apameibómenos proséphē
her Ptc. answering he-said
'Then answering her he said . . .'

Such uses are impossible in Ancient Egyptian, according to Alan Gardiner (1950:270). We may view the IE constructions as archaisms from the earlier OV syntactic patterns. As we have noted in § 4.8, Example 145, Japanese has participal forms in a wide array of meanings; like *apameibómenos* in Example 44, these are placed before the clause with the finite verb, though, like other nominal forms in Japanese, they are not inflected. We may assume that such forms were found in early PIE and that they subsequently came to be inflected, as congruence markers were extended to nominal modifiers. This assumption is supported not only by the large number of uses of participles in IE but also by the archaic inflectional patterns of *nt-* participles, as we have noted for the Latin present participle with its single nominative ending and no distinction for gender. When participles came to be viewed as nominal forms, nominal inflections may also have been extended to them because of the subjective dominance of verb forms, as noted in § 4.2.

The recent addition of inflection to nominal forms of verbs may also be observed in infinitives and supines (Delbrück 1897:440–475; Sturtevant 1951:74–75, 148–149; J. Friedrich 1960:142–144). Infinitival forms could simply be combined with nouns, as complements; see Delbrück (1897:465–467), who gives among others the following example:

45. RV 1.113.16. ā́raik pánthāṃ yā́tave sū́ryāya
she-cleared way for-going for-sun
'She cleared the way for the sun to go.'

Such a use of the infinitive is found also in Greek, Germanic, Baltic, and Slavic. In Greek the article came to be used with the infinitive (Schwyzer 1950:368–372).

By a further development the infinitive could be used alone in complementation, as noted in § 4.8; it then had the same subject as the principal verb, as in Hittite (J. Friedrich 1960:143):

46. LÚSANGA akuu̯anna u̯ekzi
priest drink he-requests
'The priest requests to drink.'

This use led to periphrastic constructions, both with participial or adjectival forms of the verb and with infinitival or nominal forms, as already in Hittite (J. Friedrich 1960:136–137):

47. hurtanteš ešir
cursed they-were
'They were cursed.'

A periphrastic construction with nouns was accompanied by *dāi-* 'place' or *tii̯a-* 'step' (see Götze and Pedersen 1934:21–22):

48. *Muršilis Sprachlähmung* I.7. nu-mu ... aši memii̯aš tešhaniškiu̯an tii̯at
Ptc.-to-me that situation appear-in-dream began
'And that situation began to appear in my dreams.'

The nominal elements of the verb thus were employed in various constructions in the dialects (Brugmann 1904*a*:603–609). These developed from uses in PIE which were like those of adjectives and nouns.

In accordance with these uses, nominal forms of verbs were normally related closely to other elements of the sentence. The various dialects however also contain absolute constructions, that is, case forms of nouns accompanied by participles in constructions which resemble independent clauses. The cases differ from dialect to dialect and also within dialects. Moreover, the uses vary considerably, from manner to time to means, and so on. From this variation we may conclude that the absolute constructions developed independently in each of the dialects. Such independent origins of parallel constructions are plausible only if we can ascribe them to typological reasons. I have proposed that absolute constructions arose as the various dialects were developing from OV to VO languages. During the transition period a participle might be related either to a preceding or to a following finite verb. Accordingly the participle and its noun were used "absolutely," without reference to a finite verb, in the Sanskrit locative absolute, the Greek genitive absolute, the Latin ablative absolute, and the Gothic, Slavic, and Baltic dative absolute. This explanation for the origin of absolute constructions receives support from the possible location of absolutes before or after the finite verb in the various dialects (Lehmann 1972*b*:987–989). The following example of a Vedic locative absolute provides a further illustration of its independence, though the relationship to other constituents of the sentence is clear:

49*a*. RV 1.16.3.	índram	prātár	havāmaha
	Indra	early	we-call-on
	índram	prayaty	àdhvaré
	Indra	going-along	sacrifice

'We call on Indra early, on Indra as the sacrifice proceeds.'

The locative *adhvaré,* accompanied by the present participle *prayatí,* is parallel on the one hand to the adverb *prātár,* on the other hand to an independent clause. And when one compares the third line of this stanza:

49*b*.	índraṃ	sómasya	pītáye
	Indra	of-soma	at-drinking

'on Indra at the drinking of soma'

the participial absolute seems parallel to a verbal noun in the dative. In this way verbal derivatives of various kinds could be used to express categories generally associated with nouns, such as the case category of time in the three lines of Example 49. Other mechanisms for expressing syntactic categories in the sentence were provided by particles and frozen forms of inflected words, generally referred to as adverbs.

5.5. The Use of Particles and Other Uninflected Words as Syntactic Means of Expression

Noninflected words of various functions were used in indicating relationships between other words in the sentence or between sentences. Some were used for modifying nouns, often indicating the relationships of nouns to verbs. Although these were generally placed after nouns and accordingly were postpositions, they have often been called prepositions by reason of their function rather than their position with regard to nouns (Delbrück 1888:433–471). Others were used for modifying verbs, often specifying more precisely the meanings of verbs; these then may be called preverbs. Others, commonly referred to as sentence connectives, were used primarily to indicate the relationships between clauses or sentences (Watkins 1964; Lehmann 1969).

5.5.1. Postpositions. Surveys of the postpositions in the various dialects are given in the handbooks, as for Hittite (J. Friedrich 1960:129–130) and Vedic (Delbrück 1888:440–470). They are found with specific cases, in accordance with their meanings. Yet in the Old Hittite texts, the genitive rather than such a specific case is prominent with postpositions derived from nouns, such as *piran* '(in) front' (Neu 1970:10, 59):

50. kuiš LUGAL-ua-aš piran ēšzi
who king's front he-sits
'whoever sits before the king'

Such postpositions came to be frozen in form, whether unidentifiable as to etymology; derived from nouns, like *piran*; or derived from verbs, like *tirás* in Example 51. Further, as the language came to be VO, they were placed before nouns. As case forms were less clearly marked, they not only "governed" cases but also took over the meanings of case categories. The preposition *tirás (tiró),* derived from the root **tṛ-* 'cross', illustrates both the etymological meaning of the form and its eventual development as preposition:

51. RV 8.82.9. yáṃ te śyenáḥ padā́bharat
what for-you eagle with-foot-he-bore

tiró rájāṅsy áspṛtam
crossing, through skies not-relinquishing

píbéd [< píba íd] asya tvám iśiṣe
you-drink-indeed of-it you you-are-master (for-your-benefit)

'What the eagle brought for you in his claws, not dropping it [as he flew] through the skies, of that drink. You control [it for your own benefit].'

The syntactic use of such particles with nouns is accordingly clear.

5.5.2. Preverbs. Rather than having the close relationships to nouns illustrated above, particles could instead be associated primarily with verbs, often the same particles which were used as postpositions. Thus in the following Hittite passage *piran* is used as preverb (Szabó 1971:24):

52. nu *ANA* ᴰIŠKUR *Ù* DINGIR.LÚ[MEŠ]-*ŠU* *ANA* ᴰUTU
Ptc. to weather-god and his-male-gods to sun-god
Ù DINGIR.LÚ[MEŠ]-*ŠU* píran zikizzi
and his-male-gods front he-lays-in-turn
'He lays before in turn [the slices of bread] for the weather god and his male gods and the sun god and his male gods.'

See also Example 15 in Chapter 2. Such combinations of particles and verbs came to be treated as units and are found repeatedly in specific uses (Delbrück 1888:433–437).

Preverbs may occupy various positions: if unmarked, they are placed before the verb; if marked, they are placed initially in clauses (Watkins 1964), as in the following examples of *úpa* and *ápa* from an Archaic hymn:

53. RV 7.71.4. ā́ na enā́ nāsatyā úpa yātam
to us with-that Nasatyas hither you-two-come
'Come hither to us with that, Nasatyas.'

And the hymn begins with the following line, in which the departure of Night is emphasized by initial placement of *ápa* 'off, away':

54. R̥V 7.71.1. ápa svásur uṣáso nág jihīte
away from-sister from-Dawn Night she-departs
'Night goes away from her sister Dawn.'

In the course of time the preverbs in unmarked position came to be combined with their verbs, though the identity of each element is long apparent in many of the dialects. Thus, in Modern German the primary accent is still maintained on some verbal roots, and in contrast with cognate nouns the prefix carries weak stress: *ertéilen* 'distribute', *Úrteil* 'judgment'. The steps toward the combination of preverb and verbal root have been described for the dialects, for example, Greek, in which uncombined forms as well as combined forms are attested during the period of our texts.

Preverbs which remained uncombined came to be treated as adverbs. Thus adverbs, as in the sequence:

55. RV 1.147.5. átaḥ pāhi
thence you-protect
'Protect us from that.'

are similar in use to preverbs like *ápa* in Example 54. Combinations of preverbs plus verbs, on the other hand, eventually came to function like unitary elements. Already in the Rigveda, compounds of frequent verbs like *i* 'go' may be regarded as independent verbs. Combinations of *i* plus *sam* 'come together, join', for example, are used with the dative or locative, and they may also be combined with other preverbs:

56. RV 6.19.9.

ā́	viśváto	abhí	sám	etu
toward	from-all-sides	hither	together	it-should-come

'It should join [us] here from all sides.'

The two different positions of preverbs in early texts led eventually to different word classes.

5.5.3. Sentence Particles. Particles were also used to relate sentences and clauses (J. Friedrich 1959:18, § 11):

57.

takku	LÚ.ULÙ^{LU}-an	*EL.LUM*	*QA.AZ.ZU*	našma	GÌR-*ŠU*	kuiški
if	man	free	his-hand	or	his-foot	someone

tuu̯arnizzi	nušše	20	GÍN	KUBABBAR	paai
he-breaks	Ptc.-to-him	20	shekels	silver	he-gives

'If anyone breaks the hand or foot of a freeman, then he must give him twenty shekels of silver.'

Particles like the initial word in this example indicate the kind of clause that will follow and have long been well described. The function of particles like *nu* is not, however, equally clear.

A generation ago Dillon and Götze related *nu* and the use of sentence connectives to similar particles in Old Irish (Dillon 1947). Such particles introduce many sentences in Old Irish and have led to compound verb forms in this VSO language. Delbrück had also noted their presence in Vedic (1888:23–24), as in the following examples:

58.

sá	hovāca	gā́rgyaḥ
Ptc.	Ptc.-he-said	Gārgya

'Then Gārgya said . . .'

59.

tád	u	hovācā́suriḥ
Ptc.	Ptc.	Ptc.-he-said-Asuri

'Then Asuri said . . .'

Since introductory *šu* and *ta* were more frequent than was *nu* in the older Hittite texts, scholars assumed that sentences in IE were regularly introduced by these sentence connectives. And Sturtevant proposed, as etymology for the anaphoric pronoun, combinations of **so-* and **to-* with enclitic pronouns, as in the well-known Hittite sequence *ta-at*, cf. IE **tod*, and so on (see Otten and Souček 1969:89–90 for the use of such particles in one text). Subsequent study has not corroborated assumptions on the consistent use of sentence connectives, even in narrative patterns. Otten and Souček found, for example, that their Old Hittite text contained far more uses of *nu* than were expected (twenty-two) and only one *šu* in contrast with thirty-two attested uses of *ta*. Moreover, sentence connectives seem to be characteristic of VSO languages. Squamish, for example, resembles Hittite in beginning its sentences with "sentence connectives" followed by other enclitics (Kuipers 1967:206–211). Since Hittite was in close contact with the VSO language Akkadian, the widespread use of *nu* and the other sentence connectives may be the result of influence from other languages. And if, as especially Szemerényi has maintained, Indo-Iranian was influenced by Semitic languages before it was carried further east, the occasional uses of *nū, sa,* and *ta* in Vedic as sentence connectives may also be the result of outside influence rather than an inheritance from PIE. The apparent similarity between Old Irish and Hittite may therefore be explained on grounds other than common origin. Further study of the role of sentence connectives in language is therefore essential before we can propose firm conclusions about their possible role in PIE.

It is clear however that sentence connectives were used in Hittite to indicate continued treatment of a given topic (Raman 1973:165). This use was illustrated in Example 59. It is also found with Hittite relative constructions. Such a function may also be ascribed to Vedic *sá* and *tád,* as in Examples 58 and 59. Yet, since this use may be accounted for through post-PIE influences, sentence connectives may have had a minor role in PIE.

Other particles, like Hitt. *takku* 'if', probably had their counterparts in PIE, even if the surface forms were completely unrelated. This is also true for emphatic particles like *íd* in Example 51; they were used after nouns as well as imperatives like *píba* (see Speyer 1896:72). Such emphatic particles combined with imperatives suggest the presence of interjections, which cannot be directly reconstructed for PIE but are well attested in the several dialects.

Although sentence-introductory particles like Hitt. *takku* can be reliably assumed, there is less evidence for coordinate sentence connectives. A coordinating particle can clearly be reconstructed on the basis of Skt. *ca,* Gk. *te,* Lat. *que,* and so on. But its primary function is the coordination of elements in the sentence rather than clauses or sentences. Moreover, when *ca* is used to connect verbs in the Vedic materials, they are parallel (Delbrück 1888:472–474); Delbrück finds only one possible exception. This situation reminds us of the OV language Japanese; for in an OV language the relating of successive verbs is carried out by means of nonfinite verbs placed before finite. We may then expect that coordinating particles had their primary use in PIE as connectors for sentence elements rather than for sentences.

Another such particle is **wĕ̄* 'or'. It is notable that, like *$*k^we$*, the particle indicating disjunctive 'or' was postposed, in retention of the OV pattern as late as Classical Latin.

We have noted above that particles in PIE may also have corresponded to verbal qualifiers. The most notable of these is **mē*, which carried a negative modal meaning. There is indication of such uses of particles in other patterns, for example, of Vedic *purā́* 'earlier' to indicate the past, as apparently Brugmann was the first to point out (Delbrück 1888:502), and also Vedic *sma*, to indicate repeated action in the past (Hoffmann 1967:201, 203). It is curious that *sma* is also found after *mā́* in Vedic (Hoffmann 1967:91, 98). As we have suggested above, such mood- and tense-carrying particles may have been transported from a postverbal to a preverbal position. Some particles may accordingly have been equivalent in an earlier stage of PIE to elements used after verbs to indicate verbal categories.

5.6. On the Generation of Sentences.

Having examined the syntactic categories of PIE and its syntactic rules, we may observe how they account for sentences.

The P rules presented in § 1.3 and subsequently amplified would produce the following underlying structures:

1. $\Sigma \rightarrow$ Conj. Σ^n (optional)
2. $\Sigma \rightarrow$ Q Prop.
3. Q $\rightarrow$ [±Dec.] [±Int.] [±Neg.] [±Mid.] [±Nec.] [±Vol.] [±Perf.] [±Mom.] [±Iter.] [±Caus.]
4. P $\rightarrow$ V (Target) (Receptor) (Agent) (Means) (Source) (Time) (Place) (Manner)

One of the possibilities generated by these rules would be as follows:

($\Sigma \rightarrow$) +Dec. –Int. –Neg. +Mid. –Nec. –Vol. +Perf. +Mom. –Iter. –Caus. V Agent Means

This string of categorial elements would generate a sentence with a middle verb in the aorist. Since the verb is unspecified for person and number, the verb form would be third singular. The +Dec. would require that it be indicative; and the following minus categories would require it to be a positive statement. The verb would be accompanied by a noun in agential relationship with the verb; such a noun might be expected to be animate, though it could also be an "active" natural force. This nuclear sentence might be accompanied by other nominal forms, possibly in adverbial relationship.

As an example of such a sentence we may cite from an Archaic hymn:

60*a*. RV 5.52.6.	bhānúr	arta	tmánā
	light	has-appeared	by-itself

The position of the adverbial instrumental indicates its facultative inclusion in the sentence; as discussed in Chapter 2, one or more such elements could be introduced in sentences. The actual line in the hymn includes a further element following *tmánā: diśáḥ* 'of the sky', a genitive modifying *bhānúr*. This nominal modifier would have been introduced by the optional P rule (P Rule 6):

$$NP \rightarrow (Det.)\ N\ (\Sigma)$$

The modifying Σ would be reduced in accordance with processes that are well known and not of interest here.

The basic sentence in Stanza 6 of this Archaic hymn then reports a sunrise, in Geldner's translation:

60*b*. von selbst bricht der Glanz des Himmels an
'the light of the heavens dawns spontaneously'

Many other such sentences that are attested in our early texts, in the Anatolian, Greek, and other dialects as well as Indo-Iranian, could be generated in much the same way as this sentence.

A further, somewhat more complex example from a Strophic hymn may provide another illustration; again the verb is based on the root *ṛ-* 'go', which will be discussed in Chapter 6.

61. RV 7.56.21.	mā́	vo	dātrā́n	maruto	nír	arāma
	may-not	your	from-gift	O-Maruts	out, except	we-will-go

[interpretation of verbal phrase with ablative = 'we will be deprived of']
'May we not be deprived of your gift, O Maruts.'

This sentence would be generated from the following categorial set: +Dec. –Int. +Neg. –Mid. –Nec. +Vol. +Perf. +Mom. –Iter. –Caus. V Agent 1 pl. Det. Source, coordinated with a nominal sentence generating the vocative *maruto*. The +Vol. category is attached to the negative particle as well as to the V, and accordingly determines the selection of *mā́*. The *agent* node is attached to the V, generating the first-person plural form. The pronominal *vo* is generated from the node Det. of the optional P rule generating nominal modifiers.

Further such examples could be given, for complex and compound sentences as well as simple sentences. Rather than an account of the generation of further sentences, some examples will be cited to illustrate the analysis of complicated sentences in accordance with the syntactic rules given above.

5.7. On the Analysis of Sentences.

As an example of a complex sentence we may take the opening of the Hittite Laws (J. Friedrich 1959:16):

62*a*.	takku	LÚ-an	našma	SAL-an	šullannaz	kuiški	kuenzi
	if, when	man	or	woman	from-quarrel	anyone	he-kills

apūn arnuzi . . .
that-one he-brings (recompense) . . .

'If anyone kills a man or a woman because of a quarrel, he gives recompense for that one . . .'

In the principal clause the verb is a cognate of Skt. *ṛ*- 'go', with causative meaning indicated by the *nu*- form. P Rules 3 and 4 would accordingly generate the categories expressed by the principal clause, which may roughly be paraphrased: 'he causes that recompense goes with regard to him on a given occasion'. The verb is accompanied by categories for the agent, the target, and time. The *agent* category is expressed in the verb form. The *target* category is expressed by the demonstrative pronoun. The *time* category is expressed by the clause introduced and made more specific by the particle *takku* 'if'.

The temporal-conditional clause introduced through P Rule 6 is a sentence consisting of a verb accompanied by an agent expressed by the indefinite pronoun and the verb form, as well as by a compound target and a source category. The arrangement of the two clauses with regard to each other is that expected in an OV language. If we view the first clause as subordinate, this sequence of clauses is an example of embedding resulting in a complex sentence.

If we parse the following clause as coordinate with the principal clause, assuming that the obscure *Ù* means 'and indeed', the sentence consists of two coordinate clauses plus the subordinate clause:

62*b*.	. . . *Ú*	4	SAG.DU	pāi	LÚna-ku	SALna-ku
	. . . and-indeed	4	heads	he-gives	man-or	woman-or

'. . . and indeed he pays the equivalent of four persons, either men or women.'

This sentence, introduced through P Rule 1, consists of an agent incorporated in the verb and a target preceded by the Det. expressed by the numeral 'four'. The noun introduced through the target category is itself modified by the disjunctive apposition. This examination may illustrate that sentences of moderate complexity yield to analysis as readily as simple sentences.

Additional complexities are simply results of further coordination or embedding. For example, relative constructions, attributive adjectives, or genitives are modified forms of embedded sentences, as may be illustrated with citations from an Archaic hymn:

63.	RV 2.33.5.	hávīmabhir	hávate	yó	havírbhir
		with-invocations	is-supplicated	who	with-oblations
		áva stómebhī		rudráṃ	diṣīya
		down with-songs-of-praise		Rudra	I-would-give (Aor. Opt.)

'With songs of praise I would appease Rudra, who is supplicated with invocations and oblations.'

The first of these two lines has a middle form in passive sense, with Rudra as target of the verb *hū-* 'call'; embedded in the main clause, this undergoes deletion of the target, with substitution of the relative marker *yo* < *yas.* Even further reduction is carried out in descriptive genitives and adjectives, as in:

64.	RV 2.33.8.	gr̥ṇīmási	tveṣáṃ	rudrásya	nā́ma
		we-sing	terrible	Rudra's	name

'We invoke the terrible name of Rudra.'

The basic sentence consists of *nā́ma* and *gr̥ṇīmási;* in it are embedded constructions corresponding to 'the name is terrible' and 'the name is Rudra's', each with reduction of the equivalent NP corresponding to *nā́ma* of the principal clause. Further analyses of complex sentences would simply repeat and amplify the processes noted here.

5.8. Marked Order in Sentences.

Elements in sentences can be emphasized, by marking; the chief device for such emphasis is initial position. Arrangement in this position is brought about by stylistic rules applied after structures have been generated by P rules and transformational rules. The sentence quoted above is a ready example. In Stanza 8 of this hymn the last two lines have initial position of the verb. The stylistic basis for this position is clear; these lines simply rephrase the content of the initial statement, emphasizing the poet's praise of Rudra:

65. RV 2.33.8.

prá	babhráve	vṛṣabhā́ya	śvitīcé
forth	for-brown	for-bull	for-whitish
mahó	mahī́ṃ	suṣṭutím	īrayāmi
of-great	great	praise	I-cause-to-move
namasyā́		kalmalīkínaṃ	námobhir
I-will-do-homage		radiant	with-obeisances

'For the brown and whitish bull I send out a great hymn of praise of the great one. I will do homage to the radiant one with obeisances.'

The last line, given as Example 64, continues the marked pattern both with initial position of the verb and selection of the present tense.

Other sentence elements may also be placed in initial position for marking. An example is the preverb *prá* in the first line of this stanza (Watkins 1964:1035–1042, Lehmann 1969:9-10). In unmarked position the preverb directly precedes the verb. Changes in normal order thus provide one of the devices for conveying emphasis.

Other devices have to do with selection, notably particles which are postposed after a marked element. These have been identified in the handbooks (e.g., Delbrück 1888:471–540; see esp. 497–501). Emphasis can also be indicated by lexical selection, as in the repetition of *mah-* in the second line of Example 65. Presumably other modifications might also be made, as in intonation, as we have noted above in the discussion of *pluti.* The various syntactic devices accordingly provided means to introduce marking in sentences.

5.9. Topicalization with Reference to Emphasis.

If we analyze sentences as consisting of a known and an unknown or new component, that is, of a theme and a rheme, segments of the theme may be sorted out as forming the more important elements. These may be said to form the topic of the discourse. They are distinguished by arrangement. For example, in the sentence from the Hittite Laws (Example 52), the topic is indicated as 'man or woman' by initial placement of these elements, rather than 'as a result of a quarrel'. Similarly in Stanza 8 of the Archaic hymn to Rudra (Example 65), the topic is indicated as 'the bull (Rudra)' rather than 'praise' by the arrangement of the two phrases with regard to each other. Like emphasis, topicalization is carried out by patterns of arrangement, but the arrangement is applied to co-equal elements rather than elements which are moved from their normal order.

Topicalization by arrangement is well known in the study of the early languages, as in the initial lines of the Homeric poems. The Iliad begins with the noun *mênin* 'wrath', the Odyssey with the noun *ándra* 'man'. These, to be sure, are the only possible nouns in the syntactically simple sentences opening both poems: *mênin áeide* 'Sing of the wrath' and *ándra moi énnepe* 'Tell me of the man'. Yet the very arrangement of *moi* and other enclitics occupying second position in the sentence, in accordance with Wackernagel's law, indicates the use of initial placement among nominal elements for topicalization.

The use of topicalization may be illustrated by a more complex set of sentences, such as the first address of Zeus in the Odyssey. Only the first lines of this will be quoted; but these indicate a shift in topic from the 'gods' to 'men', then to a particular man, Aegisthus, then to Agamemnon, and subsequently (in line 40, not included here) to Orestes.

66. Odyssey 1.32.

Ô pópoi, hoîon dḗ nu theoùs brotoì aitióōntai;
alas how indeed now gods mortals they-blame

eks hēméōn gár phasi kák' émmenai, hoi dè kaì autoì
from us for they-say evils are they but and themselves

sphêisin atasthaliḗisin hupèr móron álge' ékhousin,
own stupidities beyond fate woes they-have

hōs kaì nûn Aígisthos hupèr móron Atreídao
thus and now Aegisthus beyond fate of-son-of Atreus

gêm' álokhon mnēstḗn, tòn d' éktane nostḗsanta,
he-married spouse wedded him but he-killed having-returned

'Alas, how the mortals are now blaming the gods.
For they say evils come from us, but they themselves
have woes beyond what's fated by their own stupidities.
Thus Aegisthus beyond what was fated has now married
the wedded wife of Agamemnon, and killed him on his return.'

As this passage and many others that might be cited illustrate, the basic sentence patterns could be rearranged by stylistic rules, both for emphasis and for topicalization. In this way the relatively strict arrangement of simple sentences could be modified to bring about variety and flexibility.

6. Lexical Entries

6.1. Comprehensive Treatments of the PIE Lexicon.

During the century and a half of IE investigations, the lexicon has been thoroughly studied. A comprehensive summary of these studies was made by Alois Walde and Julius Pokorny (1927–1932; usually referred to as WP); it was based on earlier dictionaries, notably that inaugurated by August Fick (1890–1909). Pokorny's later dictionary (1959–1969) is essentially a rearrangement of the data in WP in accordance with the order of the Latin alphabet. Dictionaries for individual branches of IE and for individual dialects contain more recent findings than does WP. But like it they concentrate on etymologies and lexical meanings. They do not discuss the roles of individual lexical elements in syntactic units; WP, for example, does not indicate the cases accompanying verbs. While these dictionaries are indispensable for IE syntactic studies, they lack information which a comprehensive lexicon should include and which a subsequent compilation will presumably contain.

Information concerning some lexical features of direct importance to syntactic studies is, on the other hand, included in grammatical treatments, notably Delbrück's second volume of 1897; as its bibliography indicates, this volume in turn is based on earlier studies. Subsequent studies, such as Meillet's of the root **men-* (1897) and Emmanuel Laroche's of the root *nem-* in Greek (1950), have investigated the uses of specific lexical elements in further detail. These too need to be pursued with similar precision. Lexical analyses must be carried out in accordance with a specific theory of grammar; and lexical entries must be so described that their role in sentences is specified as fully as are the characteristic syntactic patterns of PIE. Here only a highly preliminary treatment can be included, with selected lexical items presented only as examples. In view of the central importance of the verb, a selected verbal root will be examined first in the following section, then this root accompanied by preverbs, and then other elements of the PIE lexicon.

6.2. Lexical Analysis of a Selected PIE Root: γer- 'move'.

WP includes a long entry for this root, written as *er-* (I, 136–142; see also Persson 1912:767–773). In Sanskrit grammars it is written *ṛ-*, or *ar-*. For it Walde and Pokorny give the meaning: 'sich in Bewegung setzen, erregen (auch seelisch, ärgern, reizen); in die Höhe bringen (Erhebung, hochwachsen), z. T. aber auch von Bewegung nach abwärts' ('move, arouse, raise, in part however also of downward motion'). This attempt to give the meaning of a root must be interpreted carefully, for, as examples of its occurrences indicate, the root differs in meaning in accordance with the formations it adopts. If we would set out to characterize the meaning of the unextended root, we would describe it as intransitive and punctual, in accordance with the occurrence of the third singular present in the Hittite Laws (J. Friedrich 1959:74, § 50):

1. kuitman MU.KAM-za mehuni ari
   until year in-time it-moves, reaches
   'until a year in the course of time is completed'

Further examples will permit us to describe its meanings in greater detail.

When listing the root WP gives as its "base-forms": *er-, ere-* ("thematic"), *erē(?)*, *erei-, ereu-, eras.* In accordance with the lexical analyses carried out particularly by Meillet and Benveniste, we would propose a root consisting of two consonants, which might be followed by suffixes of specific shapes (Lehmann 1952:17–18). Because of the initial vowel in Greek forms like *ôrto* 'has arisen' (Delbrück 1897:101), I assume that the initial consonant was the *o*-coloring laryngeal γ. The root and suffix combinations must be written in accordance with the patterns determined in IE lexical research; thus the PIE suffixed form written *ereu-* in WP would be cited as *γr-ew-*.

With its intransitive, punctual meaning, the simple root *γer-* would be expected to take the endings of the *h-* conjugation, as indeed its Hittite reflex does; *arhi* 'I arrive (at a place)'. Moreover, for transitive and durative uses we would expect affixed forms. These are found in Vedic and also in other dialects, including Hittite. Virtually all the present system forms of this root in the Rigveda are made in accordance with the third reduplicating class, *íyarti,* or with the fifth nasal infixing class, *ṛṇóti.* In addition there are three occurrences of present forms with the *-sk-* suffix, all in the late tenth book, and two with the suffix *-e/o-*, both in near-contiguous hymns of the seventh book. It is likely therefore that the unextended forms of the root were inflected in the aorist or the perfect; although the Rigveda contains only constructions of perfect forms with preverbs, Delbrück, on the basis of Skt. *ā́rat* and Gk. *ṓreto* reconstructs the "proethnic ạorists" **ṓret, ṓreto* (1897:101). The "similarly proethnic" Skt. *ā́rta,* Gk. *ôrto,* which he also cites, permit us to reconstruct PIE *é-γr-to* 'he moves, rises', as in the following line from an Archaic hymn addressed to Agni:

2.	RV 5.25.8.	utó	te	tanyatúr	yathā
		and	your	thundering	like
		svānó	arta	tmánā	diváḥ
		roaring	it-rises	powerfully	of-heaven

'And your roaring rises powerfully like the thundering of the heavens.'

Rather than the analysis of Delbrück (1897:94–95), according to which such aorists might be derived from perfects, the assumption that PIE roots might be inflected either in the *h-* conjugation or the *m-* conjugation clarifies the attested forms of roots like *γer-*. As a root with a lexical meaning which is intransitive and punctual, *γer-* would be expected to inflect in accordance with the *h-* conjugation.

The lexical entry of the root would then be as follows:

γer- 'move, rise' ____ Agent (K)

This entry would require an agent noun, as in Example 2. If the agent generated the first- or second-person pronoun, this would be indicated in the verb form, as in the following passage from a Strophic hymn to Agni:

3.	RV 4.15.7.	áchā	ná	hūtá	úd	aram
		upwards	as-if	summoned	up	I-rose

'I rose up as if summoned.'

Number, whether plural, dual, or the unmarked singular, would also be introduced as a property of nouns lexically inserted in sentence strings through the K nodes. For early PIE, number was not significant, as the reconstructible forms indicate (Lehmann 1958). In late PIE and the dialects, number was indicated in the verbal phrase as well as the nominal phrase, by a congruence rule requiring number and person agreement of verbs with subjects. The well-known use of singular verb forms with neuter plural subjects provides insight into this development.

The definition 'move, rise' should be analyzed for its lexical features. Such analysis is a task of the future. At present, in IE studies as well as in general linguistic studies, it is being carried out for selected nominal sets, such as the kinship terms and the names of trees (Wordick 1970; P. Friedrich 1970). In the future, similar studies should be carried out for verbs. For the time being we can indicate specific features associated with verbs, such as the requirement for *γer-* that its agent be active, usually animate; in this way it contrasts with $g^{w}em$-, which commonly has inanimate subjects, such as wagons or prayers. A set such as verbs indicating motion might well be investigated much as Paul Friedrich has investigated the set of names for trees.

Here a tentative set of features is given for the roots *γer-* and $g^{w}em$-:

γer- ____ Agent (K)	$g^{w}em$- ____ Agent (K)
'move, rise, reach'	'move, come'
<+Vb.>	<+Vb.>
<+V>	<+V>
<-Transitive>	<-Transitive>
<+Punctual>	<+Punctual>
<+Action>	<+Action>
<+Movement>	<+Movement>
<+Human agent>	<- Human agent>

These roots accordingly are highly similar. Both differ from *wegh-* 'move', which is +transitive and −punctual. They also differ from their affixed forms and their combinations with preverbs. When used in sentences, the actual forms, such as **eγrto* > Gk. *ôrto*, would be generated on the basis of categories introduced in the Q component, as well as those like –transitive, +punctual, which determine its inflection according to the *h-* conjugation.

In an OV language, roots are commonly followed by suffixes. Examples of such possibilities may be found in dictionaries like Grassmann's for the Rigveda (1872) or Ananthanarayana's for the Taittirīya Brāhmaṇa (1970*a*). The forms for the root *ṛ* listed by Ananthanarayana (1970*a*: 7–8) are as follows:

Present indicative:	Class 3	iyarti
	Class 5	ṛṇvati
	Classes 6 and 1	ṛchati
		árchati, archanti, archataḥ
	Causative, Class 10	arpáyati

In addition to the "indicative", three imperative forms are attested: *ṛṇvatu, ṛchatu, arpayatu.* As noted in § 4.1.6, the imperative was marked with affixes, such as *-u* in these forms.

Moreover, four optative forms are attested: *ṛchét, ṛchéran, archeyuḥ, arpayet.* The optative affix, like the imperative affix and other affixes which survived into the inflectional system of late PIE and the dialects, was placed after those affixes which indicated Q categories, like the causative; the difference in position and in frequency led to the subsequent distinction between derivational categories and inflectional categories.

In addition, two perfect forms of *ṛ* are attested: *ārimá* and an "imperfect" *ārchat.* The form *ārchat* illustrates the development from a verbal system with forms made from the root to a system in which forms were based on the "present" stem. This development is even more notable in dialects with late materials, such as Latin; its reflexes of the root *γer-* may be illustrated with the principal parts: *orior, ortus sum, orīrī 'arise'.* The deponent inflection of *orior* recalls the intransitive lexical meaning of the PIE root, though its structure of inflections differs greatly from that of PIE; as its principal parts indicate, it is inflected as a deponent throughout the six tense forms of the Latin verb.

Affixed forms of roots illustrate the PIE verbal system, such as forms with *-ew-*, which are maintained in Lat. *ruō, ruere* 'move down, tear down'. Because the IE verbal system has changed considerably, it is difficult to determine the meanings of the affixes like *-ew-*, which came to be derivational. In general such affixed forms must be described as separate lexical items, with distinct lexical characteristics. Thus Lat. *ruō* < *γr-ew-* is transitive in contrast with the simple root. For its PIE etymon the lexical entry would be:

γr-ew- 'move/tear down' ____ Agent Target (K)

plus its lexical features. The extended form is most widely maintained with an *n* infix, as in Skt. *ṛṇóti,* Gk. *órnumi,* Hitt. *arnuzi,* as in the following passage from the Hittite Laws, in which the object is implicit (J. Friedrich 1959:20, § 19):

4. nu Eir-šet-pát arnuzi
Ptc. house-his-Ptc. he-causes-to-move
'He makes him go to his own house.'

The *n* forms add to the extended root a factitive or causative notion; but the transitive characteristic of the form is conveyed by the *-ew-* extension, as may be noted by examining the various "meanings" of *ṛṇóti* in the Rigveda, all of which are accompanied by an accusative.

Reduplicated forms of the root have an iterative and often an intensive meaning (Delbrück 1893:16–26). Thus *íyarti* means 'to move back and forth', whether or not it is transitive, as it probably is in all of its occurrences in the Rigveda, such as the marked sentence pattern in the Strophic hymn of dialogue between Varuna and Indra, who says:

5. RV 4.42.5. íyarmi reṇúm
I-stir-up dust
'I stir up the dust [in battles].'

The same meaning, though in a transferred sense and intransitive, is found with an alternate reduplicated form: *álar-*, as in the following Strophic hymn:

6. RV 8.1.7. álarṣi yudhma
you-stir-up O-warrior?
'Are you aroused, O warrior?'

Reduplicated forms of the root, however remodeled phonologically, would then have the lexical entry:

γir-γer- 'move back and forth' ____ Agent Target (K)

One further suffixed form of the root will be noted here, with *-sk-*, as in Skt. *ṛcháti,* Gk. *érkhomai,* Hitt. *aršk-*, an iterative. Although the forms of Skt. *ṛch-* are consistently transitive in the Rigveda, with the intensive meaning 'reach, strike, harm', the forms in Greek are commonly intransitive, except in passages like Andromache's lament for Hector:

7. Iliad 22.482. nûn dè sù mèn Aḯdao dómous hupò keúthesi gaíēs
now indeed you Ptc. of-Hades domains under depths of-earth
érkheai
you-go-to
'But now you are going on your way to the domains of Hades, beneath the depths of the earth.'

The lexical entry of the root with this suffix would then be:

γer-sk- 'move steadily to' ____ Agent (Target) (K)

To such extended forms, as well as roots, the affixes could be added which expressed the meanings introduced through the Q component. Examples of such forms were cited above from the Taittirīya Brāhmaṇa. One further example is cited here, a middle form from Hittite, where the reflexive meaning 'move oneself, place oneself' often simply corresponds to 'stand', as in the following Old Hittite sentence from Otten and Souček (1969:18–19):

8. [úg]- a arhari
I- however I-stand-still
'But I remain standing.'

The combination of Q categories with verb forms and their meanings in combination with lexical items have also been discussed in Chapter 5. The Q categories simply added nuances of meaning to the lexical meanings, which could however be modified by other lexical elements.

6.3. Lexical Items Consisting of Verbal Roots and Preverbs.

Already in PIE, combinations of roots and preverbs have special lexical characteristics and are to be treated as individual lexical items. For example, in the Rigveda twelve preverbs may be used with the root *ṛ-*. The combined lexical unit made with one of these, Skt. *prá* 'forward, ahead', illustrates the constructions and senses as they differ from those of the simple root.

The combination is attested with the straightforward meaning of both constituents, and with intransitive force, as in the following Strophic passage:

9. RV 7.68.3. prá vāṃ rátho mánojavā iyarti
forward your wagon thought-swift it-moves
'Your wagon, swift as thought, moves ahead.'

But a passage in a neighboring Strophic hymn illustrates a distinct "idiomatic" meaning for the combination and its particular syntactic construction, accompanied by an accusative and a dative:

10. RV 7.61.2. prá vāṃ sá mitrāvaruṇāv ṛtā́vā
forward to-you he O-Mitra, Varuna pious
vípro mánmāni dīrghaśrúd iyarti
poet thoughts, prayer widely-heard he-moves

'The far-famed pious poet sends [addresses] to you his hymn, O Mitra and Varuna.'

In both of these passages the preverb occupies initial position in the clause, in accordance with marked order. But in Example 10 it must be taken as a member of the compound lexical item, which would be stated as follows, in addition to its lexical features:

pra ṛ 'send' ____ Agent Target Receptor (K)

It is noteworthy that such compound verbal expressions are accompanied by more than one case node, in contrast with the syntactic patterning of most simple roots, as pointed out in Chapter 2 (see also Gaedicke 1880:35–36).

The history of such lexical combinations is well known. In the course of time they came to be units, as the dialects became SVO in structure. Thus Greek has a separate lexical item *proérkhomai* 'advance', attested in post-Homeric materials, though even in Homer many such combinations were already units. And among the compounds of Goth. *rinnan* 'run', presumably a reflex of PIE *γr-n-ew-*, is *faurrinnan* 'proceed'. Yet the length of time that elapsed before such combinations became units is indicated by the difference in accent and vocalism in contemporary German between verbs like *ertéilen* and *Úrteil,* and also by earlier evidence, such as the Gothic sequences in which clitics were placed between the preverb and the verb, as in the form of *atgiban* 'give to' in Mark 14:44:

11. at-uh-þan-gaf	sa	lewjands	im	bandwon
'to'-but-then-he-gave	the	betrayer	them	sign

'But then the betrayer gave them a sign.'

See also § 4.3.1*b*. Accordingly, in PIE, combinations of preverbs and verbs must still be viewed as morphologically and phonologically distinct; but they must be treated as lexical units, much as is *pra ṛ-* in Vedic.

6.4. Nominal Lexical Units.

Among the lexical elements which may fill the K categorial positions are nouns. As noted above, Indo-Europeanists have long insisted on assuming a strict distinction between nouns and verbs. The distinction is expressed most clearly in derivation; as Benveniste pointed out (1935), nouns may have more suffixes added to roots than may verbs.

Whether or not Gk. *órnis, órnīthos* 'bird' and cognates such as OE *earn* 'eagle' are derived from the root *γer-*, as tentatively proposed by WP (I, 135) and assumed here, the forms may be used to illustrate the greater morphological complexity of nominal elements. Thus the Greek stem *ornīth-o-* has an *n* suffix, as in Germanic, and a *-th-* suffix. The dialectal

Lith. *arēlis* has an *l* suffix. Germanic has a *w* suffix, in Old Norse (ON) *ǫrn* < **arnuz*. Hitt. *haran-* 'eagle', which must be related to the forms in the other dialects, has an *n* suffix; by the etymology adopted here, the Hittite word for 'eagle' provides direct evidence for the initial *γ-* of the PIE root.

Another noun derived from the root *γer-* is Skt. *árṇas* 'streaming flood, sea', as well as *arṇavá* 'surging, sea'. These may be related to Hitt. *arunaš* 'sea', And Germanic forms, such as Goth. *runs,* OE *ryne,* ON *run* 'stream' provide further examples of nouns with the meaning 'stream, sea' derived from this root. Like ON *run,* Skt. *árṇas* is a neuter noun.

Assuming PIE *γorn-* 'eagle' and *γern-* 'sea', their entries in the lexicon would have the following features, among others:

γorn- 'eagle'	γern- 'sea'
<+n. >	<+n. >
<+m. >	<+n. >
<+Common >	<+Common >
<+Concrete >	<+Concrete >
<+Animate >	<-Animate >
<+Count >	<-Count >
<+Animal >	<+Water >
<+Flying >	<+Moving >

Nouns thus would be specified for gender, as common or proper, for concreteness or abstractness, as animate or inanimate, as count or mass nouns, and for specific lexical features.

One set of lexical items which has been thoroughly described is that of the kinship terms. The most recent description is given by Frank Wordick in his doctoral dissertation (1970). When semantic study is further developed, additional sets of nominal elements will be described with thoroughness similar to that applied by Wordick, whose work may be used as a pattern for such study. As did Wordick in accordance with his lengthy bibliography, such lexical studies will make use of many admirable treatment of the PIE vocabulary, such as Benveniste's "Vocabulary of IE institutions" (1969). Like Delbrück's monograph of 1889 on the PIE kinship terms, these treatments contain excellent information on the IE lexicon, though it is not analyzed in the detail found in the studies of Paul Friedrich (1970) and Wordick.

6.5. Pronominal Lexical Units.

The so-called personal pronouns provide us with insights into the earlier nominal system. The separate lexical elements for singular and plural forms, as well as for the oblique cases, given above, § 5.4.3, indicate that the sets of pronouns were made up of individual lexical items rather than members of a close-knit paradigm. Such a situation is also found in the *r*/*n* nominal stems, with their distinction between *r* forms in the nominative/accusative and *n* forms in the oblique cases, as in Hitt. *uttar* 'word, thing', Gen. *uddanaš*; Nom. Acc. pl. *uddār*, Gen. *uddanaš*. We assume that personal pronouns, like nouns, were introduced through the K nodes.

Presumably, at an early stage of PIE, person was not a syntactic category. When a person was to be specified, a lexical element was used, e.g., **eg-/me-* 'I'. At a subsequent period person was indicated in the verb, first with no distinction for number, but by late PIE with the inflectional markers for person and number that are listed in IE grammars (Brugmann 1911:378–427; 1916:583–666). The complicated morphological problems and the reconstructions for the various stages of PIE cannot be pursued here. Brugmann and his predecessors solved some of the problems, and others have been treated subsequently (see Seebold 1971). In a syntactic treatment the primary interest lies in the introduction of the category for person and markers for person into the sentence. This was effected through K nodes, as we have noted, both for personal pronouns and for demonstratives and interrogatives (for these, see Brugmann 1904*b*; 1911:302–377).

The lexical entries for pronouns would then be similar to those for nouns, though they would contain very few features. The lexical entry for **eg-* would only have the features *personal pronoun* and *first person* or in Brugmann's term *I-deixis* (1911:312). That for a demonstrative pronoun would have the feature *this-deixis* or *that-deixis*. Except when emphasized, these features would be associated with the verb form in late PIE, and expressed through the first, second, and third endings of finite forms. When emphatic, they would be marked with special lexical items, as described in morphological treatments.

6.6. Adjectival Lexical Units.

Adjectival modifiers in early PIE were simply nominal elements preposed to nouns, as noted with the example of Hittite *kurur* above (§ 5.3.2; see also J. Friedrich 1960:116–117). The lexical entries of the PIE etyma of works like Hitt. *mekki-* 'much, many', *kurur-* 'inimical, enemy, enmity', *takšul* 'friendly, friendship, peace' would then be given as are those of the nouns in § 6.3. Their function as modifiers or nouns would have been indicated by their position in the sentence.

The lack of distinction between adjectival substantives and nominal substantives in PIE is reflected in further characteristics of the early dialects. One such characteristic is the late introduction of gender inflection in the adjectives, as noted above (§ 5.3.2). Another is the possibility of affixes indicating comparison on nouns as well as adjectives in Sanskrit, as in the following Strophic passage:

12. RV 1.84.6.

nákiṣ	ṭvád	rathī́taro
no-one	from-you	more-charioteer

hárī	yád	indra	yáchase
fallows	when	O-Indra	you-rein

'No one is a better charioteer than you, O Indra, when you rein in the fallows.'

Further evidence for the earlier lack of distinction between nominals used attributively and those used as nouns is provided by the cardinal numerals, which for the most part are uninflected. Accordingly, lexical entries would not distinguish between PIE nouns and adjectives; these two differing functions would be indicated in the early period by order and only later by special inflections and thus distinct selectional characteristics.

6.7. Adverbial Lexical Units.

As Brugmann has indicated (1911:667–758), adverbs are words that are used in the first instance to modify verbs, though they may also be used to modify adjectives and nouns. Moreover, while they may have suffixes comparable to those of substantives, they are not inflected in paradigms; even though a frozen genitive *autoû* is used in Attic and a frozen locative *auteî* in Doric Greek to indicate the adverb 'here', the two forms and other similar forms cannot be associated in a productive paradigmatic set. Adverbs then are frozen forms, some of which came to be disassociated from paradigms.

Adverbs are constantly being "renewed" from other elements in the language, and accordingly it is difficult to reconstruct specific forms for PIE. Hitt. *parā* 'forward, away' and Skt. *parā* 'away', however, as well as Lat. *prō* 'forward', permit the reconstruction of PIE **prō*, with alternate forms **pr̥rō,* and **perō.* As generally assumed (WP:II, 29–40), the adverbial forms are derived from a word **per,* homonymous with the root **per-* 'cross over, penetrate'. Besides **perō*, other extended forms were made from this root, and used as function words: **peri, *prai, *pru, *pres, *preti,* each with possibilities of further extension, as may be observed in the long entry for the root in WP, such as Gk. *próka* 'at once' and *OCS proče* 'therefore' (see also Brugmann 1911:864–888). Which of these extended forms one should assume only for the dialects and which one should reconstruct for PIE is a difficult problem. But on the basis of Hitt. *parā* and Skt. *parā*, we may assume a PIE adverb **perō*. Its precise etymology is not of primary concern here, that is, whether it should be regarded as a case form of a root noun **per* or an extended form of a particle **per* (Delbrück 1893:536–643, esp. 641–643). The reconstructed adverb **perō* would have had uses such as the following in an Old Hittite text (Otten and Souček 1969:20, § 20):

13.	n-ašta	parā	paiu̯ani
	Ptc.-away	away	we-go
	'And we go away.'		

The Hittite adverb *parā* is similar in form to other prominent adverbs in Old Hittite: *anda* 'in', *appa* 'back', *šara* 'upward', and also *(a)šta* 'away' (see the excellent discussion in Otten and Souček 1969:82, 86–88). Its lexical entry would be parallel with that of other adverbs such as Hitt. *anda,* which is related to Skt. *ánti,* Gk. *antí* 'towards' (WP:I, 58–59, 65–67).

*perō	*henda
<+Adv.>	<+Adv.>
<+Away>	<+Towards>
(<+Forwards>)	(<+In>)

Further lexical characteristics are facultative, like the last given here. Selection of them would vary with the verb of the clause and accompanying nominal forms; these modified considerably the meanings of adverbs as the discussions of Delbrück (1893) illustrate.

6.8. Preverbs, Postpositions, and Particles.

In their discussion of *parā* and other adverbs, Otten and Souček point out the difficulty of distinguishing such words from preverbs and postpositions (1969:88). Actually the occurrences of *parā* in the Rigveda are all interpreted as preverbal by Grassmann (1872:782). The following example may illustrate the problems involved in distinguishing whether such words are to be interpreted as adverbs or preverbs.

14.	RV 3.53.2.	mā́	párā	gāḥ
		do-not	away	you-go
		'Don't go away.'		

When the adverbial element generally combined with the verbal to form a unit with distinct meaning and syntactic construction, it would be considered a preverb, and the combination would be treated as are the items in § 6.3.

As a further development, preverbs were used as postpositions. Another passage containing *parā* and the root *gā-* may illustrate such a development:

15. RV 1.164.17. kám svid árdham párāgāt
which indeed region towards she-went
'To whatever region did she go?'

Indo-Europeanists have long noted this development and also the further development of such postpositions to prepositions (Delbrück 1893:643-774). The use of preverbs as postpositions can be understood on the basis of recurrent patterning in the OV period of PIE; their further development to prepositions resulted as the dialects came to be VO.

In a similar way, preverbs could be used to introduce clauses, and they then developed into conjunctions (Brugmann 1904*a*:666). The Greek particle *per* may provide an example (Denniston 1966*b*:481–490); the various uses of *per* cannot be discussed here, but an illustration of its concessive force as a postposed particle is found in the following line:

16. Iliad 2.270. hoi dè kaì akhnúmenoí per ep' autôi
they however and troubled though at him
hēdù gélassan
heartily they-laughed

'But they, though troubled, laughed heartily at him.'

Although Denniston accepts the etymology of Brugmann, by which *per* developed an intensive meaning, 'completely', from the meaning 'around', and further a contrastive force, as illustrated in Example 16, the steps in such developments are difficult to construct in the absence of earlier records. The particles reconstructed for PIE (Brugmann 1916:969–1009) must be described to the extent permitted by our evidence and our understanding of the uses of particles; see above, § 5.5. They were ancillary elements indicating relationships between the primary words in sentences or between sentences, and in this way they developed a wide variety of uses.

Their role in the sentence structure of PIE presumably was similar to that in early Indic prose, as illustrated in Example 64 of Chapter 3. Particles, such as *ha* and *vai* of the first sentence of that example, and preverbs, such as *prá* and *sám* in Sentences 6 and 7, specified the relationships between nouns and verbs. Still other particles introduced sentences, such as *átha* in Sentence 9 and *sá* in Sentence 7, to which the sentence-introductory pronominal elements of sentences 2, 3, 4, 5, 6, 8, 10, and 12 are related. In Vedic, the particles were placed in accordance with their role in the clause, initially when modifying the entire clause, medially when modifying nouns and verbs. In Hittite, on the other hand, they came to be grouped initially, as indicated in § 5.5.3. The difference in arrangement resulted from different syntactic principles, presumably introduced into Hittite by the influence of neighboring languages in Asia Minor, as suggested in § 5.5.3. Though ultimately distinct in their uses, many of the particles, preverbs, and adverbs developed from the same lexical elements, as the variety of their uses in the early dialects suggests.

6.9. Extended Forms of Verbal and Nominal Roots; Further Development of the Lexicon.

The PIE roots are to be regarded like the roots of OV languages, such as Turkish, e.g., Turkish *gel-* 'come', *git-* 'go', and so on (see § 5.4). To these roots various affixes can be added, e.g., *gel-me-di-m* 'come-not *past*-I = I didn't come', *gel-e-bil-eceğ-im* 'come-*gerund*-can-will-I = I will be able to come'. Moreover, by means of derivational suffixes, nouns can be derived from these roots, such as the action noun *geliş* 'the act of coming'. These in turn may be the bases for denominal verbs, such as *gelişmek,* infinitive, 'grow up, develop' in contrast with *gelmek,* infinitive, 'come'. Similar processes can be assumed for PIE. As a result of these processes, not merely root nouns and simple verbs but also extended forms of roots and various formations of verbs and nouns must be treated as basic forms in late PIE. The bases of the lexicon were accordingly undergoing change.

As a result of such changes, forms that are listed as roots do not necessarily have the canonical shape of PIE roots: C*e*C-. For example, the widely attested root **weyd-* is always found with a *-d-* extension. Such extensions may be expected to specify in greater detail the meanings of roots. To ascertain their effect, Per Persson carried out his monumental studies (1912). Traditionally in IE investigations such extensions are called determinatives when they are consonantal, suffixes when accompanied by a vowel. Another notable study of a determinative, *-dh-*, was carried out by Benveniste (1935; see also Lehmann 1942). Because of the time depth involved, the meanings of the determinatives and suffixes may now be difficult to ascertain. W. S. Allen, in a detailed study of the affix *-bh-* (1950), likened such elements to the affixes marking gender classes in Bantu. Whether or not their meanings can be determined, such affixes had a marked effect on the IE lexicon.

Their effect may be best determined by thorough study of the forms in the early dialects. Thus Elmar Seebold has made a detailed investigation of the root **weyd-* (1973), finding various meanings for it in Aryan. If active and accompanied by the genitive, it meant 'come to know'; if middle and accompanied by the genitive it meant tentatively 'become aware of'. If active and accompanied by the accusative, it meant 'decide'; the comparable middle meant 'make a decision'. Further, a middle form in absolute use meant 'turn up, come'. To understand these various meanings one might examine simple roots of the shape *wey-* in PIE. WP lists three such roots: *wey-* (I, 223) 'turn, bend'; (I, 227) 'wither'; (I, 228) 'go after something'. The extended form **weyd-* might well be based on one of these; 'decide' for example might result from a modified form of *wey-* 'bend'. Or **weyd-* may be based on a root which is not attested. It would be important to account for the diverse meanings of roots like *weyd-*. Here the example is cited as an illustration of difficulties involved in exploring earlier forms of the IE lexicon.

Other difficulties result from phonological losses. Thus roots with initial laryngeal, like **γer-* have many reflexes in which only the last consonant of the original root is maintained. By means of a rigorous formal analysis, such as that of Benveniste, the PIE lexicon can, however, be determined with some precision. The various nominal and verbal affixes have been extensively investigated, as by Brugmann (1906:126–581; 1913:86–390) and in many subsequent studies, such as those cited here. Such investigations must be based on an understanding of the formal characteristics of the PIE lexicon and its possibilities for modification.

To be sure, borrowings are included in the earliest reconstructible corpus of the lexicon. Some of these may be indistinguishable from the native vocabulary and accordingly subject to false analysis. The nominal borrowings are most readily recognized. Thus the apparent archaic word for 'axe', Skt. *paraśús,* Gk. *pélekus,* may be a borrowing from Akkadian *pilaqqu;* though since this apparently means 'spindle', the borrowing would have been made in some sort of ceremonial context (Mayrhofer 1953:213–214). Another word which may have been borrowed through cultural contact with the Mesopotamian area is that for cattle, **g^{w}ōus,* cf. Sumerian *gu* (Pokorny 1959–1969:482–483).

Whatever the source of such words, they must have contributed to changes in the rules of derivation for the IE lexicon. Like that of any language, this was undergoing modification. Even the lexicons of early dialects, like Vedic and Greek, contain words which differ considerably in their structure from those that must be assumed for PIE.

7. Syntactic Developments from PIE to the Dialects

7.1. Changes in the Sentence Pattern.

By the time of Classical Greek and Latin, the OV syntactic pattern of PIE had been largely modified to a VO pattern. Yet the VO pattern was still inconsistent in the early classical period of both Greek and Latin, as is illustrated by such relic patterns as OV comparatives, and also in Classical Sanskrit. In spite of such inconsistencies, this stage of development is that "reconstructed" by comparison and represented for the parent language in the standard handbooks, such as Brugmann's. It is virtually an automatic outcome of comparative studies relying on the texts of the classical periods of the three widely studied ancient dialects, Indic, Greek, and Italic. But the Old Hittite texts and the Archaic and Strophic hymns of the Rigveda reflect a language with far more OV characteristics than are proposed for the original IE language in such handbooks. As indicated in the preceding chapters, PIE must be reconstructed as basically OV. In addition to reconstructing PIE in this way, Indo-Europeanists must determine the developments from PIE to the individual dialects. This chapter will sketch some of those developments.

Rather than by reconstructed texts, PIE may be represented by some of the most archaic Hittite materials, such as those found in the Chronicles and Laws—for example, the following sentence from the Chronicles (KBo III 28. 17f.):

1.

attaš-maš	haršanī	^{d}ÍD-	i̯a	mekkeš	papriškir
of-father-my	person-Dat.	river-god	and	many	they-were-unclean

n-uš	ABĪ	LUGAL	natta	huišnušket
Ptc.-them	my-father	king	not	he-caused-to-live

'My father, the king, had many of them killed who sinned with reference to the person of my father and the river-god.'

In this passage both clauses have final position of the verb. The relationship between the first and second clauses is not specified; yet, as the translation suggests, the first clause may be taken as a relative, indicated as such simply by preposing. Such a preposed relative construction is one of the notable characteristics of OV languages. The verb forms are in accordance with OV structure; *huišnušket* contains a *nu* causative affix added to *huiš-* 'live', followed by the *-šk-* iterative-durative suffix, which is also found in *papriškir.* Literally, then, it means: 'he continued causing to live'. As a noteworthy feature of this sentence the negative applies to the root *huiš-,* not to the entire verb form. In this way the clause represents a construction earlier than the subjective system of PIE, one comparable to the Turkish sentence cited above, Chapter 4, Example 1. If the subjective domination had been in effect, the negative of this form would have meant 'he was not causing to live' rather than 'he was causing not to live', i.e., 'he killed'. Morphological constructions like *huišnušket* must be assumed for PIE, that is, loosely constructed verb forms in which the various affixes maintained their independence.

Reflexes of such verb forms appear in other early dialects, as in the "Ionic iterative preterites" attested chiefly in Homer (Schwyzer 1939: 710–712). Two such *-sk-* forms are found with other archaisms in Odysseus's account of Tantalus's torment:

2. Odyssey 11.585.

hossáki	gàr	kúpsei'	ho	gérōn	piéein	meneaínōn,
as-often-as	for	he-wished-to-bend-down	the	old-man	drink	striving

tossákh'	húdōr	apolésket'	anabrokhén,	amphì	de	possì
so-often	water	it-disappeared	it-was-sucked-down	around	Ptc.	at-feet

gaîa	mélaina	pháneske
earth	black	it-appeared

'For as often as he wished to bend down, that old man, striving to drink, so often the water disappeared; it was sucked down; round about then, at his feet, the earth appeared black.'

Besides maintaining the PIE meaning of the *-sk-* suffix, the Ionic iterative preterites preserved the archaism of being made from "aorist" as well as "present" stems. Moreover, the lack of an augment in the preterites indicates their archaic construction. It must not be taken as evidence for a compositional derivation, with an otherwise unattested **skon* 'I was'. The explanations proposed for the Ionic iterative preterites before the discovery of Hittite must be abandoned. Rather, the forms must be regarded as reflexes of the PIE verb system, in which *-sk-* functioned as in Hittite. In addition to these archaic forms, the Homeric passage is also of interest for its preposed complement *piéein* and for other early constructions, such as the use of the optative aorist *kúpsei* in the volitional sense.

Before examination of the later constructions, another Hittite sentence may be cited, with preposed relative and complement clauses; the sentence is from the Old Hittite Proclamation of Anittaš (KBo III 22, 49–51; Raman 1973:63):

3. kuiš ammel appan LUGALuš kišar(i) nu uruHattušan appa
who my-Gen. after king he-becomes Ptc. Hattusa back

aša[ši]	n-	an	nepišaš	dIŠKUR	hazze[du]
he-settles	Ptc.	him	of-heaven	god-Iskur	let-him-strike

'Let the Storm God of heaven strike him who becomes king after me, if he resettles Hattusa.'

In this passage the relative clause, unlike that in Example 1, has a relative marker, *kuiš*. The relationship of the second clause however is unspecified; it may be interpreted as a relative, as it is by Raman: 'the [one who] resettles Hattusa'. The introductory *nu* however suggests a more specific interpretation, such as the conditional of the translation. Whatever the interpretation, the modifying clauses are still preposed, and the pattern of arrangement is OV for the clauses as well as for the postposition *appan* and the preposed genitive *nepišaš*. Other preposed complements have been illustrated in sentences cited above, such as *akuwanna* before the verb *pianzi* in the Hittite example, Chapter 2, Example 17. Later, as early as the Homeric texts, such complements follow.

Before examples of such patterns are cited, a sentence from Middle Indic will be given, from the Pali report of the Buddha's Fire-Sermon. The only finite verb in this sentence, *pakkāmi,* follows its object *cārikaṁ*; but subordinate expressions are placed after as well as before this verb.

4. Atha kho Bhagavā Uruvelāyaṁ yathābhirantaṁ viharitvā yena
then the Blessed Uruvela as-long-as-wished having-lived-in where

Gayasisaṁ tena cārikaṁ pakkāmi mahatā bhikkusaṁghena
Gayasisa (a mountain) there wandering he-went great priest-congregation

saddhiṁ bhikkhusahassena sabbeh' eva purāṇajaṭilehi
with monk-thousand all indeed previous-ascetics

'Then the Blessed One, having lived in Uruvela as long as he wished, undertook a wandering thither, where Gayasisa is, with a great congregation of priests, a thousand monks, all formerly ascetics.'

This comparatively simple example of Middle Indic prose is considerably more complex syntactically than the Vedic prose passage given above in Chapter 3, Example 64, especially in its modifiers of the principal clause. It is important to account for the basis of the syntactic changes which have taken place in Indic, as well as those in the other dialects.

Explanations for specific syntactic changes have been proposed by suggesting influences from neighboring languages or internal developments. The influence of Dravidian may well have been important in the development of morphological constructions in Middle Indic, such as the compounds in this sentence. But since the Dravidian languages are OV they cannot have brought about changes in order of complements and possibly not the gerundial and participial constructions which characterize Middle Indic prose. Such characteristics are also found in the IE dialects of Europe, as a passage from Saint Augustine's Confessions, cir. 400 A.D., may illustrate. The passage is Augustine's well-known observation of how he learned to speak, Confessions I.8:

5. nōn enim docēbant mē maiōrēs hominēs, praebentēs mihi verba certō
not for they-taught me older humans providing for-me words certain

aliquō ordine doctrinae sicut paulō post litterās, sed ego ipse mente,
some order of-teaching as little later letters but I self with-mind

quam dedistī mihi, deus meus, cum gemitibus et vocibus variīs et
which you-gave me god my with grunts and voices various and

variīs membrōrum mōtibus ēdere vellem sensa cordis meī
various members motions express I-wished senses heart my

'For older people did not teach me, furnishing me words in some certain order of teaching as [they did] a little later the letters, but I myself with the mind that you gave me, my God, tried to express with grunts and various voices and various motions of my members the senses of my heart.'

Since passages in other dialects, like this sentence of St. Augustine's, also contain the typical characteristics of VO structure, I suggest that the major cause for the shift to a VO structure, as of complements and subordinate constructions from preverbal to postverbal position, was internal. The shift to VO structure resulted from the development of the subjective quality of the late PIE verb.

7.2. Reasons for the Shift to VO Structure, Illustrated by Complements.

Section 2 of Chapter 4 has illustrated that the PIE verb, and also the entire clause or sentence, came to be dominated by the person marker. The Pali example given above (Example 4) also illustrates such domination. There is no question about the "subject" of the gerund *viharitvā,* or of the participial *abhirantaṁ,* or of the postposition *saddhiṁ*; similarly, the "subject" of *praebentēs* in Example 5 is clearly *hominēs.* Other nouns than the subjects, to be sure, had their own attributive and appositional modifiers, indicated by means of nominal inflections, as do *bhikkusaṁghena, ordine,* and so on. But the entire Pali sentence obviously relates incidents referring to the subject *Bhagavā* with its third-person singular verb. In addition to Augustine's sentence, Greek texts could be cited for further examples of such "subjective dominance," as could texts from other dialects.

With such clarity of focus, sentences could have complements follow verbs as well as precede them, as in the examples given in § 4.8. The change in position of complements has been discussed by various Indo-Europeanists, for example Sommer (1959). His compact treatment proposes that infinitives used as complements first had case forms like the accusative and dative, which in the OV period would have preceded the principal verb, e.g., Lat. *piscātum īre* 'go with the aim of fishing' (Sommer 1959:92–93). Thereupon patterns arose, like Gk. *bē̂ d'ímen* 'he set out to go', exemplifying "infinitives of purpose" (ibid.:98–99). Participles were also used as complements after verbs, as in Sommer's example (1959:103):

6. Odyssey 14.334.	túkhēse	gàr	erkhoménē	nēûs
	it-happened	for	going	ship
	'A ship happened to be going.'			

As a further development the complements were introduced by markers for infinitives and then also for finite verbs, as the following examples with *hṓste* illustrate (Smyth 1956:510–511).

7. Thucydides 5.35.

épeisan	toùs	Athēnaíous	hṓste	eksagageîn
they-persuaded	the	Athenians	"so-that"	to-pull-out
ek	Púlou	Messēníous		
from	Pylos	Messenians		

'They persuaded the Athenians to withdraw the Messenians from Pylos.'

Comparable to Thucydides's use of an infinitive after *hṓste* to indicate result is Xenophon's use of a finite verb form:

8. Anabasis 4.4.11.

epipíptei	khiṓn	ápletos	hṓste	apékrupse	
it-fell	snow	much	so-that	it-covered-over	
kaì	tà	hópla	kaì	toùs	anthrṓpous
both	the	weapons	and	the	men

'A great deal of snow fell so that it covered both the weapons and the men.'

In this last example the result clause is like those in Modern English and other VO languages, as is also the position of the objects with *apékrupse,* and other syntactic characteristics, such as the preposed conjunctions *kaì . . . kaì.*

These examples illustrate how complements postposed after the principal verb came to be expressed by means of complete clauses as well as nominal forms of verbs. Examples of the uses of postposed clauses in other dialects are cited by Delbrück (1900:319–338, 420–447; 1897: 463–475; see also Grace 1971:372–374). As Indo-Europeanists have pointed out (Delbrück 1900:295–406, 423–435), such postposed complementary clauses were also introduced by relative pronouns, or by particles based on relative markers. In this way complements came to use syntactic devices developed for nominal modifiers. Moreover, sequences of modal and tense forms also served to indicate relationships between clauses in complex and compound sentences. These sequences, like the ellipses, assimilations, and mixtures of constructions discussed by Brugmann (1904*a*:289–705), are characteristic of the dialects after they came to be VO in structure rather than of PIE.

7.3. The Postposing of Relative Clauses.

When a relative clause directly precedes its antecedent, the relationship is clear from the arrangement alone. The same is true when it directly follows its antecedent, as in English sentences in which the equivalent noun of the relative clause is the object.

9*a*. It was the color I liked.

But when relative clauses do not directly follow the antecedent, some other syntactic device must be used to identify it, as in:

9*b*. It was the cólor of the car I liked.

By means of the intonation pattern the English relative construction can be specified as referring to *color* as well as to *car,* whichever has the primary stress. The syntactic device of selection may be used similarly to specify the antecedent of a relative clause, as in German:

9*c*.	Es	war	die	Farbe	des	Autos,	die/das	mir gefiel.
	It	was	the	color	of-the	car	that	me pleased.

This example illustrates the basis for the course of development of the position of relative clauses in PIE. When a marker was introduced, the relative clause could follow as well as precede the matrix clause.

Raman has thoroughly examined the development of relative clauses in Hittite. In most passages, even in the Old Hittite texts, the relative clause accompanied by a marker already has a referent in the matrix clause, such as *-an* of Example 3 in this chapter; a referent is found also in Example 1, which has no relative marker. This sentence may be considered an example of the stage directly after that in which preposed relative clauses directly preceded their referents, as illustrated in Example 17 of Chapter 3. Specified by a marker, relative clauses could follow their matrix clauses as well as precede them. The postposed position would have been suggested by the postposed position of complements.

Already in late Hittite, relative clauses have come to be postposed, as they are in the other dialects (Raman 1973:167–201). Raman cites a particularly interesting passage which is preserved in two versions, the older with a direct statement rather than a relative clause, the later cited here with relative marker *kuit* and postposed arrangement; the passage is from ritual texts, which, according to Professor Kammenhuber, were modernized by continuous use in cult ceremonies (Raman 1973:182):

10. KUB XXIX 1 I 26f.

nu	EGIRpa	addaš-man	^{d}Uan	walluškimi
Ptc.	again	father-my	Storm-God	I-am-praising

nu	GIŠ$^{hi.a}$	LUGALuš	^{d}Uni	wekzi
Ptc.	trees	king	Storm-God	he-asks

hējawēs	kuit	tasnuškir
rains	which	they-are-causing-to-be-strong

šallanuškir
they-are-causing-to-be-large

'Again I praise the Storm God, my father; the king asks the Storm God for the trees which the rains have made to grow strong and tall.'

Raman accounts for the VO characteristics in the later Hittite text through borrowing; this explanation is especially cogent for another Hittite text with VO characteristics, which was written in Egypt, for it is quite plausible that scribes who also knew Egyptian or Akkadian would have taken over their VO patterns (Raman 1973:188). But such an explanation for the shift to VO structure is less weighty for the texts in the other IE dialects. Already in the Rigveda almost half of the relative clauses are postposed, and in later texts, such as those of Homeric Greek, the percentage increases. Concerning these we have no basis for assuming modifications by bilinguals who also knew VO languages. Unless further materials become available for the languages which Greek, Latin, and other dialects displaced, the best explanation for the shift to VO relative constructions is that of internal innovation. Such an explanation is supported by the parallel shift to VO structure of relative clauses, though with differing relative markers in the various dialects. For some of the dialects, however, as for Hittite, the shift may have been advanced by influence from VO languages.

7.4. Change in the Position of Attributive Adjectives and Genitives.

In view of their relationship with modifying relative clauses, change in the position of adjectives and genitives would be expected with that of relative clauses. The change was slow; in the Italic branch, for example, adjectives and genitives are consistently postposed only in the Romance languages, though the main clause pattern of Late Latin was VO already at the time of Saint Augustine. The position of attributive adjectives in the sentence cited from his Confessions (Example 5) is not fixed; *variīs* is postposed after *vocibus* but preposed before *mōtibus*.

During the course of the change a remarkable construction arose in the northern languages, Slavic, Baltic, and Germanic: the so-called weak adjective inflection. In this inflection the relative marker of reduced relative clauses was maintained as a suffix in Slavic and Baltic, e.g., OCS *vino novoje* 'wine (which is) new', in contrast with *vino novo* 'new wine', and Lith. *geràsis* 'the good one' as opposed to *gẽras* 'good'. The weak or definite forms of adjectives can be accounted for through their reduction from relative constructions, in contrast with the strong declensions, which continue the regular IE adjective inflection (Lehmann 1970*b*). Germanic, which lacked reflexes of the *yo* marker, generalized the *n* inflection for definite adjectives. Thus the weak inflections provide further insights into changes which took place as IE dialects moved to a VO structure.

7.5. Change in Verblike Elements and Verbal Modifiers.

After the arrangement of relative clauses was modified, the change in position of attributive adjectives and genitives is readily understandable, inasmuch as these constructions are reduced forms of relative clauses. But verblike governing elements, such as postpositions, and their patterning may seem not to be closely related to verbs. New High German however provides an example of their relationship in change. After an OV order was adopted in subordinate clauses around 1500 A.D., postpositions were introduced. The entities chosen for postpositions are not of syntactic importance, taken as they are from various sources; *wegen* 'because of', for example, used postpositionally since around 1600, is in origin a dative plural; another, *entlanc* 'along', first attested as postposition in 1751, developed from a phrase. The German phenomena therefore suggest that verblike elements, such as postpositions and prepositions, are placed in accordance with the position of the verb with regard to its object, as stated in the principle of § 1.3. Since comparative constructions are essentially verbal, they too would be remodeled in accordance with the principle.

In this way the verblike constructions of the IE dialects were changed to those of VO pattern, much as the nominal modifying constructions had been. Prepositions came to replace postpositions; comparative constructions came to have the pattern of Latin *maior quam tū* 'bigger than you' rather than the relic pattern *tē maior* ('you-from bigger'). Moreover, adverbs typically came to follow verbs, as did the verbal complements. Such changes varied in time of adoption and spread from dialect to dialect; investigations into the reasons for the variation must be pursued by specialists in the several dialects.

Among the verbal innovations of greatest interest for pursuing the changes in the verbal system are the newly introduced reflexive and reciprocal phrases with pronouns. These developed when the suffixed verb system no longer agreed with the changing pattern of arrangement of the clause to VO (Lehmann 1973*a*, 1973*b*). The OV middle formation was then lost or modified in meaning. The new verbal phrases are among the earliest analytic verbal constructions. Other analytical constructions were introduced in innovating such paradigms as the perfect passive forms of

Latin. Subsequently, as the verbal endings were weakened, analytical devices were also used for tense and mood forms. The system of verb markers thus changed from a system of suffixes, as expected in an OV language, to a system making use of auxiliaries and function words.

7.6. Changes in Selectional Categories.

Among the most significant changes in selectional categories was the thoroughgoing systematization of paradigms. Already in late PIE the three persons had distinctive endings in the plural as well as the singular, as the result of increasing systematization of category markers. But only in the dialects were verbal paradigms systematized to such an extent that grammars can propose principal parts for verbs. The Latin verb system may be the most obvious example; three of the four conjugations have parallel sets of forms that can be constructed on the basis of four principal parts, e.g., *laudō, laudāvī, laudātum, laudāre* 'praise'. Even the remaining conjugation shows few traces of the unpredictability of the PIE verb, in which a large number of forms could be made from one root, with no means of predicting the particular forms, even from principal parts, as examination of the forms given by Whitney for Vedic roots (1885) will indicate. The various later dialects systematized in this way not only verbal inflections but also those of nouns, adjectives, and pronouns. In the course of remodeling the IE forms into symmetrical paradigms, new, or weak, inflections were introduced, such as the Latin *v* perfect exemplified in *laudāvī* and the *k* perfect of Greek, the *d* preterite of Germanic, and so on. The source of most of these formations is still disputed and may never reach general agreement. In proposing theories for their origins a syntactic model is particularly important. For, as is revealed by the investigation of any one form, such as the Germanic dental preterite, scholars have often looked at apparent parallels, such as the composite forms in the Romance languages, without considering whether the syntactic situation was the same in the two differing languages. By the view of syntactic structure held here for PIE and the early dialects, such weak preterites must have arisen by generalization of suffixes rather than from periphrastic formations (Lehmann 1943*a*). Scholars who hold a different point of view must support it with arguments based on general syntactic theory and a particular framework of IE syntax, not merely with unmotivated parallels in other languages.

In the systematization of paradigms, thematic vowels were highly important. The regular verb conjugations generally involve reflexes of thematic vowels, as in *laudāre,* or parallels, as in *habēre* and *audīre.* Moreover, the most systematic and complete inflections are thematic, such as the adjective inflection illustrated in Latin by *bonus, -a, -um* 'good' in contrast with the inflection of the third declension, as in *gravis, -e* 'heavy'. Examination of the grammars of the individual dialects illustrates the pervasiveness of thematic inflections.

Phonological changes, especially the loss of the laryngeals and the realignment of the resonants, however, came to obscure the earlier parallelism between forms even in late PIE. Thus the nominative feminine ending of *bona,* < *-ah* < *-eh,* was earlier parallel with those of the masculine and neuter (*-os, -om*); but upon loss of the *h* the parallelism was lost.

Such losses of parallelism contributed to the gradually increasing analytic character of the dialects, especially those dialects in which a stress accent led to weakening of inflectional syllables. Even in the highly inflected period of Classical Latin, forms like *rosae* (feminine genitive/dative singular, nominative plural) and *rosīs* (dative/ablative plural) had to be disambiguated by function words or by arrangement; prepositions like *sub* would distinguish the ablative from among homonymous forms; its role as subject or predicate nominative would distinguish the nominative plural. In the course of time the inflectional syllables were further reduced or lost, partly through lack of distinctiveness, partly through replacement of their function by prepositions and other syntactic markers. Moreover, the development towards analytical structure correlates with departure from an OV structure with its rich possibilities of suffixation. Investigations of the extent to which these various forces were of effect in the selectional changes belong among syntactic problems of general concern. For the understanding of such problems the individual changes in each of the dialects need detailed study.

7.7. Changes in Modification.

Modification, or sandhi, played an important role in the delimitation of PIE words and of phrases consisting of an accented word followed by an enclitic. Meillet concluded that words were syntactic units in PIE, using metrical practices in Indo-Iranian, Greek, and Latin to support his conclusions (1937:136–140). Words were demarcated by the possibility of only one accent and also by features of modification of their final elements.

The final elements were modified in accordance with phonological classes. Presumably even in late PIE the modification of final stops corresponded to that of early Indic, where they consisted only of the implosive segment; without discussing other changes, it may be recalled that in Armenian, Greek, Slavic, Baltic, Germanic, and Celtic such final stops were lost. The final fricative also had a weakened form, as may be determined from its reflexes in Sanskrit, such as *ḥ* and its merger with vowels, e.g., *o* < *-as*.

These and other modification phenomena are of interest here because of the evidence they supply for assuming that the word was a syntactic and morphological unit in PIE and because of the effects of such modifications on syntactic patterning. Since the final segments of words, those subjected to weakening, consisted in large part of the markers for syntactic categories, further weakening or loss led to the greater use of analytic devices for the expression of syntactic relationships. The effects are clearest for dialects which introduced a stress accent, such as Celtic, Germanic, Italic, and Middle Indic. In contrast with the well-preserved inflectional endings of Baltic and Slavic, the dialects with stress accent underwent major losses of inflectional markers. The details of the effects of such losses and their relationships to other changes in the dialects are intricate, and by no means ascertained in spite of admirable studies of "laws of finals." For syntactic study the effect in reducing the selectional devices rather than precise details on the phonological processes concerned is of primary importance, for it led to greater reliance on function words and other analytic devices in syntax.

7.8. Changes in Intonation.

The information on intonation patterns and their uses in PIE is slight, as noted in § 2.7. Yet, at least in early Vedic and presumably in PIE as well, pitch accent on the verbs of subordinate clauses is one indicator of subordination. When a stress accent was introduced, such a use of intonation must have been disrupted. Jules Bloch states that this device for indicating subordination was lost by the time of Classical Sanskrit (1965:311). A great deal of further study is required, however, to permit more than general statements on the changes in intonation patterns in Indic and other dialects. Such study must also involve the changes in use of enclitics, that is, the loss of application of Wackernagel's law.

For Greek, Allen has made preliminary analyses in admirable investigations of the bases of Greek meter (1968:106–124). A further imaginative investigation of changes in the accent patterns of the dialects has been carried out by Paul Kiparsky (1973). These investigations promise greater understanding of PIE intonation patterns and their changes, with resultant changes in syntax. For the time being these investigations are chiefly concerned with individual accentual phenomena; as Allen states, "we know virtually nothing about 'tonal syntax,' i.e. the way in which such patterns interacted with one another and with clause- and sentence-intonations in continuous speech" (1968:118). The patient research of Indo-Europeanists like Allen and Kiparsky, based on that of earlier scholars like Kurylowicz and Hirt, may in time amplify our knowledge and provide some improved observations on the use of intonation in PIE syntax and its subsequent changes.

7.9. The Syntactic Changes, with Reference to the Community of PIE Speakers

The overall pattern of changes from PIE to the dialects is from an OV to a VO structure. Individual dialects differ in the time and extent of the changes.

The southern European dialects have become consistently VO: Albanian, Greek, the Romance languages. The group farthest to the west, Insular Celtic, with its VSO structure, has developed farthest from the OV structure of PIE.

Persian and the northern European dialects—Baltic, Slavic, Germanic—are inconsistently VO. These dialects illustrate some of the problems that complicate the understanding of the syntactic changes; for especially Slavic and North Germanic were influenced by neighboring OV languages. As a result they reintroduced OV characteristics. The dialect which, apart from Tocharian, was most heavily influenced by neighboring OV languages was Indic, which was contiguous to Dravidian. Like Slavic and North Germanic, Indic illustrates that an unbroken trend of change, or drift, cannot be assumed for any of the dialects, or even for PIE. In view of our lack of information on the early location of Armenian, we cannot account for its OV structure, whether it was maintained from that of the parent language or reintroduced. The Anatolian languages must have continued the OV structure of the parent language.

PIE itself must have been subjected to various influences. As a result its stages cannot be sketched with certainty. The common trend towards VO patterning, apparent even in Anatolian, indicates however that late PIE must have been changing from an OV structure. To what extent its earlier structure was consistently OV cannot be ascertained, at least for the present. Future possible contributions to the understanding of PIE syntactic developments will depend largely on insights into the processes of syntactic change. Improved understanding may also result from the study of its neighboring languages. Archeological investigations have provided a good measure of certainty on the location of the parent language around 3000 B.C. through identification of the community of PIE speakers with the Kurgan culture of the area north of the Black Sea. Further investigations are beginning to provide information on contacts between this community and other communities. Metallurgical data are giving information both on the spread of the Indo-Europeans and on sources of their innovations.

Gimbutas concludes that the new technique of alloying copper with arsenic or tin was devised in "Transcaucasia during the 5th millennium B.C." and "transmitted to Europe by the 'Kurgan' (Indo-European) people at the end of the 4th millennium B.C." Presumably the Indo-Europeans were in contact with the "proto-Caucasian (Kartvelian) family" at this time (Gimbutas 1973:174, 207). The contacts may permit inferences on early syntactic structure, as they have on phonological structure (Gamkrelidze 1966).

Whether or not such inferences are possible, a treatment of PIE syntax must be based on the assumption that the language reconstructed was in use at least as early as 3000 B.C. This assumption alone requires revisions of earlier statements of PIE syntax. It also readily permits an understanding of the divergent systems of the dialects, from the Anatolian to those of Europe. Since many of the conclusions concerning PIE are based on recently provided information and recent developments in syntactic and typological theory, a treatment of PIE syntax can only be preliminary at this time. It should however indicate some of the problems and opportunities for further research, while providing a general statement on the syntactic structure of the parent language of a language family for which we have one of the longest and most comprehensive amounts of data.

BIBLIOGRAPHY

The following abbreviations are used:

ABG: Abhandlungen der Deutschen Akademie der Wissenschaften zu Berlin, Phil.-hist. Klasse
APrA: Abhandlungen der Preußischen Akademie der Wissenschaften, Phil.-hist. Klasse
ASG: Abhandlungen der Sächsischen Akademie der Wissenschaften, Leipzig, Phil.-hist. Klasse
BSG: Sitzungsberichte der Sächsischen Gesellschaften der Wissenschaften zu Leipzig, Phil.-hist. Klasse
BSL: Bulletin de la Société de Linguistique de Paris
IF: Indogermanische Forschungen
JAOS: Journal of the American Oriental Society
KZ: Zeitschrift für vergleichende Sprachforschung auf dem Gebiete der indogermanischen Sprachen
MKDA: Det Kgl. Danske Videnskabernes Selskab, Hist.-fil. Meddelelser, Copenhagen
MKNA: Mededelingen van de Koninklijke Nederlandse Akademie van Wetenschappen, afdeling Letterkunde Amsterdam
MSL: Mémoires de la Société de Linguistique de Paris
PBB: Beiträge zur Geschichte der deutschen Sprache und Literatur
PhM: Philologische Monatsschrift
PMLA: Publications of the Modern Language Association
TPhS: Transactions of the Philological Society, Oxford
VJa: Voprosy Jazykoznanija
WSB: Sitzungsberichte der Akademie der Wissenschaften in Wien, Phil.-hist. Klasse

Adrados, Francisco R. 1968. Die Rekonstruktion des Indogermanischen und die strukturelle Sprachwissenschaft. IF 73.1–47.

———. 1971. On Indo-European sigmatic verbal stems. Archivum Linguisticum. n.s. 2.95-116.

Allen, W. S. 1950. The Indo-European primary affix *-b[h]. TPhs, pp. 1-33.

———. 1968. Vox Graeca. Cambridge: University Press.

Ananthanarayana, H. S. 1970*a*. Verb forms of the Taittirīya Brāhmaṇa. Poona: Deccan College.

———. 1970*b*. The kāraka theory and case grammar. Indian Linguistics 31.14–27.

———. 1970*c*. Intonation contours in Vedic: A hypothesis. Vishveshvaranand Indological Journal 8.1-19.

Anderson, John M. 1971. The grammar of case. Cambridge: University Press.

Arnold, E. Vernon. 1905. Vedic metre in its historical development. Cambridge: University Press.

Aufrecht, Theodor, ed. 1877. Die Hymnen des Rigveda. 2 vols. 4th ed. Reprint. Wiesbaden: Harrassowitz, 1968.

Avery, John. 1881. On relative clauses in the Rigveda. Proceedings of the American Oriental Society 11.64-66.

———. 1884. The unaugmented verb-forms of the Rig- and Atharva-Vedas. JAOS 11.326-361.

Bednarczuk, Leszek. 1971. Indo-European parataxis. Kraków: Wydawnictwo Naukowe.

Behaghel, Otto. 1923-1932. Deutsche Syntax. 4 vols. Heidelberg: Winter.

———. 1929. Zur Stellung des Verbs im Germanischen und Indogermanischen. KZ 56.276-281.

Bennett, Charles E. 1910-1914. Syntax of Early Latin. 2 vols. Reprint. Hildesheim: Georg Olm, 1966.
1910. I. The verb.
1914. II. The cases.

Benveniste, Emile. 1935. Origines de la formation des noms en indo-européen. Paris: Maisonneuve.

———. 1948. Noms d'agent et noms d'action en indo-européen. Paris: Adrien-Maisonneuve.

———. 1950. La phrase nominale. BSL 46.19-36.

———. 1951. Prétérit et optatif en indo-européen. BSL 47.11-20.

———. 1960. "Etre" et "avoir" dans leurs fonctions linguistiques. BSL 55.113-134. Also in idem 1966:187-207; 1971:163-179.

———. 1966. Problèmes de linguistique générale. Paris: Gallimard.

———. 1969. Le vocabulaire des institutions indo-européennes. 2 vols. Paris: Minuit.

———. 1971. Problems in general linguistics. Translation of Problèmes de linguistique générale. Translated by Mary E. Meek. Coral Gables: University of Miami Press.

Bergaigne, Abel. 1879. Essai sur la construction grammaticale considérée dans son développement historique, en sanskrit, en grec, en latin, dans les langues romanes et dans les langues germaniques. MSL. 3.1-51, 124-154, 169-186.

Bills, Garland D.; Bernardo Vallejo C.; and Rudolph C. Troike. 1969. An introduction to spoken Bolivian Quechua. Austin: University of Texas Press.

Birnbaum, Henrik, and Jaan Puhvel, eds. 1966. Ancient Indo-European dialects. Berkeley and Los Angeles: University of California Press.

Bloch, Jules. 1965. Indo-Aryan from the Vedas to Modern Times. Translated by Alfred Master. Paris: Adrien-Maisonneuve.

Bloomfield, Leonard. 1933. Language. New York: Holt.

Brugmann, Karl. 1891. Zur Frage der Entstehung des grammatischen Geschlechtes. PBB 15.523-531.

——. 1893-1894. Die Ausdrücke für den Begriff der Totalität in den indogermanischen Sprachen. Leipzig: Edelmann.

——. 1897*a*. The nature and origin of the noun genders in the Indo-European languages. Translated by E. Y. Robbins. New York.

——. 1897-1916. Vergleichende Laut-, Stammbildungs- und Flexionslehre der indogermanischen Sprachen. 2 vols. 2d ed. Strassburg: Trübner.

1897*b*. I. Einleitung und Lautlehre.

1906. II. Part 1. Lehre von den Wortformen und ihrem Gebrauch.

1911. II. Part 2. Nomina.

1913. II. Part 3.1. Verbum finitum.

1916. II. Part 3.2. Verbum finitum.

——. 1904*a*. Kurze vergleichende Grammatik der indogermanischen Sprachen. Strassburg: Trübner.

——. 1904*b*. Die Demonstrativpronomina der indogermanischen Sprachen. ASG 22.6. Leipzig: Teubner.

——. 1917. Zu den Wörtern für „gestern", „morgen" in den indogermanischen Sprachen. BSG 69.1.1-34. Leipzig: Teubner.

——. 1918. Verschiedenheiten der Satzgestaltung nach Massgabe der seelischen Grundfunktionen in den indogermanischen Sprachen. BSG 70.6. Leipzig: Teubner.

——. 1925. Die Syntax des einfachen Satzes im Indogermanischen. Berlin und Leipzig: DeGruyter.

——, and Berthold Delbrück. 1886-1900. Grundriss der vergleichenden Grammatik der indogermanischen Sprachen. 5 vols. First two volumes replaced by Brugmann 1897-1916. Strassburg: Trübner.

Buck, Carl Darling. 1933. Comparative grammar of Greek and Latin. Reprint. Chicago: University of Chicago Press, 1937.

Calbert, Joseph P. 1971. Modality and case grammar. Working Papers in Linguistics No. 10, edited by Charles J. Fillmore, pp. 85-132. Columbus: Department of Linguistics, Ohio State University.

Calboli, Gualtiero. 1966–1968. I modi del verbo greco e latino 1903–1966. Lustrum 11 (1966).173–349; 13 (1968).405–511.

Canedo, José. 1937. Zur Wort- und Satzstellung in der alt- und mittelindischen Prosa. Ergänzungsheft zur KZ 13.

Cardona, George; Henry M. Hoenigswald; and Alfred Senn, eds. 1970. Indo-European and Indo-Europeans. Philadelphia: University of Pennsylvania Press.

Carnap, Rudolf. 1958. Introduction to symbolic logic and its applications. Translated by W.H. Meyer and John Wilkinson. New York: Dover.

Carruba, Onofrio. 1969. Die satzeinleitenden Partikeln in den indogermanischen Sprachen Anatoliens. Rome: Ateneo.

Chomsky, Noam. 1957. Syntactic structures. The Hague: Mouton.

——. 1965. Aspects of the theory of syntax. Cambridge: MIT Press.

Cowgill, Warren. 1968. The first person singular medio-passive in Indo-Iranian. In Pratidānam, edited by J.C. Heesterman et al., pp. 24–31. The Hague: Mouton.

de Groot, A.W. 1956. Classification of the uses of a case illustrated on the genitive in Latin. Lingua 6.8–65.

Delbrück, Berthold. 1871. Der Gebrauch des Conjunktivs und Optativs im Sanskrit und Griechischen. Syntaktische Forschungen 1. Halle: Waisenhaus.

——. 1876. Altindische Tempuslehre. Syntaktische Forschungen 2. Halle: Waisenhaus.

——. 1878. Die altindische Wortfolge aus dem Çatapathabrāhmaṇa dargestellt. Syntaktische Forschungen 3. Halle: Waisenhaus.

——. 1879. Die Grundlagen der Griechischen Syntax. Syntaktische Forschungen 4. Halle: Waisenhaus.

——. 1888. Altindische Syntax. Syntaktische Forschungen 5. Halle: Waisenhaus. Reprint. Darmstadt: Wissenschaftliche Buchgesellschaft, 1968.

——. 1889. Die indogermanischen Verwandtschaftsnamen. ASG 11.381–606. Leipzig.

——. 1893–1900. Vergleichende Syntax der indogermanischen Sprachen. 3 vols. (= Vols. 3–5 of Grundriss der vergleichenden Grammatik der indogermanischen Sprachen, 1st ed.) Strassburg: Trübner.
1893. I.
1897. II.
1900. III.

——. 1907. Synkretismus. Ein Beitrag zur germanischen Kasuslehre. Strassburg: Trübner.

——. 1918. Germanische Syntax IV. Die Wortstellung in dem älteren westgötischen Landrecht. ASG 36.1. Leipzig: Teubner.

Denniston, J. D. 1966*a*. Greek prose style. 2d ed. rev. Oxford: Clarendon.

——. 1966*b*. The Greek particles. Oxford: Clarendon.

Devoto, Giacomo. 1958. Scritti minori I. Florence: Felice le Monnier.

Dickens, F. Victor. 1888. The old bamboo-hewer's story. London: Trübner.

Dillon, Myles. 1947. Celtic and the other Indo-European languages. TPhS 1947.15-24.
Dover, K. J. 1960. Greek word order. Cambridge: University Press.
Dressler, Wolfgang. 1968. Studien zur verbalen Pluralität. WSB 259.1. Wien: Böhlau.
——. 1971. Über die Rekonstruktion der indogermanischen Syntax. KZ 85.5-22.
Elizarenkova, T. 1960. Aorist v "Rigvede" [The aorist in the Rigveda]. Moscow: Izdatel'stvo Vostochnoj Literatury.
——. 1972. Review of K. Hoffmann, Der Injunktiv im Veda. Indo-Iranian Journal 14.247-253.
Erdmann, Oskar, ed. 1882. Otfrids Evangelienbuch. Halle: Waisenhaus.
Fick, August. 1890-1909. Vergleichendes Wörterbuch der Indogermanischen Sprachen. 3 vols. 4th ed. By Adalbert Bezzenberger, Hjalmar Falk, August Fick, Whitley Stokes, and Alf Torp. Göttingen: Vandenhoeck & Ruprecht.
Fillmore, Charles T. 1968. The case for case. In Universals in linguistic theory, edited by Emmon Bach and R. T. Harms, pp. 1-88. New York: Holt, Rinehart and Winston.
Fischer, P. 1924. Zur Stellung des Verbums im Griechischen. Glotta 13.1-11, 189-205.
Fourquet, Jean. 1938. L'ordre des éléments de la phrase en germanique ancien. Paris: Les Belles Lettres.
Friedrich, Johannes. 1959. Die hethitischen Gesetze. Leiden: Brill.
——. 1960. Kurzgefasste Grammatik. Vol. 1 of Hethitisches Elementarbuch. 2d ed. Heidelberg: Winter.
Friedrich, Paul. 1970. Proto-Indo-European trees. Chicago: University of Chicago Press.
Frisk, Hjalmar. 1941. Über den Gebrauch des Privativpräfixes im idg. Adjektiv. In Kleine Schriften, pp. 183-229. Göteborg: Elander, 1966.
Gaedicke, Carl. 1880. Der Accusativ im Veda. Breslau: Koebner.
Gamkrelidze, Thomas V. 1966. A typology of Common Kartvelian. Language 42. 69-83.
Gardiner, Alan. 1950. Egyptian grammar. London: Oxford University Press.
Geldner, Karl Fr. 1951-1957. Der Rig-Veda aus dem Sanskrit ins Deutsche übersetzt mit einem laufenden Kommentar versehen. 4 vols. Harvard Oriental Series 33-36. Cambridge: Harvard University Press.
Gimbutas, Marija. 1973. The beginning of the Bronze Age in Europe and the Indo-Europeans: 3500-2500 B.C. The Journal of Indo-European Studies 1. 163-214.
Götze, Albrecht, and Holger Pedersen. 1934. Muršilis Sprachlähmung. Copenhagen: Munksgaard.
Gonda, Jan. 1951*a*. Remarks on the Sanskrit passive. Leiden: Brill.
——. 1951*b*. La place de la particule négative *na* dans la phrase en vieil Indien. Leiden: Brill.

———. 1952. Remarques sur la place du verbe dans la phrase active et moyenne en langue sanscrite. Utrecht: Oosthoek.

———. 1954*a*. The history and original function of the Indo-European particle $k^{u}e$, especially in Greek and Latin. Mnemosyne, 4th ser. 7.177-214, 265-296.

———. 1954*b*. The original character of the Indo-European relative pronoun *i̯o-*. Lingua 4.1-41.

———. 1956. The character of the Indo-European moods. Wiesbaden: Harrassowitz.

———. 1962. The aspectual functions of the Ṛgvedic present and aorist. The Hague: Mouton.

———. 1971. Die Indischen Sprachen: Old Indian. Handbuch der Orientalistik 2.1.1. Leiden: Brill.

Goodwin, William W. 1893. Syntax of the moods and tenses of the Greek verb. Boston: Ginn.

Grace, E. C., Jr. 1971. The order of constituents in Indo-European. Austin: University of Texas dissertation.

Grassmann, Hermann. 1955. Wörterbuch zum Rigveda. 3d ed. Unchanged reprint of the 1st ed. of 1872. Wiesbaden: Harrassowitz.

Greenberg, Joseph H. 1966. Some universals of grammar with particular reference to the order of meaningful elements. In Universals of language, edited by idem, 2d ed., pp. 73-113. Cambridge: MIT Press.

———. 1966. Language universals, with special reference to feature hierarchies. The Hague: Mouton.

Grimm, Jacob. 1870-1898. Deutsche Grammatik. 4 vols. 2d ed., reprinted under the direction of Wilhelm Scherer. Gütersloh.

Guiraud, Charles. 1962. La phrase nominale en grec, d'Homère à Euripide. Paris: Klincksieck.

Hahn, E. A. 1953. Subjunctive and optative: Their origin as futures. Philological Monographs 16. New York: American Philological Association.

Hale, William Gardner, and Carl Darling Buck. 1903. A Latin grammar. Reprint. University, Ala.: University of Alabama Press, 1966.

Hartmann, Hans. 1954. Das Passiv. Heidelberg: Winter.

Havers, Wilhelm. 1911. Untersuchungen zur Kasussyntax der idg. Sprachen. Strassburg: Trübner.

———. 1924. Eine syntaktische Sonderstellung griechischer und lateinischer Neutra. Glotta 13.171-189.

Held, W. H., Jr. 1957. The Hittite relative sentence. Language Dissertation 55. Baltimore: Waverly.

Hermann, Eduard. 1895. Gab es im Indogermanischen Nebensätze? KZ 33.481-534.

Heusler, Andreas. 1950. Altisländisches Elementarbuch. 4th ed. Heidelberg: Winter.

Hirt, Hermann. 1921-1937. Indogermanische Grammatik. 7 vols. Heidelberg: Winter.

———. 1931-1934. Handbuch des Urgermanischen. 3 vols. Heidelberg: Winter.

———, and Helmut Arntz. 1939. Die Hauptprobleme der indogermanischen Sprachwissenschaft. Halle: Niemeyer.

Hoenigswald, Henry M. 1960. Language change and linguistic reconstruction. Chicago: University of Chicago Press.

Hofmann, J. B. *See* Leumann 1963-1965.

Hoffmann, Karl. 1967. Der Injunktiv im Veda. Heidelberg: Winter.

———. 1968. Zum Optativ des indogermanischen Wurzelaorists. In Pratidānam, edited by J. C. Heesterman et al., pp. 3-8. The Hague: Mouton.

———. 1970. Das Kategoriensystem des indogermanischen Verbums. Münchener Studien zur Sprachwissenschaft 28.19-41.

Hope, Edward R. 1972. The deep syntax of Lisu sentences. Canberra: Australian National University dissertation.

Hopper, Paul J. 1967. The syntax of the simple sentence in Proto-Germanic. Austin: University of Texas dissertation.

Ivanov, V. V. 1963. Chettskij jazyk [The Hittite language]. Moscow: Akademija Nauk.

Jacobi, Hermann. 1897. Compositum und Nebensatz. Bonn: Cohen.

Jakobson, Roman. 1971. Implications of language universals for linguistics. In Selected writings, pp. 580-591. The Hague: Mouton.

Jansky, Herbert. 1954. Lehrbuch der türkischen Sprache. Wiesbaden: Harrassowitz.

Jensen, Hans. 1959. Altarmenische Grammatik. Heidelberg: Winter.

Jespersen, Otto. 1922. Language. London: Allen and Unwin.

———. 1924. The philosophy of grammar. London: Allen and Unwin.

Jolly, Julius. 1872. Ein Kapitel vergleichender Syntax: Der Conjunktiv und Optativ und die Nebensätze im Zend und Altpersischen. Munich: Ackermann.

Jucquois, Guy. 1970. Les postpositions du hittite et l'accentuation des préverbes en indo-européen. Muséon 83.533-540.

Kammenhuber, Annelies. 1969. Hethitisch, Palaisch, Luwisch und Hieroglyphenluwisch. Handbuch der Orientalistik 1.2.1 and 2.2. Leiden: Brill.

Kent, Roland G. 1953. Old Persian. 2d ed. New Haven: American Oriental Society.

Kiparsky, Paul. 1968. Tense and mood in Indo-European syntax. Foundations of language 4.30-57.

———. 1973. The inflectional accent in Indo-European. Language 49.794-849.

Krahe, Hans. 1972. Grundzüge der vergleichenden Syntax der indogermanischen Sprachen. Edited by Wolfgang Meid and Hans Schmeja. Innsbrucker Beiträge zur Sprachwissenschaft 8. Innsbruck.

Krause, Wolfgang. 1955. Tocharisch. Handbuch der Orientalistik 4.3. Leiden: Brill.

———, and Werner Thomas. 1960. Grammatik. Vol. 1 of Tocharisches Elementarbuch. Heidelberg: Winter.

Kronasser, Heinz. 1966. Etymologie der hethitischen Sprache. Wiesbaden: Harrassowitz.

Kühne, Cord, and Heinrich Otten. 1971. Der Šaušgamuwa-Vertrag. Wiesbaden: Harrassowitz.

Kuiper, F. B. J. 1951. Nṓropi khalkôi. MKNA 14.5.201-227. Amsterdam.

Kuipers, Aert H. 1967. The Squamish language. The Hague: Mouton.

Kurylowicz, Jerzy. 1935. Etudes indoeuropéennes. Kraków: Gebethner and Wolff.

———. 1964. The inflectional categories of Indo-European. Heidelberg: Winter.

———. 1968. Akzent; Ablaut. Vol. 2 of Indogermanische Grammatik. Heidelberg: Winter.

Lambertz, Maximilian. 1948. Grammatik und albanische Texte. Vol. 1 of Albanisches Lesebuch. Leipzig: Harrassowitz.

Laroche, Emmanuel. 1950. Histoire de la racine nem- en grec ancien. Paris: Klincksieck.

Lees, Robert. 1960. The grammar of English nominalizations. Bloomington, Ind.: Research Center in Anthropology, Folklore, and Linguistics.

Lehmann, Winfred P. 1942. The Indo-European *dh*-determinative in Germanic. Language 18.125-132.

———. 1943*a*. The Indo-European *dh*-determinative as Germanic preterite formant. Language 19.19-26.

———. 1943*b*. The Germanic weak preterite endings. Language 19.313-319.

———. 1952. Proto-Indo-European phonology. Austin: University of Texas Press.

———. 1956. The development of Germanic verse form. Austin: University of Texas Press. Reprint. New York: Gordion, 1972.

———. 1957. A syntactic reflex of the Indo-European laryngeals. In Studies presented to Joshua Whatmough, edited by Ernst Pulgram, pp. 145-147. The Hague: Mouton.

———. 1958. On earlier stages of the Indo-European nominal inflection. Language 34.179-202.

———. 1969. Proto-Indo-European compounds in relation to other Proto-Indo-European syntactic patterns. Acta Linguistica Hafniensia 12.1-20.

———. 1970*a*. The Nordic languages: Lasting linguistic contributions of the past. In The Nordic languages and modern linguistics, edited by Hreinn Benediktsson, pp. 286-305. Reykjavík: Vísindafélag Íslendinga.

———. 1970*b*. Definite adjective declensions and syntactic types. In Donum Balticum, edited by Velta Rūķe-Draviņa. Stockholm: Almquist and Wiksell.

———. 1971. On the rise of SOV patterns in New High German. In Grammatik Kybernetik Kommunikation, edited by K.G.Schweisthal, pp. 19-24. Bonn: Dümmler.

———. 1972*a*. Converging theories in linguistics. Language 48.266-275.

———. 1972*b*. Contemporary linguistics and Indo-European studies. PMLA 87.976-993.

———. 1972*c*. Descriptive linguistics: An introduction. New York: Random House.

———. 1973*a*. A structural principle of language and its implications. Language 49.47-66.

———. 1973*b*. Explanations for some syntactic phenomena of Proto-Indo-European. Glossa 7.81-90.

———, and Solveig Pflueger. Forthcoming. The structure of compounds in Proto-Indo-European.

Leumann, Manu. 1952. Morphologische Neuerungen im altindischen Verbalsystem. MKNA 15.3. Amsterdam.

———. 1963-1965. Lateinische Grammatik. 2 vols. Handbuch der Altertumswissenschaft 2.2.1-2. Munich: Beck.

1963. I. Lateinische Laut- und Formenlehre. Reprint of first edition (1926-1928).

1965. II. Lateinische Syntax und Stylistik. By J. B. Hofmann, revised by Anton Szantyr.

Levy, Ernst. 1942. Der Bau der europäischen Sprachen. Dublin: Hodges-Figgis. Reprint. Tübingen: Niemeyer, 1964.

Löfstedt, Einar. 1956. Über einige Grundfragen der lateinischen Nominalsyntax. Vol. 1 of Syntactica: Studien und Beiträge zur historischen Syntax des Lateins. 2d ed. Lund: Gleerup.

Lunt, Horace G. 1955. Old Church Slavonic Grammar. The Hague: Mouton.

Macdonell, Arthur A. 1910. Vedic grammar. Strassburg: Trübner.

———. 1916. A Vedic grammar for students. Oxford: University Press.

———. 1917. A Vedic reader for students. Oxford: University Press.

Margulíés, Alfons. 1924. Die Verba reflexiva in den slavischen Sprachen. Heidelberg: Winter.

Mayrhofer, Manfred. 1953. A concise etymological Sanskrit dictionary, vol. 1. Heidelberg: Winter.

McQuown, Norman A., and Sadı Koylan. 1945. Spoken Turkish, 2 vols. New York: Holt.

Meid, Wolfgang. 1963. Die indogermanischen Grundlagen der absoluten und konjunkten Verbalflexion. Wiesbaden: Harrassowitz.

Meillet, Antoine. 1897. De indo-europaea radice *men- "mente agitare." Paris: Bouillon; Champion successeur.

———. 1906-1908. Les alternances vocaliques en vieux slave. MSL 14.193-209.

———. 1913. Altarmenisches Elementarbuch. Heidelberg: Winter.

———. 1936. Esquisse d'une grammaire comparée de l'arménien classique. Vienne: Mekhitharistes.

———. 1967. The comparative method in historical linguistics. Translated by Gordon B. Ford, Jr. Paris: Champion. First published as La méthode comparative en linguistique historique (Oslo: Aschehoug, 1925).

———. 1937. Introduction à l'étude comparative des langues indo-européennes. 8th ed. Paris: Hachette.

Miklosich, Franz. 1868-1874. Vergleichende Grammatik der slavischen Sprachen. Reprint. Heidelberg: Winter, 1926.

Mitchell, T. F. 1973. Aspects of concord revisited, with special reference to Sindhi and Cairene Arabic. Archivum Linguisticum, n.s. 4.27-50.

Monteil, Pierre. 1963. La phrase relative en grec ancien: Sa formation, son développement, sa structure dès origines à la fin du Ve siècle a[vant] [J.] C. Paris: Klincksieck.

Munro, D. B. 1891. A Grammar of the Homeric Dialect. 2d ed. Oxford: Clarendon.

Narten, Johanna. 1964. Die sigmatischen Aoriste im Veda. Wiesbaden: Harrassowitz.

Neu, Erich. 1967. Die Bedeutung des Hethitischen für die Rekonstruktion des frühindogermanischen Verbalsystems. IF 72.221-238.

———. 1968. Das hethitische Mediopassiv und seine indogermanischen Grundlagen. Wiesbaden: Harrassowitz.

———. 1970. Ein althethitisches Gewitterritual. Wiesbaden: Harrassowitz.

Nida, Eugene A. 1949. Morphology: The descriptive analysis of words. 2d ed. Ann Arbor: University of Michigan Press.

Nygaard, M. 1905. Norrøn Syntax. Kristiania: Aschehoug.

Otfrids Evangelienbuch. *See* Erdmann 1882.

Otten, Heinrich, and Vladimir Souček. 1969. Ein althethitisches Ritual für das Königspaar. Wiesbaden: Harrassowitz.

Parry, Milman. 1971. The making of Homeric verse: The collected papers of Milman Parry, edited by Adam Parry. Oxford: Clarendon.

Paul, Hermann. 1920. Prinzipien der Sprachgeschichte. 5th ed. Halle: Niemeyer.

———; Hugo Moser; and Ingeborg Schröbler. 1969. Mittelhochdeutsche Grammatik. 20th ed. Tübingen: Niemeyer.

Pedersen, Holger. 1909-1913. Vergleichende Grammatik der keltischen Sprachen. 2 vols. Göttingen: Vandenhoeck & Ruprecht.

———. 1938. Hittitisch und die anderen indoeuropäischen Sprachen. MKDA 25.2. Copenhagen: Munksgaard.

———. 1941. Tocharisch vom Gesichtspunkt der indoeuropäischen Sprachvergleichung. MKDA 28.1. Copenhagen: Munksgaard.

Perel'muter, I. A. 1969. K stanovleniyu kategorii vremeni v sisteme indoevropeiskogo glagola [On the formation of the category of tense in the system of the Indo-European verb]. VJa 1969.5.11-21.

Persson, Per. 1892. Über den demonstrativen Pronominalstamm *no-*, *ne-* und Verwandtes. IF 2.199-260.

———. 1912. Beiträge zur indogermanischen Wortforschung. Uppsala: Almquist & Wiksell.

Pflueger, Solveig; George Saad; and W. P. Lehmann. Forthcoming. The causative, especially in Arabic.

Pinnow, Hans-Jürgen. 1960. Über den Ursprung der voneinander abweichenden Struktur der Munda- und Khmer-Nikobar-Sprachen. Indo-Iranian Journal 4.81-103.

Pokorny, Julius. 1959-1969. Indogermanisches etymologisches Wörterbuch. 2 vols. Bern & Munich: Francke.

Polomé, Edgar C. 1967. Swahili language handbook. Washington: Center for Applied Linguistics.

Porzig, Walter. 1932. Die Hypotaxe im Rigveda, 1: Die durch das Pronomen *ya* charakterisierten Sätze und syntaktischen Gruppen in den ältern Büchern des Rigveda. IF 41.210-303.

——. 1942. Die Namen für Satzinhalte im Griechischen und im Indogermanischen. Berlin: DeGruyter.

——. 1954. Die Gliederung des indogermanischen Sprachgebietes. Heidelberg: Winter.

Puhvel, Jaan. 1969. "Perfect tense" and "middle voice": An Indo-European morphological mirage. Actes du Xe Congrès International des Linguistes 4.629-634. Bucharest: Editions de L'Akadémie.

Raman, Carol F. 1973. The Old Hittite relative construction. Austin: University of Texas dissertation.

Reichelt, H. R. 1909. Awestisches Elementarbuch. Heidelberg: Winter.

Renou, Louis. 1925. Les formes dites d'injonctif dans le R̥gveda. In Etrennes Benveniste, pp. 63-80. Paris.

Richter, Oswald. 1898. Die unechten Nominalkomposita des Altindischen und Altiranischen. IF 9.1-62, 183-252.

Ries, John. 1932. Was ist Syntax? 2d ed. Prague: Taussig & Taussig. First published 1894.

Risch, Ernst. 1944-1949. Griechische Determinativ-Komposita. IF 59.1-61, 245-294.

——. 1971. Die griechische Sprachwissenschaft nach der Entzifferung der mykenischen Schrift. In Donum Indogermanicum, edited by Robert Schmitt-Brandt, pp. 107-117. Heidelberg: Winter.

Rosenkranz, Bernhard. 1953. Die hethitische ḫi-Konjugation. Jahrbuch für kleinasiatische Forschung 2.339-349.

Saussure, Ferdinand de. 1879. Mémoire sur le système primitif des voyelles dans les langues indo-européennes. Reprint. Paris: Vieweg, 1887.

Schmid, Wolfgang P. 1963. Studien zum baltischen und indogermanischen Verbum. Wiesbaden: Harrassowitz.

Schmidt, Gernot. 1971. Altirisch *ro-fitir* und Verwandtes. KZ 85.242-272.

Schmidt, Johannes. 1889. Die Pluralbildungen der indogermanischen Neutra. Weimar: Böhlau.

Schmitt, Rüdiger. 1967. Dichtung und Dichtersprache in indogermanischer Zeit. Wiesbaden: Harrassowitz.

Schmitt-Brandt, Robert. 1971. Die Herausbildung der slavischen Gemeinschaft. In Donum Indogermanicum, edited by Robert Schmitt-Brandt, pp. 224-243. Heidelberg: Winter.

Schwyzer, Eduard. 1942. Zum persönlichen Agens beim Passiv, besonders im Griechischen. APrA 1942.10. Reprint. Berlin: DeGruyter, 1943.

——. 1939-1953. Griechische Grammatik. Handbuch der Altumswissenschaft 2.1. 1-3. Munich: Beck.
1939. I. Allgemeiner Teil, Lautlehre, Wortbildung, Flexion.
1950. II. Syntax und syntaktische Stilistik.
1953. III. Register, by D. J. Georgacas.

——. 1947. Zur Apposition. ABG 1947.3. Berlin: DeGruyter.

Seebold, Elmar. 1971. Versuch über die Herkunft der indogermanischen Personalendungssysteme. KZ 85.185-210.

——. 1973. Die Stammbildungen der idg. Wurzel **u̯eid-* und deren Bedeutungen. Die Sprache 19.20-38.

Seiler, Hans-Jakob. 1960. Relativsatz und Apposition. Wiesbaden: Harrassowitz.

Senn, Alfred. 1966. Grammatik. Vol. 1 of Handbuch der litauischen Sprache. Heidelberg: Winter.

Smyth, Herbert W. 1956. Greek grammar. Revised by Gordon M. Messing. Cambridge: Harvard University Press. First published 1920.

Snyder, D. Paul. 1971. Modal logic and its applications. New York: Van Nostrand Reinhold.

Solta, Georg R. 1970. Der hethitische Imperativ der 1. Person Singular und das idg. *l*-Formans als quasi-desideratives Element. IF 75.44-84.

Sommer, Ferdinand. 1959. Vergleichende Grammatik der Schulsprachen. 4th ed. Unchanged reprint of the 3d ed. of 1931. Darmstadt: Wissenschaftliche Buchgesellschaft.

Specht, Franz. 1947. Der Ursprung der indogermanischen Deklination. Göttingen: Vandenhoeck & Ruprecht.

Speyer, J. S. 1886. Sanskrit syntax. Reprint. Kyoto: Rinsen-Shoten Bookstore, 1968.

——. 1895. Vedische und Sanskrit-Syntax. Strassburg: Trübner.

Stang, Chr. S. 1966. Vergleichende Grammatik der baltischen Sprachen. Oslo: Universitetsforlaget.

Streitberg, Wilhelm. 1920. Gotisches Elementarbuch. 5th and 6th ed. Heidelberg: Winter.

Strunck, Klaus. 1967. Nasalpräsentien und Aoriste. Heidelberg: Winter.

——. 1968. Zeit und Tempus in altindogermanischen Sprachen. IF 73.279-311.

Stumpf, Peter. 1971. Der Gebrauch der Demonstrativ-Pronomina im Tocharischen. Wiesbaden: Harrassowitz.

Sturtevant, E. H. 1942. The Indo-Hittite laryngeals. Baltimore: Linguistic Society of America.

——. 1947. An introduction to linguistic science. New Haven: Yale University Press.

——. 1951. A comparative grammar of the Hittite language. New Haven: Yale University Press.

Szabó, Gabriella. 1971. Ein hethitisches Entsühnungsritual. Heidelberg: Winter.

Szantyr, Anton. *See* Leumann 1963-1965.

Szemerényi, Oswald. 1960. Studies in the Indo-European system of numerals. Heidelberg: Winter.

——. 1970. Einführung in die vergleichende Sprachwissenschaft. Darmstadt: Wissenschaftliche Buchgesellschaft.

Thomas, Werner. 1957. Der Gebrauch der Vergangenheitstempora im Tocharischen. Wiesbaden: Harrassowitz.

Thommen, Eduard. 1905. Die Wortstellung im nachvedischen Altindischen und im Mittelindischen. Gütersloh.

Thurneysen, Rudolf. 1885. Der indogermanische Imperativ. KZ 27.172-180.

——. 1946. A grammar of Old Irish. Revised and enlarged edition translated from the German by D. A. Binchy and O. Bergin. Dublin: Institute for Advanced Studies.

Traugott, Elizabeth Closs. 1969. Toward a grammar of syntactic change. Lingua 21. 1-27.

Ureland, Sture. 1973. Verb complementation in Swedish and other Germanic languages. Stockholm: Skriptor.

Vaillant, André. 1936. L'ergatif indo-européen. BSL 37.93-108.

Van Coetsem, Frans, and Herbert L. Kufner, eds. 1972. Toward a grammar of Proto-Germanic. Tübingen: Niemeyer.

van der Meer, M. J. 1901. Gotische Casus-Syntaxis. Leiden: Brill.

Van Nooten, Barend A. 1969. Pāṇini's theory of verbal meaning. Foundations of Language 5.242-255.

Van Wijk, N. Jan. 1902. Der nominale Genetiv singular im Indogermanischen in seinem Verhältnis zum Nominativ. Zwolle: de Erven.

Verkuyl, H. J. 1972. On the compositional nature of the aspects. Foundations of Language Supplementary Series 15. Dordrecht: Reidel.

Verner, Karl. 1875. Eine Ausnahme der ersten Lautverschiebung. KZ 23.97-130.

Vondrák, Wenzel. 1924-1928. Vergleichende slavische Grammatik. 2d ed. Göttingen: Vandenhoeck & Ruprecht.

Wachowicz, Krystyna. 1974. On the syntax and semantics of multiple questions. Austin: University of Texas dissertation.

Wackernagel, Jacob. 1892. Über ein Gesetz der indogermanischen Wortstellung. IF 1.333-436.

——. 1896-1957. Altindische Grammatik. Göttingen: Vandenhoeck & Ruprecht.

1896. I. Lautlehre. 2d ed., with supplements by Albert Debrunner, 1957.

1905. II.1. Einleitung zur Wortlehre: Nominalkomposition. 2d ed., with supplements by Albert Debrunner, 1957.

1954. II.2. Die Nominalsuffixe, by Albert Debrunner.

1930. III. Nominalflexion; Zahlwort; Pronomen, with Albert Debrunner.

1957. Introduction générale, by Louis Renou.

1964. Register zur Altindischen Grammatik, by Richard Hauschild.

——. 1908. Genetiv und Adjektiv. In Mélanges F. de Saussure, pp. 125-152. Paris.

——. 1926-1928. Vorlesungen über Syntax. 2d ed. Basel: Birkhäuser.

1926. I. Erste Reihe.
1928. II. Zweite Reihe.

Wagner, Heinrich. 1956. Zu den indogermanischen ē-Verben. Zeitschrift für Celtische Philologie 25.161-173.

——. 1959. Das Verbum in den Sprachen der Britischen Inseln. Tübingen: Niemeyer.

Walde, Alois. 1927-1932. Vergleichendes Wörterbuch der indogermanischen Sprachen, edited and revised by Julius Pokorny. 3 vols. Berlin und Leipzig: DeGruyter.
1927. II.
1930. I.
1932. Register or Index, prepared by Konstantin Reichardt.

Warmington, E. H., ed. and trans. 1959. Archaic Inscriptions. Vol. 4 of Old Latin. Loeb Classics. Cambridge: Harvard University Press.

Warren, Minton. 1881. On the enclitic *ne* in early Latin. American Journal of Philology 2.50-82.

Watkins, Calvert. 1962. The sigmatic aorist. Vol. 1 of Indo-European origins of the Celtic verb. Dublin: Institute for Advanced Studies.

——. 1963. Syntax of the Old Irish verb. Celtica 6.1-49.

——. 1964. Preliminaries to the reconstruction of Indo-European sentence structure. In Proceedings of the IX International Congress of Linguists, edited by H. G. Lunt, pp. 1035-1045. The Hague: Mouton.

——. 1967. Remarks on the genitive. In To honor Roman Jakobson, pp. 2191-2198. The Hague: Mouton.

——. 1969. Geschichte der indogermanischen Verbalflexion. Part 1 of Formenlehre. Vol. 3 of Indogermanische Grammatik. Heidelberg: Winter.

Wheeler, B. I. 1898. The origin of grammatical gender. Journal of English and Germanic Philology 2.528-545.

Whitney, William D. 1885. The roots, verb-forms and primary derivatives of the Sanskrit language. Leipzig: Breitkopf und Härtel.

——. 1896. A Sanskrit grammar. 3d ed. Boston: Ginn.

Wienold, Götz. 1967. Genus und Semantik. Meisenheim: Hain.

Windisch, Ernst. 1869. Untersuchungen über den Ursprung des Relativpronomens in den indogermanischen Sprachen. Curtius Studien 2.201-419. Leipzig: Hirzel.

Winkler, Heinrich. 1896. Germanische Casussyntax I. Berlin: Dümmler.

Wistrand, Erik. 1941. Über das Passivum. Göteborgs Kungl. Vetenskaps- och Vitterhets-Samhälles Handlingar, 6 sec. A, part 1.

Wordick, Frank. 1970. A generative-extensionist analysis of the Proto-Indo-European kinship system with a phonological and semantic reconstruction of the terms. Ann Arbor: University of Michigan dissertation.

Wyatt, William F., Jr. 1972. Review of Geschichte der indogermanischen Verbalflexion, by Calvert Watkins. Language 48.687-695.

Yamagiwa, J. K. 1942. Modern Conversational Japanese. New York: McGraw-Hill.

INDEX

Hymn and stanza numbers for Rigvedic citations and line numbers for other citations are in boldface type; page references are in roman type.